Horia Ion Groza

Discovering the Sacred Time of Our Life

Doamnei Virginia Stănescu,
cu adâncă admirație pentru nobila muncă
de cultură pe care o face cu exemplară dăruire,
o carte de gânduri despre adesea ignorata
sacralitate a existenței noastre

Horia Ion Groza
25 mai 2017, Înălțarea Domnului

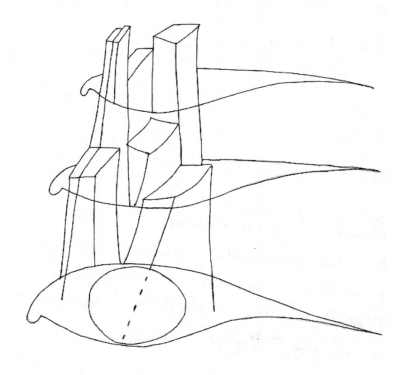

"Look upon me and hear me, O Lord my God.
Enlighten my eyes, lest I sleep in death"
(*Psalm 12/13:4*).

Horia Ion Groza

Discovering the Sacred Time of Our Life

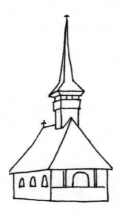

Reflection Publishing

Title: Discovering the Sacred Time of Our Life
Author: Horia Ion Groza
On the cover: Monastery of Voronetz, Romania. Picture taken by
Alexis Norauski
Cover Artist: Ioana Onica
Line drawings: Horia Ion Groza

ISBN: 978-1-936629-46-6

Reflection Publishing. P.O. Box 2182
Citrus Heights, California 95611-2182
E-mail: info@reflectionbooks.com
www.reflectionbooks.com

Contents

A Detailed List of Contents

    1.1. Should We Believe in God? *[A life without faith in God is a sad life. The Spirit Comes Before Matter. Happiness and Perfection. Wisdom of Philosophers. Power of Thinking. Laws of the Lord. The Voice of Conscience. Vulnerability of Human Ethics. Risks and Consequences. The Unknown of the Events. Tolls of Life. Life Length is Unknown. Need of Contemplation. Being Alone with Oneself. Meaning of Life. The Inner Life. To Live with God. Understanding God and Life. Some Still Wonder. Knowledge and Mysteries. Cataphatic and Apophatic. Prayer as a Tool. Belief and Prayer. Urgency of Soul. Faith Strengthens the Soul. The Spiritual Growth. The Peace Given by the Lord.]*

    1.2. What is the Sense of Our Daily Life? *[Life's Ups and Downs. Philosophy of Life. Is There a Human Fate? Role of Conscience. Trust in God. Human Mind and Miracles. Believe What Is Hard to Explain. Miracles in Daily Life. Religion and Church. Live and Die in the Lord. What Counts the Most. Fruitful with Lord's Help. Wise Stories. Real Stories. A Scary Story. End of Earthly Life. Meeting Death. Time of Death. Suicide is a Serious Sin. Life Beyond Death. Our Hidden Sins. Do it Before Departure. Do not look for revenge. Judgment and Forgiveness. Charity and Hospitality. Lord*

Letter of Hieromonk Petroniu Tanase from Mount Athos

March 1, 2007

Dear Mister Groza,

Receive, please, heartfelt thanks for the precious present, the book "Trepte de văzduh..." with which you honored me causing a big joy. It is a spiritual Philokalia, gathered from the wisdom and life of the Holy Fathers of our Holy Church and from the fruitfulness of a Christian life inspired by them. I am confident that, in this time of deep disintegration of the human person, your book will help many to climb up the ascending ladder to the heights of salvation, and will award its laborer with the joy of being a faithful servant.

I wish the Holy and Great Lent that we entered to be for you of much use and spiritual achievement.

With best wishes from the Good Lord: health and salvation.

Hierom. Petroniu

Romanian Skete Prodromu
Saint Mount Athos, 630 86 Kareia, Greece

Note. This letter is referring to the book entitled "Treptele de văzduh ale sufletului şi setea de Dumnezeu" (*The Ladder of the Inner Sky and the Thirst for God*, published in Romanian in 2006). The present book, "Discovering the Sacred Time of Our Life", is based on the first half of the above-mentioned Romanian version.

SCHITUL ROMANESC PRODROMU
SF.MUNTE ATHOS - 630 86 KAREIA - GRECIA
☎: 0030-23770-23294 ☎ / FAX: 23788

1. martie 2007

Mult stimate Domnule Groza,

Vă rog să primiți călduroase mulțumiri pentru prețiosul dar: volumul „Trepte de văzduh..." cu care m'ați bucurat și cinstit. Este o filo-calie duhovnicească, adunată din înțelepciunea și viața Sfinților Părinți ai Sfintei noastre Biserici și din rodnicia unei vieți creștine, însuflețită din acestea. Sunt încredințat că, în aceste vremi de adâncă destrămare a persoanei umane, lucrea dvs. va ajuta multora să pășească pe trepte suitore în văzduhul cel mântuitor, și va învrednici pe ostenitorul ei de bucuria răsplătirii slujitorului credincios.

Sfântul și marele Post în care am intrat vi-l doresc cu mult folos și împlinire duhovnicească.

Cu cele mai bune doriri de la Bunul Dumnezeu: sănătate și mântuire.

Ieromonah Petroniu

Forward Foreword

It gives me great joy to see that Horia is publishing his reflections on the spiritual life in a form accessible to English readers. Many conversations and reflections through the years have gone into this book. It stands in continuity with the writings of the great fathers, through the experience of the Romanian elders, into the modern Orthodox spiritual-intellectual tradition.

I advise the reader not to be misled by the straightforward simplicity of this work. We live in a chaotic and impulsive age that claims to be spiritual without discipline and intellectual without logic. We are not used to systematic, authentic, philosophical reflection.

This is the work of a patient thinker, who is first and foremost an Orthodox believer. Horia started this work with the passionate desire to pass on to his family, and then to a world in need, the great treasure he has received. Anyone who desires to approach the spiritual life with sincerity will find treasure here.

Rt.Rev.Arch. Mark Melone
St. Joseph Melkite Greek Catholic Church,
Lawrence, Massachusetts

The essayist, poet and novel writer Horia Ion Groza (born in Romania and established in USA in 1986), has a PhD in plant genetics and breeding. He worked 40 years in this domain of scientific research, at a plant research institute in Romania, for several bioengineering companies and for the University of Wisconsin-Madison in U.S.A. He authored three books of essays on philosophical and social themes, three books on Christian faith and tradition, one volume of poems, one novel and one book of literature critique. All of them have been published in Romanian and were very well received. He was awarded the LiterArt XXI Prize for journalism (1999) and for essays (2002).

Introduction

This book is addressed to the Christians of our modern time. They are under a continuous attack from the materialistic scientists and from the so-called "free" thinkers. The Christians are also confronted daily with the misunderstanding and denial of a society based on a large consumption of goods that do not last long but bring "fun," a society interested in all means possible to achieve maximum comfort. The Christians face a society trending toward a life style that intermingles right and wrong, comparing and confusing relativity with the principles of ethics. André Malraux was right when he said several decades ago that the twenty-first century will be religious or will not be at all. As Pascal-Emmanuel Gobry commented, after the twentieth century that reached a very high level of secularism, we already notice several significant changes in the first two decades of the new century (Gobry, 2015). Christianity became stronger in the East-European countries where the atheist communist regime was abolished, in South America and even in some countries of the Oriental Asia like China and South Korea. In the same time, an unprecedented movement that affects West Europe, U.S.A. and several other countries is the Islamism. I think religion ensures the spinal column of the ethics of a society and therefore it is necessary more today than in previous times.

The Christian's life journey follows a road unswervingly directed toward God, and only God knows at what milestone the road ends for each of us. Trying not to miss the trail and walking onward, despite all the obstacles, we grow spiritually with the goal of approaching perfection without ever reaching it, because perfection is only the Lord's attribute. The road toward God corresponds to an ascending movement of the spirit. All Orthodox Christians are called to follow a process of deification. Man was created by God in His image and in His likeness (*Genesis 1:26*). By sinning, Adam lost the likeness. Striving to regain that likeness is actually a process of deification.

Here is a part of the book that I have written thinking of my sons and, in a way, it is a call to discover the eternal sacred time that is hidden behind the temporary historic time of our life. It is a call to the young people to begin a life of faith. However, this introductory book, written for the youth, thirsty for knowledge, might suit all of us, regardless of age. If we have in mind the real length of the spiritual trip everybody has to take in his life, we can say that, regardless how far we have managed to walk with God's help toward Him, we actually remain at the beginning stage. I remember a story of the Patericon, known also as *Egyptian Patericon* or *Apophtegmata Patrum* (Patericul, 1996a), about an elder who was dying. His disciples asked the Abba why he looked so nervous before meeting with Christ, for he was already a saintly person. He answered them with a sigh, "Because I am just at the beginning of my work of repentance." These profound words of wisdom should not discourage us. Certainly, God appreciates any effort of ours. However, the elder's words give us the right measure that we should consider when we estimate the accomplishments of our own spiritual life.

Saint Anthony the Great said, "Life and Death come both from our neighbor. If we bring a spiritual benefit to our neighbor, we gain Our Lord's love. If we hurt our neighbor, we hurt Christ" (see Patericul, 1996a). This book was written with love for the neighbor. I pray God that the book might not do any spiritual harm and, to the contrary, that it might be a suggestion for a better life in faith.

The author of the book is far from being a theologian. He is simply a humble layman who tried to understand and live what the theologians teach. Far from making any comparison, one can mention that there are at least two examples of lay-authors in the literature of the Orthodox Church. One is very famous: Nicholas Cabasilas. He lived in the fourteenth century and was a close friend of the Byzantine Emperor John VI Cantacuzenus who eventually retired to a monastery. Despite the false legend that he succeeded his uncle Nilus Cabasilas as Archbishop of Thessalonica and the fact that he was once a candidate for the position of Patriarch of Constantinople, Cabasilas remained a layman for his entire life (see the R.M. French's Foreword to Nicholas Cabasilas, *A Commentary on Divine Liturgy*). Nevertheless, his writing about the Liturgy is a very fundamental book for the Church, and it is read and studied today with the same great interest and respect as it was in the fourteenth century. Nicholas Cabasilas is a Saint.

A much more obscure author, Sergei Fudel, who lived in the years 1901-1977, provides the other example. The prestigious Saint Vladimir's Seminary Press published a book of his (Fudel, 1989). He was the son of a Moscow parish priest (a disciple of the elders at Optino Monastery) and had no formal theological education. He was arrested by the Soviet regime at the age of twenty for his religious activities, and he spent a total of twenty-five years in prison, labor camp, and exile. He had a wife and two sons and finished his long-suffering earthly life in Russia in the peace that faith gives to all Christians. His book, rich in deep and pious thoughts, is significantly entitled "Light in the Darkness."

I defected from a communist country at a mature age in 1985 and immigrated to the United States for the sake of civil liberty and religious freedom. My native country, Romania, has a long Christian tradition. Saint Apostle Andrew spread the

Gospel in Scythia Minor (Dobrogea of today). This region, neighboring the Black Sea, was a part of the Roman Empire and now is one of the provinces of Romania. Its capital was Tomis (or Constanța in today's terms). The first Christian martyrs in the history of the Romanian territory were in the third and fourth centuries. The Barbarians killed them.

Saint John Cassian was born and raised in Scythia Minor, a region of Dacia Pontica. Saint John Chrysostom ordained him as a priest. Saint John Cassian founded two monasteries in Marseille (France), and had a major influence on the future development of monasticism in Western Europe. When Saint John Chrysostom was exiled, Saint John Cassian and his good friend from Scythia Minor, Saint Germanicus, went to Rome to ask the Pope Innocent to intervene to the emperor and make him call back Saint John Chrysostom to the Patriarchal Throne of Constantinople (see Bălan, 1996).

Romania has a long monastic tradition. The flourishing of hesychasm that reached its peak in the eighteenth century attracted many foreigners (see Joantă, 1992). The well-known Saint Paisius Velichkovsky was among them. He came from Ukraine. While he was the Abbot of the Romanian Monasteries Dragomirna and Neamț, he worked on the translation of the Greek Philokalia - a book assembling the Holy Fathers' writings about the Prayer of Mind. The most important Russian Monasteries, including the monks from Valaam, later used the Slavonic version authored by him. Abbot Nazarius was Abbot at Valaam Monastery and his direct disciple was Saint Herman of Alaska, the first Orthodox Saint of America, who lived in the years 1756-1837. Saint Herman brought Paisius' Philokalia version to the American land.

The Orthodox Church was not persecuted in Romania by the atheistic communist regime as much as it was in Russia. It is true though that in the late '50's and early '60's tens of thousands priests and faithful laymen were imprisoned for their belief. Many monasteries were closed at that time and the monks were exiled. In addition to this, in the '60's and '70's, many churches were demolished in Bucharest due to the communist dictator's regulation of urban systematization. However, the majority of churches continued to function. The attendees were mainly old people because the working people risked losing their jobs if they were seen in churches. Anyhow, the few monasteries left continued to have their secret life. People, especially from villages, went to the elders to listen to sermons, to have confession and to ask for advice.

Many extraordinary spiritual persons were formed under this time of restrictions like Dumitru Staniloae (one of the greatest Orthodox theologians of the twentieth century), Cleopa Ilie, Joel Gheorgiu, Paisius Olaru, Benedict Ghius, Sofian Boghiu, Constantin Galeriu, Gheorghe Calciu-Dumitreasa, Vasile Vasilachi, Roman Braga, Daniil Teodorescu (Sandu Tudor), and many others (see the articles written about them in *The Orthodox Word*, published by St. Herman of Alaska Brotherhood at Platina, California). Most of these great elders suffered much in the communist prisons. I was fortunate to meet a few of them, to listen to their words of deep wisdom in the '60-'80's, and to read their writings published after the '89 Revolution. Christian literature was rarely available in communist times and it was circulated secretly. These were books written by the Russian theologians Lossky, Evdokimov, and Berdiaeff (published in French, before WWII), and manuscript versions of the writings of the Holy Fathers.

This book is part of a modified English version of the book published in Romanian (see Groza, 2006). While the Romanian version, entitled "The Ladder of the Inner Sky and the Thirst for God", emphasized aspects learned in the United

States, this present version tries to make known the Romanian fathers' thoughts to the American readers.

The main message of the book is a call to start discovering the sacred time of our life or, in other words, to begin feeling and seeing God's presence around us every minute. Someone asked Abba Anthony the Great what should be done in order to please God. The elder's reply was, "<u>Have God in front of you wherever you go</u>; rely on the Holy Scripture's words in whatever you do; and do not hurry to leave the place where you live. Keep these three rules and you will be saved."

The hieromonk Petronius Tanase from Prodromos Romanian Monastery on Mount Athos, who made reference to this Abba Anthony's wise teaching from the Patericon, added another example relating to the necessity of realizing the Lord's unceasing assistance. A monk asked a Father what thing is the most helpful in all the spiritual struggles a man faces in his earthly life. The elder replied that the most helpful thing is a strong belief that God is a permanent witness to everything man does. Without this certitude, all our efforts and labor are in vain. Father Petronius emphasized the fact that simply living in "the light of God's face" can save our souls. "The Lord is closer to us than ourselves," said Saint Augustine. Let us think of the words of an Orthodox prayer that begins the most services: "O Heavenly King, the Comforter, the Spirit of Truth, <u>Who art present everywhere and fillest all things</u>…" Saint Apostle Paul wrote, *"In Him we live and move and have our being"* (*Acts 17:28*). We have to remember God more often than we breathe as St. Gregory of Nazianz wrote.

The English Father Kallistos Ware, bishop of Diokleia and Spalding Lecturer at the University of Oxford, said that, while he was a simple young monk at St. John's Orthodox Monastery in Patmos, some American Protestants visited the

Monastery. Talking in English, in order not to be understood by the Greek monks, they said to each other with obvious superiority, "These people do not read and know the Bible because they are too busy with their unceasing prayers and their extremely long services." The visitors were surprised when Father Kallistos, sitting in a corner and doing a physical work, told them, with a mild smile and a humble voice, in pure English, "Actually we read it from time to time, and we try to obey its word."

The reader will find numerous Bible quotes in this book. The author hopes that he did not disturb with his noisy voice the harmonious sound of the Bible's Sacred Word. The version used was *The Orthodox Study Bible* issued in 2008 by St. Athanasius Academy of Orthodox Theology, based on the Septuagint version of the Old Testament (SAAS™) and on the New King James Version of the New Testament (NKJV®). Very seldom, for the Old Testament quotes, the author of this book preferred to use the King James Version (Ivy Books, New York, 1991) or the Revised Standard Version (Thomas Nelson and Sons Ltd, 1952). In this latter case, the source is specified in parentheses. The Psalms are numbered according to *The Orthodox Study Bible*, e.g. Psalm 50/51, where the first number corresponds to the Greek translation (Septuagint) and the second number to the Masoteric Text (Hebrew, translated in English in New King James Version).

Acknowledgments. The author thanks Fathers Mark Malone, Anthony Michaels, Vladimir Lecko, Ian McKinnon, and Dane Popovich for their precious suggestions and useful clarifications, Father Petronius Tanase and writer Vasile Andru for their trust and moral support, Anna Garner and Gwen Schoen for their important help in editing the manuscript, and my family and friends for their continuous love and encouragement.

1. What's Good in a Christian Life?

Every ordinary life is full of trials and tribulations. It does not matter how strong, clever and healthy we are, and it does not matter how many efforts we make, we succeed to control our life only partially, and even that fraction looks illusory at a more careful analysis. The Christian philosophy of life will not avoid all the suffering, trials, and tolls, but it will arm us with the weapons of peace, love, and hope and will make the odyssey of our life easier for our mind and heart, and what it matters the most, for our soul. The confidence in God will give us a steady peaceful joy in all moments of our life.

Let us recheck our fundamental principles. Should we believe in God? What is the sense of our daily life? Should we live in faith? These are hard questions and deserve a careful answer. Let us be wise and cautious and avoid from the very start the possibility of finishing entangled into a thick jungle of thoughts. As the ancient mathematicians needed sometimes *the reductio ad absurdum* method for being able to reach the truth of their theorems, we need the help of a knowledgeable tutor for catching the right spark of heart and mind that will ignite the fire of understanding.

Let us open the Book of Psalms. Their beauty is one of the pearls of the Old Testament and their spiritual wisdom inspires both the beginners and the advanced. The Psalms are a school of prayer and a continuous dialogue with the Lord. In monasteries, all of them are read during the Great Lent from the very first to the very last. Let us put a good start to our spiritual conversation with a prayer before confronting the difficulties of the subject and defining clearly our position. It might open our eyes in the right direction. *"Unveil my eyes, and I shall understand the wonders in Your law"* (*Psalm 118/119:18*). *"I made known my ways and You heard me; teach me Your ordinances"* (*Psalm 118/119:26*). *"Cause me to understand and I shall search out Your law, and I shall keep it with my whole heart"* (*Psalm 118/119:34*). *"Turn away my eyes that I may not see vanity; give me life in Your way"* (*Psalm 118/119:37*). *"O Lord, You test me and know me; You know my sitting down and my rising up; You understand my thoughts from afar; You search out my path and my portion, and You foresee all my ways... If I should ascend into heaven, You would be there; if I should descend into Hades, You would be there; if I should take up my wings at dawn and pitch camp at the furthest part of the sea, even there Your hand would lead me, and Your right hand would hold me"* (*Psalm 138/139:1-3, 8-10*).

Father Kallistos (known also by his name as author, Timothy Ware) one day started his sermon at Holy Trinity Church in San Francisco with the verse, *"Direct my steps according to Your teaching and let no lawlessness rule over me"* (*Psalm 118/119: 133*). All the above-quoted verses might introduce us effectively into the nature of the discussion proposed in this book.

1.1. Should We Believe in God?

A LIFE WITHOUT FAITH IN GOD IS A SAD LIFE. The trials, annoyances, failures, and losses painfully grind the heart, exhaust the energy sources, and destroy the enthusiasm. Even all the pleasures can end in a bitter way. A cartoon by Jules Feiffer, published by an Italian newspaper, tells the story of a young woman, in a string of sequences. In my translation from Italian, it sounds like this: "I drive to work - I am tested if I am under influence. I go shopping - I notice everywhere guardians who watch me. I have a new date - I check if I did not catch

AIDS. I drive home - a police officer stops me to see if I am drunk. I cannot find my driver's license to identify myself; the officer becomes suspicious and does not allow me to enter my house. I go to sleep at mom's house. Finally I can relax in my childhood room, in a warm bed. I feel thirsty at three o'clock in the morning and go downstairs to drink a glass of milk. Unknowingly I trigger the alarm. Mom jumps from her bed, grabs a gun, and shoots me." Dry and sad humor.

Filled with the bitterness of vanity the wise man of Ecclesiastes wondered, *"What advantage does a man have in all his labor in which he toils under the sun?"* (*Ecclesiastes 1:3*). Our Lord Jesus Christ gave more weight to this thought by adding the concern for man's soul in contrast with his worldly goals: "*For what profit is it to a man, if he gains the whole world and loses his own soul? Or what will a man give in exchange for his soul?"* (*Matthew 16:26*).

THE SPIRIT COMES BEFORE MATTER. As Father George Calciu (his complete name is George Calciu Dumitreasa) wrote, it is time now for science to be in accord with theology and not theology with science. We learn from scientists that energy comes before matter. In the Church's terms, this means the spirit comes before matter (Calciu, 1997).

Let us listen to the psalmist's words: *"He shall not take pleasure in the strength of a horse, nor be pleased with the legs of a man."* God enjoys not the physical performances but the spiritual ones. *"The Lord is pleased with those who fear Him and with those who hope in His mercy"* (*Psalm 146/147: 10-11*).

"Even the youths shall faint and be weary, and the elect shall be without strength. But those who wait on God shall renew their strength; they shall mount up with wings like eagles; they shall run and not be weary; they shall walk and

not hunger" (*Isaiah 40: 30-31*). Saint Paisius Velichkovsky from the Romanian Neamț Monastery said that if we put our hope in God, even if we live only one day and then we die, it is much better than to live very many years but always with doubts in our mind, heart, and soul.

Elder Raphael Noica, now a well-respected hermit living in the Romanian West Carpathians, entered the monastic life in Essex (England), in 1961, at the Saint John Baptist's Monastery, under the Abbot Sophrony Sakharov. He was only 19 years old at that time. His father, the famous Romanian philosopher Constantin Noica, who remained in communist Romania, suffering political prison, wrote him a highly emotional letter. The philosopher was very sad that his son decided to retreat from the world so early, missing the chance of learning first a fraction of the gigantic progress the scientific and philosophical knowledge humankind had achieved by the middle of the twentieth century. The philosopher opposed the phrase "Know and then do what you like," characterizing the contemporary thirst for knowledge, to Saint Augustine's phrase "Love and then do what you like." He metaphorically said that, if the Lord should decide today a new deluge in the entire world and ask Noah to save that which can perpetuate the living creation, the latter would not crowd the ark with a multitude of animals but with a computerized collection of DNA's and some important technologies for using it. The philosopher ended his letter to his son with his own conciliatory conclusion. He considered that beyond love and knowledge there is an "ordo gaudii" (a line of joy) that ties them in a supreme unitary principle. Therefore, he suggested the following formula satisfactory for both, irreligious father and religious son: "Enjoy and then do what you like." The father did not disapprove of his son's option but he wanted it to come at an older age, after the son had felt the satisfaction of materialistic knowledge. It is true: the son of the highly respected philosopher did not use his youth to taste the heights of human thinking. He preferred from the very beginning to enter deeply into a dialogue with God, into the idealistic simplicity and pure devotion, proper to a teenager. Today Elder Raphael is a person of profound Orthodox spirituality, whom many faithful people ask for spiritual advice. Behold, something to reflect about - an extreme example of living with God in our present world!

HAPPINESS AND PERFECTION. The famous Nobel prize-winning Russian writer Alexander Solzhenitsyn said in his speech at Harvard in June 1978, "if, as claimed by humanism, man were born only to be happy, he would not be born to die. Since his body is doomed to death, his task on earth evidently must be more spiritual."

The classical question of the philosophers "What is happiness?" has not been satisfactorily answered yet. Therefore, it still provides a very attractive subject for intellectual debates. Perhaps the reason consists in the fact that nothing is perfect. When we attain a certain state of joy and good feelings, life brings new problems and invades us with new nuisances. However, if by an absurd mechanism, everything becomes perfect, and the extraordinary becomes ordinary, life will eventually become *boring* to our human nature.

The Sacred might be the solution for the philosophers' debate. A state specific to the Saints is achievable only through God Who is perfect. However, Saints are not God; therefore, their state still remains imperfect. Knowledge of God and belief in Him as a "touch" of eternity can stimulate us and make sense of our existence, needed for the continuously ascending trend of our spiritual development. This sense is never discouraging, never disappointing.

WISDOM OF PHILOSOPHERS. Dr. Charles Habib Malik, a former president of the UN, a devoted orthodox Christian, wrote that the Greek philosopher Aristotle was in search of Jesus of Nazareth when he thought of the design and purpose of the universe (Malik, 1974). Similarly, according to Malik, Plato had Jesus of Nazareth in mind when he pleaded for the supreme good existent behind all the phenomena. Anaxagoras had the same idea when he asked questions about the Supreme Mind responsible for the order in the universe.

Philosophy can lead us toward God. Plato and Aristotle are present among the Saints painted on the outside-wall frescos of the churches of the North Moldavian monasteries. However, the road of philosophy will always finish in a dead end, at a tall fence. The miracles are in fact the particular logic of faith. They are events or phenomena the human mind cannot sufficiently explain. The Orthodox faith is apophatic and, as Father Staniloae emphasized, a negative theology that does not imply a lazy mind and an abdication of the faculty of reasoning, but exactly the opposite, a continuous rise up the ladder of knowledge (Staniloae, 2002). Despite the fact that man always discovers something new within the created world, the unknown remains as vast as the ocean, and the only way to make sense of the whole created world is faith in the Creator.

"Beware lest anyone cheat you through philosophy and empty deceit, according to the tradition of men, according to the basic principles of the world, and not according to Christ" (*Colossians 2:8*). We can read about the risks brought on by the vulnerability of personal interpretations in the instructions given by the Apostle Paul to his young disciple Timothy: *"But avoid foolish and ignorant disputes, knowing that they generate strife"* (*2 Timothy 2:23*). About those who love this

kind of debate Saint Paul said, *"Remind them of these things, charging them before the Lord not to strive about words to no profit, to the ruin of hearers"* (*2 Timothy 2:14*).

POWER OF THINKING. The French metaphysician René Guénon wrote that man is essentially a thinking being and he cannot reach God without thinking. By meditation, man learns that he is God's image on one hand and God's reverse shadow on the other hand. Therefore, man is able to think of God through himself, i.e. through his natural perfection provided by the divine image and through his specific imperfection provided by the shadow.

In reference to the Pauline epistles, the Romanian Father Constantine Galeriu noticed that "we see now God as in a mirror; He is more of a guess. Only at the moment of our death we will be face to face with Him and will be able to see His real image." In other words, here on earth, we know God within limits; He is mirrored in that which is good inside us, while in the afterlife we will see Him directly and much closer.

Voltaire, the philosopher, had complained that the world annoyed him and looked like a watch without a watch repairer to take care of it. His words sounded humorous, to the delight of the free thinkers. Nevertheless, despite its wit, Voltaire's thought is false and even dangerous, because it includes in its structure a truth improperly used - the order and harmony of the creation.

LAWS OF THE LORD. God is order and harmony as His whole creation is. *"Your truth continues from generation to generation; You laid the foundation of the earth, and it continues. By Your arrangement each day continues, for all things are Your servants. If Your law were not my meditation, I would have perished in my humiliation"* (*Psalm 118/119: 90-*

92). We discover these in the form of physical and chemical laws and of moral laws – the laws of the spirit. Immanuel Kant felt a great admiration and awe for the starry heavens on the outside and for the Moral Law inside his soul.

Because of our ignorance, some of the laws of the spirit, despite the fact that the Bible has them firmly formulated, seem not to make much sense. If we do not respect them, we suffer the consequences not as a punishment, as many might think, but as a natural effect of ignoring the organizing principles of the creation. The parent tells his toddler that the flame will burn his finger if he touches it. The toddler does not believe it, and he touches the flame and suffers the consequences.

Not paying attention to the laws can lead to the destruction of our spiritual person. However, God may pull us to safety from the effect of the law because <u>God is not punishment but love</u>. He helps, rebuilds, and resets us in the proper place. If we put under the sign of eternity this entire equation, containing our rescue from the disaster induced by all the disrespected laws and from the tragedy of perpetual torture, and we add the reentrance into the original perfect order and harmony, we come to the term that the faithful call <u>salvation</u>.

"The law of God is in his heart, and his steps shall not be tripped up" (*Psalm 36/37:31*). *"If you love me, keep My commandments"* (*John 14:15*). God does not punish. He is just, which means He lets the laws of nature work. Nevertheless, He is also love because, even if we ignore it, He can save us from perishing, from falling away. We call this, with our earthly words, "mercy" and "forgiveness." Saint Isaac the Syrian expresses these meanings in his specific way, "Never say that God is just. If He were just, you would be in hell. Rely on His injustice which is mercy, love, and forgiveness" (see Coniaris, 1998).

THE VOICE OF CONSCIENCE. A rational manner of speaking about our responsibilities in relationship with God might be as follows. (**i**) The events and the structure of this world lead to the idea of the existence of a Universal Conscience above us who coordinates everything. Even the "chaos" and the "vague" were recently described in mathematical models. Nothing in this universe is fortuitous. (**ii**) Figuring out the imminent existence of this Universal Conscience, who governs the world, we can conclude that there is an inevitable interaction between Him in the heavens and us, who are part of this world. (**iii**) This relationship requires a certain responsibility from each side for its good functioning. Because our mind does not have the capacity to understand God's part of the responsibility, we have to be concerned only about our part. (**iv**) The way we will assume and, consequently, exercise our responsibility will eventually be examined at the Last Judgment, in a dialogue between our personal conscience and the Universal One.

Responsibility toward God does not mean self-justification for our daily activities as we usually do. "I take what is not mine or what I did not pay for, because no one notices"; "I take something from his belongings because he took much more from mine"; "I take because all people take"; "I take this thing from a store, I use it and I return it claiming that it is not good." All these excuses are condemning us.

A woman was detained in a psychiatric hospital in Russia because she was caught making the sign of cross and praying in a public place. She confessed that, while people are there in the hospital, deprived of liberty and lacking anyone whom they can trust, the only hope and friend is Our Lord Jesus. Unfortunately, after being released from the hospital, people change. They start to trust only their own forces again and forget God completely.

VULNERABILITY OF HUMAN ETHICS. Dmitri Karamazov is one of the main characters of the classic Russian writer Fyodor Dostoyevsky's novel "The Brothers Karamazov." When he was sentenced to twenty years of hard labor in Siberia, he talked with his younger brother, Alyosha Karamazov, before his departure. He asked, "What would happen if God does not exist and is merely an idea, invented by man? Then, if He does not exist, man is the master of the earth and the universe. Wonderful! How could then man be *good* without God? This is the question. To whom will a man address his love? To whom will he be grateful? To whom will he sing praise? Rakitin [the atheist] laughs; he says that you can love humanity without God's existence... Life is simpler, according to Rakitin. 'You had better to think of expanding civil rights or of keeping a low price on meat. This way you will show your love to humans much more directly than you can do with philosophy', he said. I replied, 'All right, but certainly you, without God, will raise the price of meat if you succeed in earning an additional ruble for each kopek'. He got angry. However, in fact, what is goodness? Answer me, Alexei. Goodness might mean something to me and another thing to a Chinese, so it is relative..." Do not these latter words sound like a strangely postmodernist and "politically correct" answer? Dostoyevsky prefigured that, with his visionary genius, when he wrote his novel "The Brothers Karamazov," a long time ago, in 1880!

Today in order to justify many ethical compromises we use a new terminology that apparently diminishes their deeply damaging effect. As Father Coniaris pointed out, nowadays we say "escorts" instead of prostitutes, we say "affair" instead of adultery, and we say "living together" instead of fornication (Coniaris, 2001). Living with a concubine is now named simply co-habitation or living together. Mia Farrow, defended the libertine behavior of Roman Polanski after his wife Sharon Tate's burial, by saying that, concerning men, we have to distinguish between "having an affair" and "having sex." Adultery is now excusable if it is used for obtaining a promotion or another kind of favor. Homosexuals congratulate themselves when they have the courage to declare publicly their choice of sexual life because they consider their option is something natural due to "their particular genetic structure."

Let us remember the parable of the prodigal son. When he decided to leave his home and family and to spend the money received from his father, he probably declared that he desired to see the world. While he was spending his time in debauchery and "prodigal living" (see *Luke 15:13*), he was very likely defining his style of life as a little spicy and piquant. However, the process of recuperation of his soul started as soon as he recognized the cause of his failure and told his father, "*I have sinned against heaven and before you*" (*Luke 15:18*).

It is very important for our spirit to cease floating in the *relativity* of our time. People say, "your good is good, and my good is good, regardless that it is different from yours." People forget that American society was built not on the confusion between good and evil and on tolerance for the lack of principles, but on a solid ethical attitude. As Father Coniaris commented, "If you disclose today an abuse, an unfair treatment, an injustice or an act of cheating, you risk being called a whistle blower and losing your job (Coniaris, 2001). The contemporary society has trended toward using what C.S. Lewis called *verbicides* - a kind of pesticides that destroy the word and especially *the truth* of the word.

As Father Coniaris wrote, by citing Paul Evdokimov, "If for the Greek philosopher Plato the opposite of truth was <u>error</u>, for the Gospel the opposite of truth is <u>lies</u> (i.e. the negation of the true nature of the human being). They *"exchanged the truth of God for the lie, and worshipped and served the creature rather than the Creator"* (*Romans 1:25*).

RISKS AND CONSEQUENCES. Father Thomas Hopko, who loved true short stories, told us that a priest was repeating in his sermons the appeal to sobriety and moral vigilance in order to avoid being *"cast out into the outer darkness"* where there *"will be weeping and gnashing of teeth"* (*Matthew 8:12*). Many people became tired of his insistence and stopped listening. A little old woman even protested, "Please, Father, let us alone with all these stupid threats about gnashing the teeth. Actually, if you want to know, I do not even have any teeth left. How could I still gnash?" With a kind smile the priest replied, "Madam, teeth will be provided."

There is nothing here to laugh about. This image about the darkness, torments, and *"furnace of fire"* (*Matthew 13:50*), appears several times in Our Lord's sermons. He mentioned it at least three times. The first was when He referred to those Jews, among the sons of the Kingdom, who disrespected the word that was given to them, in comparison with the many Gentiles who believed in Christ (*Matthew 8:12-13*). The second was when He spoke about the guests who came at the wedding dinner without a proper garment (*Matthew 22:12-14*); these words inspired the beautiful hymns at the Monday Vespers in Holy Week, "The bridal chamber I see adorned, O my Savior, and I have no wedding garment that I may enter. O Giver of Light, enlighten the vesture of my soul, and save me." The third was when He talked about the lack of multiplication of talents (*Matthew 25:29-30*). We have to respond to His call by living in faith, growing virtues, being never tired in prayers, keeping our soul clean, and being ready at any time to face the Savior.

THE UNKNOWN OF THE EVENTS. *"But I cried out to God; and the Lord heard me"* (*Psalm 54/55:17*). Who would think that the very powerful and sophisticated communist system would collapse one day? I cannot fully explain this even now after more than twenty-five years. It does not make sense at all and it is against any possible logic. It did not come as the effect of a revolution or of a catastrophic event. In many countries, it did not cause even a single droplet of blood. It did not result from the inner force generated by an extremely unbearable situation and it was not the consequence of the action of an overwhelming power from outside. In all the East European countries this radical change was produced by a simple coup d'état involving very small military forces, a coup d'état skillfully staged in a protest-like movement, happening as suddenly as a gust of wind that breaks tree limbs.

Many miracles can be described on a rational basis, and we might look for some reasons for this miraculous change of regime. One strong argument might be the great decline of a non-productive economic system, which made Gorbachev attempt to replace the old guard with one more flexible and receptive to the logistics of a capitalistic market, an attempt that turned against him and broke the entire communist pyramid. Who could imagine that such a solid construction built on terror during several decades, with such a giant self-protective structure, in which no one, from inside or outside, noticed the existence of a barely visible crack?

TOLLS OF LIFE. Everybody has to go through a trial during his life: the death of a dear person, a serious illness or a handicap, a catastrophic flood, a disastrous earthquake, a frightening accident, etc. At that moment, we feel our confidence blown to the wind. We are in despair. We pray to God with ardor in that emotional moment. Gradually our entire heart warms up and acquires an unknown strength from an unseen Power. We stop feeling that everything is unbearable. The soul leaves the difficulties behind and with courage remains on the rock of faith. It is like the experience a scientist has, launching himself in abstract hypotheses trusting the veracity of his conclusions. Then he begins comfortably to imagine the atoms and mesons in a microcosmic scale or the evolution of galaxies in a macrocosmic scale. Faith in God is the matter of life. People, even the ones closest to our heart, have weaknesses and limits and therefore we can count on them only partially. *"It is good to trust in the Lord, rather than to trust in man"* (*Psalm 117/118: 8*). We pray God for help when we are in danger, when we enter the unknown, when we are struck by an illness, a tragic event, or a misfortune. Despite the fact that we remain anxious, we feel a solid arm and shoulder we can lean on and this way we acquire the courage to go farther. We renounce our pride in being able to explain everything and we are joyful any time God reveals to us a deeper insight and understanding. We acquire the strength to stand the unpredictability of life.

LIFE LENGTH IS UNKNOWN. The church reminds us very frequently of the parable of the rich man who had an abundant yield on his land. He decided to enlarge his warehouses and, with enough food to store for many years, to take a break in order to enjoy a good and secure life (*Luke 12: 13-2*). A colleague of mine retired. His wife was very happy that, from that time on, they would be able to spend their annual vacation wherever they wanted and not in the boring places where he had "dragged" her in order to attend his professional conferences. Two years elapsed. The doctors discovered that her husband had colon cancer. The community hurried to honor him and inducted him into the local Hall of Fame. After a short while he died.

Another colleague retired with the great joy that he would passionately dedicate his entire time to his wooded acres. He planned gradually to cut down his pricey trees (around a thousand dollars each). This would enable him to live in peace without worrying about his income. He had worked that way half a year, but he was called back to his previous job for a temporary assignment. While he was at work, a terrible tornado destroyed the forest, blowing down the trees, breaking their branches and trunks, scattering and entangling them. After he returned to his retirement on his tree farm, he could recuperate only ten percent of the value of the wood after great effort. Very depressed, without the money he had so much counted on, he decided to move to another location.

Old age slows down the physical movements, wrecks the body, weakens the memory, trims the number of the living relatives and friends, and increases the loneliness. The intervals of suffering, pain, and weakness alternate with the intervals of quiet solitude, when the only sound in the room is made by the tic-tock of the clock and by the faint murmur of the TV set. God gives us this time for preparing our soul for the great departure. Little by little, the soul separates itself from the body and the surrounding world, and keeps only what it needs for entering eternity in the great beyond.

NEED OF CONTEMPLATION. The United States has a short history. Although less noticeable, the rhythm imposed by the Americans to their life in the last century, does not "create" history anymore. Living in the present is so intense that the news of yesterday speedily becomes the past. Unfortunately, this past turns quickly into irrelevancy because actually no one has time to analyze and incorporate it into the history of the nation. The reporters mention records of the football or ' ¬ball players or flood the media with details from the life of the rock singers or movie stars, but very few people really look behind appearances to understand the road the society has gone down and to use this in order to seize the deep meaning of the present.

In this sense, the catholic priest James Kinney commented that technology took giant steps from one day to the next in saving time and in increasing the efficiency of every positive action. However, ironically, the Americans of today have less time to catch and contemplate the very moment they are in, than the time they had before, when the work was physically very hard, the day was long and exhausting, and there was no break. James Kinney said that, despite the fact that we are the most productive country in the world, joy and peace are strangers to us. We need leisure for thinking in peace of the values that absorb and blot out ceaselessly the life of the present, and for envisioning a future that never arrives.

BEING ALONE WITH ONESELF. Father Roman Braga (deceased in 2015) suffered much persecution under the Romanian communist regime, being detained eleven years. He confessed, in an interview, to Father Dinu Cruga, "Before going to prison I had not decided about what to do with my life, and I think that's why God put me into prison" (Braga, 1996).

He was alone for very long periods in a bare bones cell, "surrounded by four walls," like a solitary. I wrote somewhere about the great happiness of a prisoner who managed to pull a knot out of the wooden door and to put it back carefully as soon as he heard the approaching steps of the guardian. Through the knothole, he could see a little bit of the outdoors! It was a matter of loneliness and solitude. Life often brings people into a state of loneliness. This leads to depression because the human being is a social being. Every political prisoner will say that no physical or psychological torture is more unbearable than the punishment in being alone, when you cease to know what day and hour it is, when you start to float in the unknown, when a huge uncertainty floods your mind, and a violent desire for seeing something alive devours your heart. The privilege to see a fly or a cockroach gives you torrents of hope, greater incentives to live. The solution for survival is to keep your mind active, to discipline the memory, and to maintain agility of thought. But, as Father Roman Braga said, the people who "tried to kill time thinking of theories and philosophies, mathematics and so on, went crazy" after a while. This is because, despite the fact that they did not allow themselves to fall into laziness and into a slow death of the mind, heart and body, their mental exercise was still oriented outwards. Father Braga said that it is a good thing that you have to direct your mind somewhere pulling you out of the killing inertia, but first "you have to go inside and <u>find who you are</u>."

This means, I think, to transform the loneliness into solitude, into a state of introspection, analysis and creativity. Solitude is, as I wrote in other places, a part of a cyclic process a person has to go through during his life span. A social episode is followed by an episode of solitude before entering the social episode again. The solitude assimilates our own experience acquired in the interactive social environment, enlarges the knowledge of ourselves, reevaluates our strengths and weaknesses, analyzes our goals, clarifies the meanings of life, defines the responsibilities, and returns our renewed, soul-enriched person to society. Father Roman extended the depth of introspection into spirituality, into our very being. He wrote, "There is no way of understanding yourself if you do not discover God there, because <u>God is the seal of our personality</u>."

MEANING OF LIFE. By discerning the presence of God in ourselves, we can discover our actual mission in this world and it depends on us if, with our own free will, want to accomplish it. Father Roman wrote, "I believe in God. When He brought someone into this world, He had determined in advance, what he would become. He said to Jeremiah the Prophet, *'I consecrated you as a prophet before you were conceived in your mother's womb' (Jeremiah 1:5)*."

It is true that faith helps us to pass easier through our life, but the main contribution of faith is to lead us to a better understanding of the meaning of life. As we grow in this world, our parents teach us how to avoid dangers. We learn what we should eat and drink, and how to maintain a healthy mind in a healthy body. We are taught good ethical principles and we start to apply and defend them, accomplishing our social duty in a decent and honest way. Later we hear the Lord's call and we realize that what we learned is not enough for a good life. We hear that there is another life beyond the life we live now and, if we do not change our life style, we are condemned to a very difficult future after the end of this earthly life. We are warned that we will be facing Judgment and it depends on us how we prepare ourselves spiritually *here* in this world for the defense *there*, and that it is the Supreme Judge's decision how we should spend our eternal time – in peace or in torment.

"For behold, I was conceived in transgressions, and in sins my mother bore me" (Psalm 50/51:7). "For I know my lawlessness, and my sin is always before me... Behold, You love the truth, You showed me the unknown and secret things of Your wisdom" (Psalm 50/51: 5 and 6). The Revised Standard Version stresses in a wonderful way that all these things happen in the depth of our own soul: *"Behold, thou desirest truth in the inward being; therefore teach me wisdom*

in my secret heart" (*Psalm 51:6*). Listening to Our Lord Jesus Christ, we discover that the body, mind, and heart trespass even without our knowledge. Saint Apostle John wrote, "*If we say that we have not sinned, we make Him a liar and His word is not in us*" (*1 John 1:10*). By faith, we understand the state of the first man's existence and the actual structure of the human being that man lost by the original sin. We find out that, as we are now, we retain a denatured structure and the meaning of our life is the struggle to regain the initial human nature. This restored nature will be enriched by the consequences of the Son of God's incarnation, sacrifice, and victory over death.

We look at the monastic "podvig" (the Orthodox Russian term for "spiritually righteous struggle"), at the terrible deprivation and at the ascetic rules that the monks and nuns voluntarily obey. These ascetics, who are God's angels on this earth, accept much suffering such that, by its great dimensions, seems to be overwhelming for our ordinary manner of living, but it actually reflects the correct measure of how far our present denatured human soul has fallen from the state in which it was created. The monks mortify their body in order to liberate their spirit, to let it ascend toward God. They do not battle with the body itself but with the temptations that the body has to endure, with the evil spirits that attack the soul through the weakness of the body.

In his letter to Simeon Yanovsky, Saint Herman quoted the words of Saint Apostle Paul: "*For we do not wrestle against flesh and blood, but against principalities, against powers, against the rulers of the darkness of this age*" (*Ephesians 6:12*). The ascetics' prayers help the laymen's own spiritual work. The power of the spiritual work of the monastic laborers and hermits are the secret heart of the human population of this world and straighten our road to the Lord and advocate for us, asking Him to make our cross endurable and to help us in our own restoration of the soul.

THE INNER LIFE. Fortunately, the theology of the traditional Christian church did not suffer from the powerful erosion that the elapse of time usually causes. Here prayer plays an important role. On one hand, during the storm of the day's action, we say the Jesus Prayer using the short form or we just call Jesus' or Theotokos' name, with the specific emotion, hope, care, concern, or panic of the moment. On the other hand, in the silence of our home after work or as we fall asleep at night, we say our prayers with a slow pace. We also pray within the Christian community at the Sunday Liturgy, as a weekly breath for our soul. All these bring peace into the heart, keep clearly in mind the goals of our spiritual being, and fill us with the mysterious joy of life and the fortifying thrill of eternity. God's attributes are love, light and peace, and they never leave our inner universe.

Despite their fragility, being shorter than a fraction of a second, the subliminal commercials on TV or in movies succeed, by a steady repetition, to influence our subconscious and eventually our consciousness. Likewise, the short prayer that calls God's name, repeated many times will end by conferring a much desired force and comfort to our soul. It is similar to the short pauses of a fraction of a second between the heart's pulsations that provide the energy necessary to our heart to keep us alive over two billion seconds – the length of a ninety-year life.

TO LIVE WITH GOD. If we deny God's presence, our "gods" will be the movie stars or the sport champions. The communist regime knew very well the need of the human soul to venerate something. Therefore, the atheism that the Russian government fed the simple people was the imposed idolatry for Lenin and for the leader of the époque. The newlyweds adopted the tradition of having a picture taken in front of Lenin's mausoleum or, if they did not have enough money to fly to Moscow, in front of the Monument of the Soviet Soldier in the city they lived in. To the more sophisticated people, the communist regime offered for veneration classic poets and musicians, whose literary and musical creations could be easily presented according to the Marxist principles, since the composers and writers were already dead and unable to protest the misinterpretations of their writings or compositions.

To live with God and to die with God – this should be the goal of any Christian. Thomas, the disciple of Jesus, showed much courage and devotion when he decided to follow his Master, despite all the dangers (*John 11:16*). We should live with God not as with an equal fellow, as with a partner, but as with a parent who is the master of the house. "*The fear of the Lord increases days, but the years of the ungodly will be shortened*" (*Proverbs 10:28*). Indeed, if we live, we live with Him and if we die, we die with Him. The real length of our life is, as Saint Paisius of Neamţ noted, the very period we were with Him. Life can be rich even if its number in calendar years might be short.

UNDERSTANDING GOD AND LIFE. Our Lord said, "*He who has seen Me has seen the Father... Do you not believe that I am in the Father and the Father in Me?*" (*John 14:9-10*). In this regard, Pascal wrote that through Jesus Christ we understand not only God, but also *ourselves.* More than that, through Jesus Christ, we also understand the real sense of life and death.

Without the incarnation of the Son of God, we would not have been able to find our mission, to decipher our own nature and to define the meaning of life. Let us try to find, without stumbling, the meaning of the double nature of Our Lord Jesus who is at the same time 100 percent God, and 100 percent man. Saint Paul said, "*[He] made Himself of no reputation, taking the form of a bondservant, and coming in the likeness of men. And being found in appearance as a man, He humbled Himself and became obedient to the point of death, even the death of the cross. Therefore, God also has highly exalted Him and given Him the name which is above every name, that at the name of Jesus every knee should bow, of those in heaven, and of those on earth, and of those under the earth, and that every tongue should confess that Jesus Christ is Lord, to the glory of God the Father... For it is God who works in you both to will and to do for His good pleasure*" (*Philippians 2:7-11 and 13*). This Epistle text is rich and deep, full of satisfactory answers, but also of very dangerous traps for those who are daring to read and interpret the message by themselves without listening to the Holy Fathers' teachings.

Without Our Lord Jesus Christ's resurrection, we cannot understand the meaning of death and we cannot transcend its limits. The Easter hymn is always alive in the Christians' heart: "Christ is risen from the dead trampling down death by death."

SOME STILL WONDER. The teenagers ask often, "How can I trust something that I do not see?" The physicists talk about mass and energy, but while we can see the first we cannot see the latter. Basically, the thermodynamic principles are extremely abstract if we do not extrapolate with hypotheses and audacious logic the very little we can apprehend with our senses. We trust the geologists who teach us about the past of earth, the seismologists about the subterranean plates, the cosmologists about black holes and the big bang. How much can we <u>actually see</u> of all these?

Saint Dionysius the Areopagite said, "God is <u>invisible</u> because He is everywhere," and, because we cannot look at the same time in all directions around us, it is impossible to see Him. Saint Paul comes with another argument: *"For we were saved in this hope, but hope <u>that is seen</u> is not hope. For why does one still hope for what he sees? But if we hope for what <u>we do not see</u>, we eagerly wait for it with perseverance"* (*Romans, 8:24-25*). Saint Augustine sent us a very powerful message that was accepted by both traditional churches - Orthodox and Catholic: "Faith is to believe what <u>you do not see</u>; truth is <u>to see</u> what you believe."

"The Lord is my helper; I shall not be afraid of what man will do to me" (*Psalm 117/118: 6*). Is it not so how we should feel Theodore Roethke's verse "In a dark time <u>the eye begins to see</u>"? His well-known poem "In a Dark Time" ends with the verses: "A fallen man, I climb out of my fear. / The mind enters itself, and God enters the mind, / And one is One, free in the tearing wind."

KNOWLEDGE AND MYSTERIES. Father Coniaris, mentioned the example of the renowned American philosopher Dr. Mortimer Jerome Adler (Coniaris, 2001). He became Christian in 1984 when he was 82 years old and renounced searching anymore for a complete explanation of all mysteries. If the mysteries could have been fully understood, his brilliant mind would have elaborated a new philosophy. However, religion is not a philosophical system. The things that faith promotes are beyond logical proofs, but not beyond disproving. So are the mysteries of the Christian tradition: The Holy Trinity, the Incarnation of the Son of God, and the Resurrection of Our Lord Jesus.

The Bible is apparently full of unclear details. Jesus' existence unfolded exactly as it was predicted in the Old Testament, but this was not obvious at first sight. For instance the leaders in the synagogue knew that the Savior, the Messiah, had to come from Bethlehem but Christ, Who was born in Bethleem, eventually came from Nazareth, where the Holy Family had settled after returning from Egypt (see *John 7:40-42*).

A protestant church commentator said, "We have to learn to live with mysteries, doubts, and incertitude." However, as we will advance in our inner work of faith and prayer, we will start to see life as a manifestation of a rich, ubiquitous, and continuous presence of God, and this will increase our degree of certitude. Saint John Chrysostom wrote that we should be happy with the little that we can comprehend, which is like the lightning that, although it is not a consistent light, it provides us sufficient amount of light to see for a moment in the darkness of the night. The revelation experienced only for an instant then will feed our spirit, mind, and heart for a long time.

CATAPHATIC AND APOPHATIC. According to Lossky, the theology of the Catholic Church is affirmative and proceeds cataphatically in knowing God through reasoning, bringing God down to the level of discursive demonstrations (Lossky, 1997). By contrast, the theology of the Orthodox Church is negative and apophatic, refusing the logic of the limited mind as an exclusive tool, because to know God fully is possible only by faith that eventually can attract the Lord's gift of the necessary grace of knowledge of the Truth. The negation of the negation can take us beyond the limits of our human reasoning. Even the great Catholic theoretician Saint Thomas Aquinas considered it necessary to complete the cataphatic procedure of logical explanations with the apophatic procedure through living the divine mysteries. This way, the affirmative manner will express "res significata," while the negative manner will try to express the "modus significandi."

The stage of knowing God can be achieved cataphatically with the mind and apophatically with the heart, but despite our efforts many meanings will remain hidden.

PRAYER AS A TOOL. The Metropolitan Anthony Bloom of Sourosz, wrote that while meditation is an activity of thought, prayer is the rejection of thought (Bloom, 1970). Prayer is our main way of being closer to God. It is our communication with Him by faith. Father Kallistos concluded that man is not only an animal armed with the power of a logical mind that makes him very creative in manufacturing necessary tools. He is also an animal able to pray - "a Eucharistic animal" who controls the world and returns it with gratitude and supplications to God. Because, as Father Kallistos said, the Lord did not create the human person only to think and talk, but also to pray, prayer being the main means of communication between man's soul and God.

We search for God's Word that is *"not as the word of men, but as it is in truth, the word of God, which also effectively works"* in those who believe (*1 Thessalonians 2:13*). In our prayers, we try to catch the rich meaning in the shadow of the words, the silent pause behind the words, making the effort to reach a complete concentration and alertness of our soul. There are hidden things in these words. We cannot treat them carelessly; we cannot play with them and we cannot change them. We have to listen to them attentively and, if we obey what they ask for, they will strengthen us. Christ said, *"Whoever hears these sayings of Mine, and does them I will liken him to a wise man who built his house on the rock; and the rain descended, the floods came, and the winds blew and beat on that house; and it did not fall, for it was founded on the rock"* (*Matthew 7:24-25*).

BELIEF AND PRAYER. The French philosopher and mathematician Blaise Pascal brought forth an interesting argument of an apologetic philosophical nature. In his "Pensées" he suggested a bet about the benefit the belief in God can offer to our ordinary life. In his argumentation, Pascal considered the answer to two questions: *"Does God exist?"* and *"Do I believe?"* He concluded that if God exists, any reasonable person should believe in God. He also concluded that if, in the contrary case, God does not exist, the believing person will still benefit because he will not lose anything essential but will keep his spirit in a certain balance.

Back in communist Romania, a colleague, the son of a colonel highly approved by the government, passing by an orthodox church, made the sign of cross according to an old Christian custom. We asked him very surprised, "How come, do you believe in God?" He answered shyly, "I know what we are taught in school. Theoretically, God does not exist. However, I have a faint doubt. Therefore I decided that I had better cross myself." Here he was! Depending on Pascal's famous wager! If you lose, you do not lose anything important but if you win, you win everything.

Let us replace the question "Do I believe" with one with a practical purpose, meaning action: "Should I pray?" Then Pascal's wager will lead us to the conclusion that we should pray, no matter what others say. If God exists, we benefit, without risking eternal punishment. If God does not exist, we just do a mental exercise, which does not bring us any harm, keeps our brain in good shape and gives us a moral support in our life. Father Kallistos said that man is a "praying being."

Our life is short and fragile. The hope in the Lord nurtures us and we feel like Saint Paul – when we are weaker in ourselves, we are stronger in God by prayer and trust. *"For God has not given us a spirit of fear, but* [a spirit] *of power and of love and of a sound mind" (2 Timothy 1:7).*

URGENCY OF SOUL. Having in it the breath of God, our soul longs for Him. Unfortunately, we often are unaware of this continuous thirst. However, as soon as the mind makes the connection to God's call, a state of urgency animates the heart. Saint Augustine was baptized by Saint Ambrose, bishop of Milan, on Easter night in the year 387, but he bitterly regretted that he had been far from God for a very long time. In his "Confessions" Saint Augustine wrote, "I was slow in turning to God. I postponed from one day to the other my decision to set my life on You, but I did not scare away the death that was killing daily something in me. I was in love with the idea of a happy life but I was afraid to search for happiness in her very place. I wanted her by running from her. I thought I would be unendurably unhappy if I should be deprived of the women's embraces and I never thought of Your love as of a drug to heal this weakness, for the simple fact that I never tried. I am sending these bitterly sad words to You above: How long? How long? Why not now?" (see St. Augustine, 1984)

Saint Herman of Alaska felt the same urgent need of God as the lungs needed air, when he told the sailors, "For our own good, for our own luck, let us at least promise that from this very day, very hour, very minute, we shall try to love God more than anything else and to obey to His Holy Will!"

Is not the speed of the response the disciples had at Christ's call a significant fact? *"And Jesus, walking by the Sea of Galilee, saw two brothers, Simon called Peter, and Andrew his brother, casting a net into the sea; for they were fishermen.*

Then He said to them, 'Follow Me, and I will make you fishers of men.' They immediately left their nets and followed Him" (*Matthew 4:18-20*). The same happened with the other two brothers, James and John. He called them and *"immediately they left the boat and their father, and followed Him"* (*Matthew 4:22*).

FAITH STRENGTHENS THE SOUL. Despite the fact that we cannot foresee any possible way the Lord could rescue us, He will do it. Even if He does not rescue us, He will give us the necessary fortitude to endure, and He will not let us lose our soul. Shadrach, Meshach, and Abednego told the king Nebuchadnezzar, *"There is a God in the heavens, Whom we serve, and He is able to save us from the burning fiery furnace; and He will deliver us from your hands, O king. But if not, let it be known to you, O king, that we will not serve your gods, nor worship the golden image you set up"* (*Daniel 3: 17-18*). Their words sounded, in a real sense, like a deep and ardent prayer. As Father Thomas Hopko from Saint Vladimir's Seminary commented, regardless what God decides for us, it will be for our good. This way of thinking provides to any Christian the needed strength for going through the trials of life with an undamaged soul.

When the American soldiers were fighting in the world wars on European territory, their interior support was many times their faith in God. During WWII, the cunning Stalin opened the churches to the people, in order to strengthen the courage of the civilians and soldiers for their retaliation against the Germans. This decision sounds extremely odd, if we think of the harsh persecution the clergy and believers had suffered in the Soviet Union before the war. When I defected from the communist regime of my native country, going into a completely unknown world and risking everything including my life, someone reminded me that my faith in God would keep me strong and would provide the best way for a better life for me and my family, and he was right.

Sometimes, after celebrating a religious Holiday preceded by a rather severe fasting period, we feel a certain force in us. This force is not caused much by the fact that our soul acquired a greater ability in the battle against temptations, but by a mysterious and silent Presence different from our own being. This Presence abides persistently in us as a steady encouragement and a caring support.

THE SPIRITUAL GROWTH inside us takes place by blending our life experience with what we are learning from God's teachings. Our doubting mind illuminated for one second and our cold heart warmed up for another second knock often but unsuccessfully at the gate of our soul's fortress. However, at the very time the Lord decides it is appropriate, the gate opens, the fortress is shaken, and our soul ignites on fire. This revelation occurs for some people in their youth making them fervent Christians, while others need to pass through many trials in order to reach the firmness of faith. Prison or deportation in the Eastern European communist countries, defection from them to the free West, illness, death of a dear person - all these events make our soul tremble and bring it nearer to God, preparing the ground for the time of revelation.

The words that had a tremendous impact on Saint Augustine's soul, setting it on fire, were those Saint Paul wrote to the Romans: *"And do this, knowing the time, that now it is high time to awake out of sleep, for now our salvation is nearer than when we first believed"* (*Romans 13; 11-14*). It happened in the garden in August 386. Saint Augustine was 32 years old. How powerful was this moment for Blaise Pascal!

"Certitude, heartfelt joy, peace…" was written in his Memorial piece of paper on the 23rd of November 1654, sewn in the lining of his vest, in order to be with him everywhere and at all times. At that time, his age was 31.

THE PEACE GIVEN BY THE LORD is more than a lack of anxiety, more than a wall protecting us from any outside aggression. It is more than the simple words "peace" and "non-aggression" suggest. It is the beneficial light of the Kingdom of God, which restores harmony within the creation. It is the joy of perceiving the beauty and the order of things. It is a relief from worrying about evil. It is the peace that spreads out from the altar, from the holy sacrifice of the Savior, from the Eucharist at the Divine Liturgy. It flows out from the Word of God. "Let us listen to the Holy Gospel. Peace be unto all," we hear at the Liturgy. This peace comes by reciprocity from our response to the act of offering praise. The priest says, "Let us stand aright! Let us stand with fear! Let us attend, that we may offer the Holy Oblation in peace." And we reply, "A mercy of peace! A sacrifice of praise!" It is the peace coming from prayer – "Again and again in peace let us pray to the Lord"; from the humility - "Peace be to all… Let us bow our heads to the Lord"; and from the love for our neighbor - "Peace be to all… Let us love one another, that with one mind we may confess." It is the peace that remains with us after the Liturgy ends: "Let us depart in peace…In the name of the Lord."

Trials of life become more endurable if we commit ourselves to faith in God, the. "*Therefore, having been justified by faith, we have peace with God through our Lord Jesus Christ through Whom we have also have access by faith into this grace in which we stand, and rejoice in hope of the glory of God. And not only that, but we also glory in tribulations, knowing that tribulation produces perseverance; and perseverance character; and character, hope. Now hope does not disappoint…" (Romans 5:1-5)*. Gradually and unknowingly, the journey of our life will build up strength in our spirit and will let us feel the bliss of the bright shadows of God. *"The Kingdom of God is as if a man should scatter seed on the ground, and should sleep by night and rise by day, and the seed should sprout and grow, he himself does not know how"* (*Mark 4:26-29*).

1.2. What is the Sense of Our Daily Life?

LIFE'S UPS AND DOWNS. Sometimes it is difficult to figure out the real sense of our life. We cannot see the forest because of the trees. *"As you do not know the way of the wind or how the bones grow in the womb of her who is with child, so you do not know the works of God even all things whatever He will do"* (*Ecclesiastes 11:5*). One can study and describe the growth of a fetus but not actually explain (and reproduce) it. We can feel and live the events of our lives but we might not comprehend why they occur. Very likely, we might remain in this state of ignorance, if we continue to shape our lives according to our will and not to the will of God. By doing so, we fail in maintaining the health of our spirit and we risk losing our soul. The greatest danger is not outside but within us.

Life's ups and downs can lead us to a hardly escapable confusion. In order to have a clear view we have to ascend above the trees of the forest. The Lord fills our existence with a huge variety of events. Those who complain that life is boring are not paying enough attention to the nuances of their own daily events and to what happens to the other people around them. *"The Lord makes poor and rich. He brings low is up"* (*1 Samuel/1 Kingdoms 2:7*). It is remarkable that changes in our life come from Him, the Lord, who *never changes*. This is why, when invaded by successive events in harmony or in contradiction with each other, we can find stability by contemplating the unmoved Divine Source of our movements. We learn to know Him by faithfully contacting His emanating energies. These energies are present in the Creation but they are not part of the Creation. They are "uncreated" as Saint Gregory Palamas wrote, because they belong to God who is the Creator Himself.

The suffering that God gives us throughout our life (obstacles, poverty, injuries, sickness, handicaps, losses, death of our friends, prison, hurricane, earthquakes, etc.) warns us about the need to direct our existence toward Him, and to accelerate the process of our spiritual maturation. Often we do not pay attention to this warning. Therefore, the Lord as a good teacher repeats it patiently, but at the same time he careful avoids any risk of overloading us or causing an irreversible damage to our spirit.

PHILOSOPHY OF LIFE. Surely, a well-balanced humanistic philosophy of life considers that a less favorable event will always find a counter weight in a more favorable one. This kind of philosophy provides the energy the spirit needs in order to survive in difficult times. However, this philosophy is based on the logic of the mind, and we know that one of the human mind's main tools used in acquiring knowledge is the process of doubt. "Dubito, ergo cogito, cogito, ergo sum" (I doubt, therefore I think, I think, therefore I am). This is how the philosophical statement proposed by René Descartes sounds. Unfortunately, doubt can act as a boomerang and destroy the scaffolding of our thinking. The result is a deep sadness, leading to an attitude of giving up or despair. Let us think of the strength of the Christian martyrs that had to undergo the most unimaginable and horrifying tortures. They had no doubts. They had faith and that gave them strength and wisdom!

"How precious also are Thy thoughts unto me, O God! How great is the sum of them! If I should count them, they are more in number than the sand. When I awake, I am still with Thee" (*Psalm 139: 17-19*, King James Version). The way our life unfolds is a secret that is known only by God. Many of us suffer terrible diseases or heavily damaging losses, become handicapped or victims of atrocities, undergo unstoppable physical pain. All these can be a natural consequence of our sins and this is why a physical healing is granted only if we are forgiven for our trespasses. They also can represent our part of martyrdom decided by God for our salvation.

IS THERE A HUMAN FATE? Some of us would like to know ahead of time what life has in store for us as in the Romanian folk tales wherein the emperor hears everything from the fate-determining fairies gathered around the cradle of his newborn son. Certainly, this thing is impossible in our ordinary life and the Church reproves us when we try to learn about our future by approaching fortunetellers and astrologists for our own amusement while also wondering about consulting palm readers or interpreters of dreams, or worse, consulting witches about seriously evil matters. The Church is not happy either when we are interested in spiritualism. Some saints and others that the Lord loves have the gift of foreseeing and they warn us about future dangers. However, even if miraculously, an old and wise person calls us aside and tells us our whole destiny in order to help us to be prepared, it is not the best for us. We can read in *Acts 16:16-18* about *"a certain slave girl"* who had *"a spirit of divination"* and *"brought much profit by fortune-telling."* She followed Saint Paul, annoying him. The Apostle *"turned and said to the spirit, 'I command you in the* *name of Jesus Christ to come out of her'."* And *"it came out that very hour."* It is not our business to know our destiny. This belongs to God. We only pray and act as we feel in accordance with His will, being ready to receive and live with whatever He sends us.

The Romanian writer Pericle Martinescu meditated about "human fate" in one of his diaries, when he described a dramatic event that his friend, an officer in the Romanian army, experienced during WWII. It happened in the night of the seventh of May 1944 during the bombardment by the American airplanes on Bucharest. The officer was rushing in a car to the military headquarters when he saw a woman scared to death, dressed only in a nightgown, running in great despair along the street to the shelter. He asked the sergeant who was driving to stop the car and they took her with them. Almost instantly thereafter, a bomb fell right in front of them, so all three jumped out and ran into the basement of a house. Another bomb destroyed the car. The woman became hysterical, crying and shaking. Holding tight the officer's arm she repeatedly thanked him that he saved her life. Nevertheless, not before long, a bomb fell on the very house they took as a shelter, and a beam collapsed killing the woman and the sergeant. The officer escaped untouched and reached the headquarters without any other problems.

As it will be discussed in the following chapters "the human fate" is a result of the co-action of the man's independence of decision and God's will. However the Lord can see forward what will happen and it is for the good of man not to know the future.

ROLE OF CONSCIENCE. Origen emphasized the fact that, besides the exterior testimony of our mind, there is *"the testimony of our conscience that we conducted ourselves in the* *world in simplicity and godly sincerity, not with fleshy wisdom but by the grace of God"* (*2 Corinthians 1:12*). Our conscience is the voice of God. The parents know that their children will rebel when they reach the teenage years, and will not apply anymore the rules of life they were taught. However, the parents have planted and grown a conscience in the soul of their children, and they are confident that this conscience will remain inside them to watch over the purity of their children's future life.

TRUST IN GOD. Saint Apostle Paul wrote, *"For me to live is Christ and to die is gain"* (*Philippians 1:21*). This does not mean that we should want our death. It means that dying to all other things that are not related to Our Lord is highly beneficial. Let us not forget that our life spent a Christian way means, as St. Paul wrote, to be *"hard-pressed between the two"* - the fruit of our labor and the care for our neighbor on one hand, and the love for Christ on the other.

Walking with His words in our mind and with His light in our heart, we acquire courage. Our Lord said to His disciples, *"Are there not twelve hours in the day? If anyone walks in the day, he does not stumble, because he sees the light of this world. But if any one walks in the night, he stumbles, because the light is not in him"* (*John 11:9-10*). With this in mind, Thomas, despite the fact that all the Apostles had to go into Judea where there was an imminent danger to be stoned to death, audaciously told the others, *"Let us also go, that we may die with Him"* (*John 11:16*).

Let us also go confidently into risky places, with our interior eyes pointing firmly toward the heavens, if we know that what we are going to do is good. I remember the American movie "A Bridge Too Far", made in 1977, based on the outstanding book with the same name, written by Cornelius Ryan. It was about the Operation Market-Garden in the

Netherlands in WWII. Crossing the Waal River, under the frighteningly dense fire of the Germans, the American officer who was in command of the troops in the boats called unceasingly the name of the Mother of God at each stroke of the oar and arrived unhurt at the shore despite the fact that the wind had dissipated the protecting smoke cover. The importance of prayer is a serious matter. In another sequence of the movie, we hear an interesting dialogue between two Germans, "We are in a battle and we are going to win it," said one, and the other replied, "We do not care about winning or losing but about living or dying."

A good friend of mine told me that many times, being on the verge of falling to his death while climbing in the mountains, he repeated in mind the Jesus Prayer, in the rhythm of his heavy breathing and under the effect of an adrenaline high. This helped him to concentrate on each step and pulled him safely out of trouble. *"Fear not, for I am with you. Do not go astray, for I am your God who strengthens you; and I will help and secure you with My righteous right hand"* (*Isaiah 41:10*). *"For thou hast been a strength to the poor, a strength to the needy in his distress, a refuge from the storm, a shade from the heat, when the blast of the terrible ones is as a storm against the wall"* (*Isaiah 25:4*, King James Version. See also *Psalm 9:10*). Lord *"will shepherd us unto the ages"* (*Psalm 47/48:15*).

The well-known Christian moralist Charles Spurgeon emphasized the importance of having a cicerone in our life: we want him while we are young; we enjoy him while we are in middle age and we find comforting peace in him when we are old. In the Akathist Hymn to Our Lord we address Christ with the following words: "Jesus, Protector of mine infancy/ Jesus, Guide of my youth/ Jesus, Boast of mine old age/ Jesus, my

Hope at death/ Jesus, my Life after death/ Jesus, my Comfort at Your judgment."

HUMAN MIND AND MIRACLES. The human mind very often can progress in knowledge by a mechanism where doubts force the retesting of an old hypothesis and generate a new one. *Dubito ergo cogito, cogito ergo sum* is the formula promoted by the philosopher René Descartes. But God's spiritual world is a world very different from the deformed one in which we have been raised and in which we have learned to live. God's realm has a different logic and its "arguments" sound strange to us. Therefore, we call them miracles. The Romanian neuroscientist Gheorghe Marinescu, tried to explain, as a process of self-suggestion and hypnosis, all the miraculous healings that occurred in Maglavit in 1935, in the presence of the illiterate shepherd Petrache Lupu, a very humble man who claimed that he talked in a vision with God.

The human mind cannot stay long in the same place. The mind checks every moment to see if things are in accord with what it has previously concluded. Jesus asked the crowds, *"O faithless generation, how long shall I be with you? How long shall I bear with you?"* (*Mark 9:19*). He was exasperated that people remained restricted to their weak logic and did not want to make the jump to faith. *"Unless you people see signs and wonders, you will by no means believe"* (*John 4:48*. See also *John 12:37* and *Matthew 13:58*).

Even when it is awe-stricken and convinced by the uncommon healing of the sick or by the multiplication of loaves and fish, the human mind does not delay its doubts for long. Perhaps it was the same people who had heard about Lazarus' resurrection and had come to celebrate Our Lord's entrance into Jerusalem who later shouted, "Crucify him!" Not only the crowds but also the disciples themselves, direct witnesses of

Christ's miracles, had their hesitation and lack of receptivity. *"They had not understood about the loaves because their heart was hardened"* (*Mark 6:51-52*). Before reading in the Gospel about Thomas' doubts (see *John 20:25*), we find out that the other disciples had their own doubts about the appearance of Our Lord in their midst after His Resurrection, *"They were terrified and frightened, and supposed they had seen a spirit."* Seeing the Savior's very hands and feet, *"They still did not believe for joy, and marveled"* (*Luke 24:37, 41*).

"He could do no mighty work there, except that He laid His hands on a few sick people and healed them. And He marveled because of their unbelief" (*Mark 6:5-6*). This did not happen because Our Lord Jesus was incapable of miracles (as evidence He healed the sick), but because the people were not receptive to the transcendental meanings of His work. Miracles occur often in our common life but they pass unnoticed due to the insensitivity of our spirit. Someone once said that not only the favorable coincidence between two events, but also the time a certain event happens is actually a miracle, if we look back at it from the perspective of our lifespan.

BELIEVE WHAT IS HARD TO EXPLAIN. Let us remember that in an American court the jury can dismiss the defendant, not only because his lawyer proved that he is innocent but also because the accusation, brought by the district attorney, is not convincing enough and remains within a reasonable doubt. Yes, it might appear to be unreal that Peter walked on water. In fact the Gospel says that after a very short while he started to sink (*Matthew 14:30*). It might also seem unreal that Moses could split the Red Sea in two with a pathway through the middle. But what if this actually happened by the strong will of God? Do we have proofs that can demonstrate the opposite? Why not give these stories the benefit of the doubt?

We use the TV set and the computer without being able to explain in details how they function, but we trust the few people with knowledge of microprocessors and electronic systems. We press some buttons and follow their instructions and we can utilize these devices with visible results. Even more, we believe the explanation given to things that affect us but we cannot control such as earthquakes and hurricanes. We trust the geologists, geographers and meteorologists, for the mere fact that their arguments seem to be "logical." We also do not cease to believe in the theory of black holes and the big bang that do not affect us at all and that does bring very few concrete proofs. We believe it, due to the mere fact that we are genuinely passionate about the scientific novelty itself.

In the same way, the Athenians, always very eager to have new philosophical debates, gathered to listen to Saint Paul's sermon on the Areopagus' Hill (see *Acts 17:19-21*). However, they left him immediately when he began to talk about the resurrection of the dead. They considered that the chain of logical arguments exceeded a certain limit of credibility because these arguments did not appear to be as realistic to us as the visible earthquakes and hurricanes shown in today's television images. But what about the healings that Our Lord did? Did they not appear to be tangible evidence?

Then why not accept what the Savior and His Apostles said, as long as we do not argue to prove the contrary but merely present simple opinions based on our own limited experience? Why not consent to what they have told us, to pass over the threshold where we had stopped, to enter the "intangible" and *to believe*?

MIRACLES IN DAILY LIFE. The probability of the occurrence of the phenomena or events we call "miracles" might be around one in a million. The small ones, with a much higher frequency, are usually not noticed. The remarkable miracles occur at a very low rate but *they occur*. I remember something that I witnessed. One day, the moving axle of an agricultural machine caught a farm worker's cloth and, in a few moments, his neck was pulled into the rolling axle. Strangled, he lost his consciousness. The two-inch long safety nail of the machine axle was digging in his neck at each rotation, deeper and deeper. Someone saw him, disengaged the machine, stopped the tractor engine, cut the cloth, pulled him out, and applied PCR pressing his chest. The farm worker started to breathe, without regaining consciousness. After he was taken to the emergency room, the doctors noticed, with great astonishment, that the moments of suffocation did not damage the brain at all. Even more, to the doctors' great surprise, the tight pressure from the strangling cloth and the axle's digging action that had produced a large hole did not affect anything in the complex structure of a human neck. The trachea, esophagus, carotid artery, jugular vein, nerves, and cervical vertebrae - all were intact. The doctors refused to believe that nothing was harmed. They checked everything very carefully again and again. Yes, there was no harm or damage. Maybe there was an explanation of this miracle. The farm worker was a pious man, humble, God-fearing. His family and friends gathered in the waiting room, in that very frightful night while he slept in the emergency room, deep under the effect of sedatives. They spent all that time in intense prayers. These prayers proved to be answered prayers.

RELIGION AND CHURCH. A youth said, "Belief is something personal, religion is a system, church is an institution, and I do not have anything to do with them. I believe in God and this is enough." Simple faith can be genuine and can lead to ‾ ˩ but walking alone, by oneself, without religion and chur very risky because one's personal faith has ultimately to choose among many alternatives already existent and these alternatives, except one, are false in the manner they represent God. Man might be misled and might create a God for himself, a God who is according to his own taste and comfort, far from the real One. This makes his faith inefficient, useless and even disintegrating for his spirit. Faith without religion has no horizon, and does not cover every principle. It does not answer the questions that haunt us in the difficult moments of our existence, like those concerning the reason for being, moral values, significance of events, happiness, comfort, responsibility for the world around us, etc. We need a coherent system of understanding the world in order to place our particular faith within it. We do not need a philosophical system, despite its power of seduction. We need a system through which our faith can achieve a real and incontestable sense and be fruitful.

Church is not an institution. It might look so, by its physical presence and historical existence. However, it is actually an assembly of people united in spirit. It is, as the Christians used to say, "Christ's Body." Church is not an institution. It is the life of the community in Christ, the Son of God. It is a living organism, *it is a Christic conscience.*

One might wonder why there are no official commitments, no written obligations, no promises, and no vows, between two people who marry each other within the Orthodox Church. Does that mean that these people are not actually tied together and that they can very easily separate from each other because there is no constraint or coercion? The worldly way of reasoning requires well-justified measures of precaution such as prenuptial contracts. Our society learned from its bitter experience and made laws and rules that coordinate people's life within a community. It institutionalized marriage. By contrast, the orthodox Christian wedding does not impose any obligation between the bride and groom. However, such a religious marriage does not risk becoming a weak link, because it is not done between two persons but, actually, among three - man, woman, and God. It is the Lord Who ties the spouses together and, when the thought of separation comes because they do not like each other anymore and argue all the time, they hit that bridge between them, hard like a rock, which is God's presence and involvement. It is the Christic conscience that stops them from separation.

Again, faith alone is powerless and we deceive ourselves when we think it suffices by itself. Faith needs a "system" for understanding the world and assembling all the meanings in a harmonious unit, and needs an "institution" where it learns how to pray efficiently and to be closer to God, with the supplementary benefit of collective prayer.

LIVE AND DIE IN THE LORD. A catholic hymn says: "To live in the Lord is also to die in the Lord." Saint Marcelinus (deceased in 304) became Pope of Rome in the time of Diocletian's reign. During the terrible period of thirty days when the emperor's soldiers killed seventeen thousand Christians in Rome, the soldiers arrested Pope Marcelinus and brought him in front of the emperor. Frightened by the threat of abominable tortures and death, the Pope compromised and made a sacrifice to the idols' altar. Consequently, he was rewarded, dressed in expensive clothes, and installed among the highest rank of people around the emperor.

However, returning home, full of remorse, he cried bitterly that he had denied the Lord, as Saint Peter did while Our Lord Jesus was being prosecuted (*Luke 22:62*). The Pope dressed himself in coarse sackcloth and covered his body with ashes and went in deep humbleness to the synod of one hundred eighty bishops and priests from Sinuesa (Campania).

He repented with tears, received their severe judgment, and asked, as a punishment for his sin, not to be buried after his martyrdom. He strengthened his request by cursing those who, feeling pity for him, would try to take care of his dead body. Then he ran to Rome. He tossed the expensive clothes in front of the emperor. He witnessed his faith in God and audaciously criticized the emperor for paganism. He was tortured and beheaded together with other three Christians. Their bodies were left in the field outside the city, prey to the scavenging dogs and beasts.

God fearing people secretly took the bodies of the three other martyrs and buried them, but they were afraid to touch Saint Marcelinus's body because of the curse. Thirty-six days later, Saint Peter came in a dream of the new Pope, Marcellus, reproving him that they did not take care of Saint Marcelinus' corpse. Saint Peter said, "Do you not remember the Gospel words that the man who humbles himself will be raised up? Go and bury his body with honor." The Christian people piously went and buried the holy remains of the martyr in the cemetery of Priscilla.

We ask forgiveness from God for all the numerous people who were arrested for their faith and died in the communist prisons, including the weak ones who, destroyed by atrocious suffering, fell prey to doubts or lost their hope.

WHAT COUNTS THE MOST. According to the Patericon, some monks went to Abba Agathon and tried to make him lose his temper (Patericul, 1999a). They scoffed at him saying, "Are you not Agathon the fornicator full of pride?" He calmly and humbly replied, "Yes, I am." "Are you not Agathon the slanderer and gossiper?" Abba replied, "Yes, I am." They continued: "Are you not Agathon the heretic?" But Abba said, "No, I am not a heretic." Then they asked him why he accepted everything but the accusation of heresy. Abba told them, "I received the first accusations with gladness because they are helpful to my soul. However, heresy separates me from God and I do not want to be separated from Him." This can also be read in an English partial version of the Patericon (The Sayings of the Desert Fathers, 1975).

FRUITFUL WITH LORD'S HELP. After a man lives in faith for a while, he starts to uncover many previously hidden meanings. This happens suddenly, like the revealing light of the lightning in the dark, in the very instant when man experiences God's goodness and care in his life. *"Behold, thou desirest truth in the inward beings; therefore teach me wisdom in my secret heart" (Psalm 51:6,* Revised Standard Version). The Holy Spirit will open our eyes. *"No one knows the things of God except the Spirit of God. Now we have received not the spirit of the world, but the Spirit who is from God, that we might know the things that have been freely given to us by God" (1 Corinthians 2: 11-12).* Faith will lead us to comprehend matters otherwise inaccessible to the mind. *"I will give you understanding, and I will teach you in the way you should walk; I will fix My eyes on you" (Psalm 31/32:8).* We can ask God: "O Lord, enlighten me to grasp Your Will and give me strength to follow It."

"I am the true vine, and my Father is the vinedresser. Every branch in Me that does not bear fruit He takes away; and every branch that bears fruit He prunes, that it may bear more fruit... I am the vine, you are the branches. He who abides in Me, and I in him, bears much fruit, for without Me you can do nothing," said Our Lord Jesus Christ *(John 15:1-2,5).* The pruning and cleaning are done on us, the scions, by the events that invade us. The role of the events is to maintain and improve our spiritual yield. *"The Lord makes poor and rich; He brings low and lifts up" (1 Kingdoms/1 Samuel 2:7).*

All the changes we suffer as a person come from <u>a Person who never changes</u>. This Person has a Mind and a Heart that are above our limited knowledge. He cares for us and watches the evolution of our spirit, <u>making decisions for the necessary changes.</u> By spreading warnings along the road of our life, the Lord tries to warn us of the danger of losing our soul. Ignoring our soul might make us exercise our given freedom of choice in a wrong way and to follow a self-destructive direction. Consequently, we can risk being condemned at the Last Judgment. That time it will be too late to change anything and the sentence will be pronounced irrecusably. Jesus Christ said, *"Even now the ax is laid to the root of the trees. Therefore, every tree which does not bear fruit is cut down and thrown into the fire"* (*Luke 3:9*). When the people heard Our Lord's words, they were frightened and asked, *"What should we do then?"* The answer was a warm call to a virtuous life and to a good performance in everyone's work, to be done with conscientiousness and diligence, and with deep love for their neighbor (*Luke 3:11-14*).

Sometimes life is harsh. There is no bridge to pass over the tribulations. We have to go through the tempestuous river of life and confront its waves and depths. In this case, God's protecting presence is better than a boat. *"If you pass through water, I am with you; and the rivers shall not overflow you. If you pass through fire, you shall not be burned up. Nor shall the flame consume you"* (*Isaiah 43:2*).

Saint Gregory of Nyssa reminded us of Our Lord Jesus' call: *"Follow me"* (*John 1:43*). By walking in front of us, the guide shows us the way. Who follows him has only to keep to the trail, looking always at the guide's back. Moses was not able to see God's face but only His back. God said, *"You cannot see My face; for no man can see My face and live"* (*Exodus 33:20*).

WISE STORIES. An old story that I was told in Europe is about a big flood. A man standing on top of the roof of his house unceasingly prayed, with all his heart, to God to rescue him. In the mean time, he was noticing, extremely worried, how the water level was rising up to the window sills, up to the tops of the windows, then up to the gutters. He saw people in boats passing by and inviting him to jump in, but he systematically refused all, thinking of God's supreme help. When the house disappeared completely under water and the water started to fill his shoes, he cried in despair, "Lord, You forgot me! Please don't let me drown." Not hearing any response, he suddenly felt a huge doubt piercing his soul and asked, "O, Lord, do You exist?" That very instant, he heard a big voice coming from above, "Poor you, who do you think has sent all the rescue boats to you?" Many European people interpreted this wise story with a nuance of pessimism and even with partial denial: "Help yourself and God will help you." However, American thinking is more vigorous and optimistic: "Grab the chance that it is given to you from Above."

Another story, heard in the United States, is told in the same sense but deeper in the domain of doubts. A man, hiking in the mountains, slipped down into a precipice. While falling, he grabbed a little tree growing on the cliff. Frightened to death and hanging in the air, he cried for help. Someone, above, answered, "No problem. Let yourself fall. The angels will catch you and everything will be all right." The man stopped yelling, thought for a few moments, and then yelled again as loud as he could from the depth of his lungs, "Is anybody else there?" This story brings something new: very often, the problems require another solution than we think is adequate. It is important not to lose hope and to abandon the action, but to continue struggling and, at the same time, to persevere in prayers, letting God decide the end. Even if this alternative should lead to a tragic end, the spirit will not lose anything but instead, it will gain the peace of faith.

I heard a story from Father Constantine Lăpuştea. An old man, with the fear of God, called his son to his deathbed and told him, "Son, I do not have much to leave you – this modest house, my Bible and my blessings. Please, every time you are in trouble, open the Holy Scripture and read. The words of it will encourage and help your soul." He died and his son, soon after that, put the Holy Book somewhere on the top of a cabinet. He had a tempestuous life with ups and downs and, in the end, after losing all his assets and investments one by one, he became so poor and so deep in debt that he decided to sell the house, the last asset he had. Cleaning the house and trashing all the things he did not need, he found a dusty Bible and tossed it in the trashcan. Before landing in the trash, the pages of the book fluttered in the air and a big bunch of one hundred dollar bills flew out and dropped on the floor. The young ran around very happy and gathered up the money. Unfortunately, the bills were not good any more – the financial reform done a few years ago made them worthless. With tears in his eyes, the man understood the lesson of his father: he had to look in the Bible at the time of each trouble. He picked up the Bible from the can and the Bible opened in his hand at the following pages of *Matthew 7:7-8*: "*Ask and it will be given to you; seek and you will find; knock and it will be opened to you. For everyone who asks receives, and he who seeks finds, and to him who knocks it will be opened.*" We ought not to forget Our Lord - if not always at least at a time of woe.

In his sermons, Father Kallistos reminded us, with his pleasant and fine humor, of a certain little story. An impetuous young student picked up the phone that had just rung and started to speak in an uninterrupted flow, "Hello, this is John. Hello, hello, this is John. Hello, hello, this is John, who is there, who is talking?" The reply came in the little pause that followed the very long string of John's words, "*You* are talking." The young man said, "Ah, I was wondering why the voice sounded so familiar." With a warm slight smile on his lips, Father Kallistos concluded: we have *to learn to listen*, to listen to God's words.

I would like to finish with the story of a dream, included in a very well-known Brazilian poem. A man dreamt how happy he was while walking on the beach, hand in hand with God. Behind them, one could see their footprints in the wet sand. The man realized that they actually marked the history of his life - a long journey through many years. He looked back and noticed that, in some places, there was only one pair of footprints. He turned toward God and said with a reproaching nuance in his voice, "Lord, you were not with me all the time! Why did you abandon me in some moments of my life?" The reply came with a soft, warm voice and surprised him: "I carried you in my arms during the difficult periods of your life."

REAL STORIES. If we read how the alpinist Joe Simpson climbed out of an abominable crevasse with one broken leg, we can realize how many times he relied on the unknown. He trusted the slimmest chance, despite the fact that he was perfectly aware that a fatal fall followed by an imminent death could occur any moment (Simpson, 1988). The alpinist did not mention God at all, but the way he thought and struggled, showed clearly his trust in Him.

Father Anthony Coniaris made an eloquent comparison in his beautiful book on the Philokalia (Coniaris, 1998). The radio operator on the Titanic had ignored all messages warning about the immanence of the icebergs and had placed the messages somewhere on a table without reporting anything to the captain because he was too busy listening to the results of a sailing boat race. The Lord sends us warnings through the events of our life and His Bible Word, about the spiritual icebergs that threaten to vanquish us. By persevering in growing the Christian virtues demanded by God, we will acquire the necessary alertness to hear the Lord's voice when He speaks to us.

A SCARY STORY. Another little story, in very modern terms, circulates among people. Two menacing men, covered with black ski caps, rushed into a big cathedral packed with over 2,000 Christians. Holding automatic weapons in their hands, they yelled at the crowd, in a very frightening tone, "We are here to shoot all those who believe in Jesus Christ!" Scared to death, everybody ran away as fast as possible: the laymen, the deacons, and the choir. Only twenty-four people remained in the huge empty cathedral. Then one of the two terrorists pulled off the cap covering his face and said to the priest, "Sir, we got rid of the hypocrites. Now you can begin the Mass. See you later." And, with a sinister laugh, both exited the cathedral. This is a very uncomfortable story. Without doubt, those who remained were truly faithful. Nevertheless, are we sure that those who ran away had a shallow, formal and weak faith? It is hard to say. There are many crazy people in this world and some of them have fun terrorizing others and by playing with their feelings and beliefs. We, who are weak in spirit but many in number, have to learn from the monastic wisdom. The Holy Fathers say that the evil spirit, the Tempter, can appear under the most unexpected forms. Therefore, we should always be very cautious.

Yes, it is very possible that the remaining twenty-four persons, if shot to death, would have gone directly to Paradise. However, after all, no one there was asked to sacrifice his life

1. WHAT'S GOOD IN A CHRISTIAN LIFE? | **69**

in order to save the life of the others, which would have been a test of conviction, paid for with one's own life. I do not think that this is the way the martyrs of earlier times reacted to the challenges imposed on them by the pagans. They did not want to be killed. They first had to do their missionary work. They had a goal in life. Why did Our Lord Jesus not reply to the mockers who asked Him to prophesy who slapped and struck Him (*Matthew 26:68*)? Why did He not answer Pilate's questions about the charges brought against Him and did not try to save His life (*Matthew 27:14*)? We have to discern, to not forget our real goal and, consequently, to choose the right attitude in front of the mockers.

A Romanian friend was arrested by the Communist Security Police under the accusation that he wanted to defect from his country. In the midst of all psychological tortures, they threatened him that he would be punished for the little Bible he had with him at the time he was caught. To carry a Bible is not compatible with a member of the Communist Party. He should be an atheist. As had the majority of people, my friend had joined the Party not by conviction but by pressure and necessity, because otherwise he would not have been allowed to work as a scientist. He defended himself against the accusations, by alleging that the Bible belonged to his deceased mother and, because the book was a souvenir dear to his heart, he carried it wherever he went. However, he was ready in the depth of his heart, if confronted, to assume all the risks and to confess openly his faith. Fortunately, the Security Police officers did not think to ask him directly, "Do you actually believe in God?" In that case, he would have had no choice and could not have hidden his belief anymore. Fortunately, they did not ask and my friend's job, family, and freedom were not endangered. It is true that Our Lord said that who denies Him on earth will be denied by Him in heaven

(*Matthew 10:33*). Maybe the terrorists' threat at the cathedral was a simple temptation inspired by the Evil Spirit aiming to destroy the human body and spirit, leading the faithful to a kind of suicide. Maybe that moment, the remaining twenty-four people prayed intensely inside their heart and God gave them the certitude of the right action. Maybe yes, maybe not. When we say the words of the Lord's Prayer, "*And lead us not into temptation but deliver us from evil,*" (*Matthew 6:13*), we make reference to this kind of cunning and malicious temptation that can lead to our self-destruction.

We pray to God to give us the needed power of discernment to understand His will. The first man, Adam, was spiritually immature at the time he discovered that there is good and evil in the world. Therefore, he did not fully understand the real meanings of this new knowledge. This is why he was ejected from Eden: he was given the chance to learn the correct distinction between good and evil by living on earth. He had therefore to confront himself with harmful events during his life, and to be subjected to disease and death. We need to pray to God to help us acquire, through our own experience, the sense of right discernment between good and evil and to overcome them.

We find another point in the Gospel to think of, and we can connect it with the story regarding the great temptation brought by the two terrorists who "wanted to get rid of the hypocrites." Our Lord told Peter that the Evil Spirit asked to be allowed to sort the disciples by the temptation test - to sift them as wheat (*Luke 22:31*). Christ knew the potential damage of this temptation. Christ asked God the Father to make Peter stronger in faith in order to protect him from the risk of being lost. He said, "*I have prayed for you that your faith should not fail; and when you have returned to Me, strengthen your brethren.*" Peter answered in a way similar to that of the twenty-four people left in the church: *"Lord, I am ready to go with you, both to prison and to death."* But the Lord, Who knows everything, including the human weakness, said with a sad voice, *"I tell, you Peter, the rooster shall not crow this day before you will deny three times that you know Me"* (*Luke 22:31-34*). The very numerous people, who, in the story of the masked terrorists, ran away from church, apparently denied Jesus Christ, as Peter, in front of the guards, denied the Savior. So, should we conclude that Peter was not a good Christian? Was not he, who was named by the Lord, the rock upon which the Church will be built and whom will be given the keys of the Kingdom of Heaven (*Matthew 16:16-18*)?

END OF EARTHLY LIFE. Many die at the end of a course of deep suffering. Christians do not want a sudden death (heart attack, accident etc). We pray in the evening to the Lord not to take us away while sleeping. We also pray to be protected from a calamitous death. We want to be prepared to accept the end, to have time to confess and have communion, or at least that the arrival of our death finds us at prayer. We say, "Give us Lord a Christian death, in peace and without pain." We are afraid of aches and pains, of being atrociously hurt, of the "unbearable" condition of being handicapped, of the heart-rending distress that is the prelude to passing over the threshold of death. The martyrs suffered unimaginable pain. Their death was *in extremis*. They prayed continuously, consciously and unconsciously; they clung to God and He gave them strength to endure the torture and to forget their excruciating pain. It is a tragedy to be ill with Alzheimer's, without the memory's help to gather thoughts into an ardent prayer. The same for the people in a coma. Maybe the Lord communicates with them in a mysterious way, imperceptible for us, because certainly He is with them every moment.

One day, in the '50's, my mother told me, with great emotion, about an event that occurred during her business trip. In the railroad station of Focsani (a Romanian city), a huge crowd was rushing impatiently, pushing and kicking, in a hurry to board the train that was just entering the station, in order to occupy a better place in the compartments or in the corridor. A man slipped and fell in front of the moving steam-locomotive. He died in an instant, cut in pieces by the wheels. The very second he fell he yelled with all his power: "Jeeeeeesus!" The sound of his voice covered everything, floating above the overheated crowd. Everybody stopped, astounded, in a chill of fear. The next minute the craziness resumed with even more intensity, with the tempestuous people crowding the ladder of the railroad cars. A friend told me that, visiting the noisy Jamaican jungle, he clapped his hands and a sudden silence of alertness froze the wood for a second before resuming the chaotic uproar. In that Romanian railroad station, everyone's heart reacted for a minute to the warning of God, but immediately the crush of worldly impetuous worries started again with increased fury.

MEETING DEATH is a terrible event. It happened that I fell asleep for a fraction of a second while driving my pickup truck, and I hit a huge metal trailer with a bulldozer on it, pulled by a giant semi-trailer truck. While continuing driving and following the curve of the road, I needed a couple of minutes to realize that I had had an accident. I miraculously missed hitting the big sharp blade of the bulldozer. I was safe, just with a few glass pieces in my hair, a big dent in my door and a badly bent fender. The great Russian theologian Vladimir Lossky changed profoundly when, child being, he witnessed how, in an outrageous trial, the Soviets sentenced Metropolitan Benjamin of St. Petersburg to death

(Metropolitan Benjamin was later canonized a Saint by the Orthodox Church). The child of that time was shocked but he had seen how much strength the faith in God could give to a person. This kindled in him the fire of belief.

A good American friend died of cancer. He fought his illness two and a half years with the same courage he had shown in the Vietnam War where he had volunteered as a Red Cross worker. When the doctors detected the tumor, the disease was already spread in all the bones in his body. They predicted the end in a couple of months. The body weakened, and Bob needed a wheelchair, but his mind remained clear and active. He continued supervising work by phone and his computer and did not stop writing scientific papers.

After one year, undergoing a theoretically useless treatment, Bob started to acquire vigor and he could walk with a stick. Then a tumor formed under his maxillary and after two years and a half from the diagnosis, i.e. five times longer than the doctors' expectations, he left this life. His faith in God never faded.

His face was always calm and joyous. He talked in good humor about his pain. He encouraged the worried people around him. He was ready to go any moment "with his luggage well packed," but he was also waiting patiently to pass through all the potential trials God had in store for him. He endured all with confidence that everything is to the good of his soul and of the loved ones around him. He trusted Our Lord's words, *"The very hairs of your head are all numbered. Do not fear therefore" (Matthew 10:30-31).*

Anthony Bloom brought to the reader's attention a Russian comment meant to strengthen those who fear death: "Do not worry. When death will be there you will not be anymore, but while you are still there death is not with you." A monk from Mount Athos said that death is a joy, because it is the ticket for the journey to meet Our Lord. Surely, he added, the ticket is rather expensive and we have to pay for it with the tribulations of our life.

TIME OF DEATH. A story is told about a traveler who missed the train and complained that he was totally confused by the clocks in the village he had visited. The time shown by each of them – that of the church, that of the city hall and that of the railroad station, differed significantly. The rigid dispatcher said that, regardless, the trains go according to the station's clock. This is also our case as we travel through our life. The death hour comes not according to our clock but to the Lord's. Therefore, we have to be prepared for departure any moment.

An idea about understanding that *the time when man dies* is in conjunction with God's will was given by the case of the Russian elder Ambrosius the abbot of Optina monastery who lived in 1812-1891. His sanctity and wisdom has attracted thousands of pilgrims. Famous men as Tolstoy, Leontieff, Solovieff, and Dostoyevsky were among these pilgrims. Dostoyevsky described Father Ambrosius, under the name of Zosima, in the novel "The Brothers Karamazov."

Father Ambrosius tried to answer the question how can humans know exactly what is in God's mind. His idea might not be the best or the most complete answer, but it is good to take it into account.

He said, "the Lord cuts short a man's life when He sees that either he is prepared to pass into the eternity or there is no hope left for him to change into a good person." I would say because he might become, in the latter case, a source of evil contamination for the others around him. However, man has to leave this decision to God and not to politicians who promote the death sentence.

SUICIDE IS A SERIOUS SIN. It is murder. The Church refuses to serve funerals for those who died that way. Father Cleopa Ilie was very strict in this regard. However, as Father Vladimir Lecko of Minocqua said, the majority of the suicides did not commit the act from pride, as the evil angel wanted, but from a deep suffering, from an unbearable physical and mental pain. Emily Dickinson wrote a highly emotional poem entitled "The Mystery of Pain": "Pain has an element of blank; / It cannot recollect/ When it began, or if there were/ A day when it was not. // It has no future but itself, / Its infinite realms contain/ Its past, enlightened to perceive/ New periods of pain." By its persistence, a rather minor pain can become habitual but also can exceed the limits of endurance.

The American physician David Kuhl, in his book "What Dying People Want: Practical Wisdom For The End Of Life" (Kuhl, 2002), mentioned that Albert Schweitzer considered that pain is more terrible to the world than death itself and the doctor should have the privilege to save the sick from days of physical torture. However, the ethical issue of this way of ending life was questioned even by the modern and liberal society of today. Suicide is a hard problem for the conscience, and the conscience is the fingerprint left by God inside of everyone.

Saint Cassian the Roman narrated the story of an elder, named Iron, who was tempted by the evil spirit to jump in a deep well with the reassuring thought that his strong faith would save him from drowning. This reminds me of the challenge given to Our Lord Jesus by the evil angel who asked Him to throw Himself from the roof of the temple (*Luke 4:9-12*). The elder Iron jumped into the well and, naturally, he died. But Abba Paphnutius, who knew well this elder, decided to pray for him in all the memorial services held in the Monastery. Abba Paphnutius did that out of his great love for the elder Iron and his respect for the many years spent by this elder in the desert, in fasting, prayer, and spiritual struggle. Abba Paphnutius did so, also fearing that elder Iron's death could be considered a suicide.

If I am not wrong, the French writer Henri de Montherlant killed himself as a philosophical demonstration that man has absolute control over his life. This sounds like a sin of pride.

None of the reasons offered by the self-murderers for doing what they did, should keep us from praying for them to be forgiven as a human being created by God, even though the Church does not allow mentioning them in prayers and services. I asked Father Petronius Tanase, from the Prodromou Romanian Skete on Mount Athos, how one is supposed to pray for these brothers of ours. He could not indicate any traditional text but he encouraged me to pray with my own words. I remember that, during a Saturday service for the departed of this life, one of the sheets of paper with names of the deceased caught on fire from a candle. The priest extinguished the little fire immediately. We noticed that only the right half of that paper burned. It was the half that among others included the name of a person that had committed suicide.

It is written in the Patericon that an Abba, in his great love for the Creation, prayed the Creator even for pardoning the evil spirits (Patericul, 1999a). Saint Isaac the Syrian wrote, "What is a merciful heart? It is a heart on fire for the whole of creation, for humanity, for the birds, for the animals, for demons, and for all that exists. By the recollection of them the eyes of a merciful person pour forth tears in abundance...For this reason, such a person offers up a tearful prayer continually even for irrational beasts, *for the enemies of the truth*, and for those who harm her or him, that they be protected and receive mercy" (adapted from Alfeyev, 2000).

LIFE BEYOND DEATH. Death comes like a cold wind over our sweet torpor. There is a life beyond death, a life much longer than that spent on earth. This is the actual truth for which Our Lord Jesus came among us - to bring a warning about eternal life and to prepare us for it. Here we are. A Man comes all of a sudden into our life and world. We gradually learn, together with others, that this man is in fact the Son of God. We hear His voice calling our attention to avoid being lazy and sinking into the passions of our body, because the short while of this life was given us just to work to avoid a frightening Beyond. This other world will come with a harsh judgment and we have to face it.

Some of us would say: here on earth it is everything - heaven and hell, joy and sadness, victories and defeats, accomplishments and disappointments. We should live with intensity every moment of our life in such a way to be sure that we did not miss anything good that life could offer. And, of course, we should pay attention not to hurt ourselves while enjoying life. Christians also approach life with the idea of an interior balance as otherwise people do, but they keep a certain serenity, moderation, and purity. Christians look always toward God in Whose shadow they prepare themselves to be ready when they will be called to the other life that is eternal. Our Lord told the disciples, *"Let your waist be girded and your lamps burning; and you yourselves be like men who wait for their master, when he will return from the wedding, that when he comes and knocks they may open to him immediately"* (*Luke 12:35-36*).

Those, who deny the existence of a life beyond death, say with a triumphant sarcasm, "No one has come from there to tell us his story." Here we could bring up a very valid point from the Holy Scripture. A rich man, who was suffering in Hades, begged Abraham to send someone back from the dead to his five brothers still alive on earth, and to suggest them to repent in order to avoid the same torment in flame. Abraham replied, *"If they do not hear Moses and the prophets, neither will they be persuaded though one rise from the dead"* (*Luke 16:31*). Even if a dead person brought his testimony to them, the deniers who confronted Christians would still doubt and *not believe*. When the Sanhedrin said to Our Lord Jesus, *"If You are the Christ, tell us,"* He replied, *"If I tell you, you will by no means believe."* In fact, they asked Him that question not to learn but to have a reason to charge Him with a crime that would convict Him to death (*Luke 22:66-71*).

OUR HIDDEN SINS. Very often, it is extremely hard to see our sins if they are not obvious as those specified in the Ten Commandments or in the civil laws. We need God's grace as a response to the perseverance, steadiness, and patience of our unceasing prayers, in order to detect our sins. We also need to realize that all the commandments carved in Moses' stone tablets are actually contained by the two commandments on love that Christ carved in our soul's tablets. Our Lord said, *"You shall love the Lord your God with all your heart, with all your soul, and with all your mind"* and *"You shall love your neighbor as yourself"* (*Matthew 22:37, 39*).

We read in the Gospel, *"For which is easier, to say, 'Your sins are forgiven', or to say, 'Arise and walk?'"* (*Matthew 9:5*). Our Lord's words are very terrifying! Even a miracle like that of the healing of the paralytic is less difficult than forgiving sins! This explains why the ascetics, who embody the most powerful expression of the full awareness of our sinful human nature, chose to go through an outstanding privation and suffering, proper to a life in the desert. They wanted to make the process of being forgiven much easier by preparing their body and soul to receive the word of God, as the farmers prepared the ground to have it fertile, loose, and moist for a good germination of the seeds. Therefore, they strove, as much as they could, to acquire the gift of seeing their own sins in order to repent for them.

The ascetics do not let the inner voices, which usually dominate our philosophy of living and instigate us to procrastination, to become loud and to affect their soul. They know, as well as we do, that a disease or an accident can cut the thread of life at any time but they do not want to be taken by surprise, unprepared for the moment of departure. *"As the lightning comes from the east and flashes to the west, so also will the coming of the Son of Man be"* (*Matthew 24:27*). *"Therefore you also be ready; for the Son of Man is coming at an hour you do not expect"* (*Matthew 24:44*).

DO IT BEFORE DEPARTURE. The time of life is running inexorably. We cannot stop it. "Life is like a taxi. The meter just keeps a-ticking whether you are getting somewhere or just standing still," are the words of a popular saying of Lou Erickson. Father Cleopa Ilie urged the faithful to think of the eternal time instead of hanging on the transient one. He advised a young monk, who was enraptured by the beauty of a girl, to look at her face with eyes that can see how wrinkled she would be in old age and how ugly her skull would be after death. Saint Isaac the Syrian taught us that, at the evening prayer, we have to think that the bed might be our grave and we might fall into eternal sleep without having a chance for penitence required by God's grace of forgiveness. He wrote, "As long as you have legs, follow the narrow path, before you are tied with ropes and unable to move. As long as you have arms, stretch them out in prayer, before you hang on death's cross. As long as you have eyes, fill them with tears, before they are filled with dust."

DO NOT LOOK FOR REVENGE. *"Love suffers long and is kind; love does not envy... does not rejoice in iniquity but rejoices in the truth; bears all things, believes all things, hopes all things, endures all things"* (*1 Corinthians 13:4-7*). *"Then Peter came to Him and said, 'Lord, how often shall my brother sin against me, and I forgive him? Up to seven times?' Jesus said to him, 'I do not say to you up to seven times, but up to seventy times seven"* Matthew 18:21-22). *"And forgive our debts as we forgive our debtors"* (*Matthew 6:12*).

Therefore we should control ourselves and transfigure our first reactions. *"Do not say 'I will repay evil'; wait for the Lord, and He will help you"* (*Proverbs 20:22*). The people who suffered and survived the communist gulag did not want revenge on their torturers. The brilliant Romanian philosopher Mircea Vulcănescu died in prison of pneumonia because he chose to be a living mattress on the wet and cold cement floor for a young cellmate very ill with tuberculosis. However, he sent a message to those outside the gulag, saying, "Please, do not avenge us."

Today Romania and other former communist countries are in the process of canonizing the martyrs from the political prisons. The prisoners wrote poems and prayers on pieces of soap with the risk of very severe punishments. In order to avoid being caught, they preferred to memorize the poems and prayers despite their poor physical condition. After coming out of prison, they secretly wrote them down and, in this way, a huge library was formed after the collapse of communism in 1989. Two beautiful Akathist hymns authored by hieromonk Daniil (known under his name of poet, Sandu Tudor) were saved, published, and spread in the Christian world: the Akathist for Saint John the Evangelist and the Akathist for Saint Calinicus of Chernika. The author died in the Aiud prison. Many people in the Romanian communist prisons survived physical and mental torture due to their faith in God.

The popular novel "Count of Monte Cristo" by Alexander Dumas is full of human justice, and therefore we, as teenagers, loved it but, due to its methodic revenge, it is not at all of a Christian nature. My mother did not pursue the punishment of the man who tortured and killed my father arrested during the period of political persecutions. She heard several years later that that man died in terrible pain due to an accident: he was, by mistake, covered with hot asphalt during a street paving operation. Although my father's loss produced a deep wound in her heart that never healed, her grief for him eventually caused a disease that killed her seven years later, yet my mother was very sad when she heard the news about the death of the man who had caused her husband's death.

JUDGMENT AND FORGIVENESS. Our Lord told Peter the parable of the unforgiving servant (*Matthew 18:21-35*). The king let the servant in debt to him go, but the servant in turn punished the person who owed him a much smaller sum of money. By enduring the cross, Our Lord Jesus forgave us for our sins, but we do not forget those who made mistakes that impacted us, exactly as did that servant who lacked compassion. Moreover, we are ready to judge others while we beg for mercy for ourselves.

Maybe that period of darkness between the sixth and ninth hour (12 to 3 P.M., in our terms), while the Lord Jesus suffered on the cross (see *Matthew 27:45*), was the dramatic time when He defended our sins in front of the Supreme Judge, God the Father. Christ was not <u>judged</u> for our sins, as some protestants say with awe and gratitude about that period of darkness, because <u>the Son of God cannot be put on trial</u>. Our Lord is an intimate part of the Holy Trinity's being and, if within the mystery of the Holy Trinity's reciprocity the Son of God obeys

God the Father, He who is <u>God's Word cannot be judged</u>. To the contrary, because Christ accomplished His work of salvation through His Incarnation into a human being, He will be the Judge of man. He will be an understanding, just and loving Judge at the very frightening Last Judgment. Very likely, at that time of tragic darkness, between the sixth and ninth hour, all the sins of the world were reviewed, one by one. As Father Anthony Michaels said, at that time one could see on Our Lord's face wrinkles caused by suffering for all the evil deeds committed by every one of us.

CHARITY AND HOSPITALITY. Our life has its natural flow and often we are not able to predict its direction. While I was in the first grade, I heard about Saint Martin who, in his unceasing mercy for beggars, in the harsh winter season cut his cloak in two and gave half of it to a poor man who was trembling and shaking with cold. One day, I saw a little old woman who was resting on a bench. I thought she was a beggar so I gave her some money. I discovered immediately that I had made a big mistake and, very embarrassed, I was afraid that I had offended her. Nevertheless, she looked at me with a bright warm light in her eyes full of tears and, with a shaking voice drawn in emotion, said, "O, my dear son, how did you know that my pension is discouragingly low?" God made me meet her humble needs without knowing her situation. Deeply touched, with my heart aching and wondering about the impact of my modest alms, I remembered then Abraham who went to welcome the three men that were passing by the oaks of Mamre. He washed their feet and invited them to eat and refresh themselves from the heat of the day (Genesis 18: 1-8). Saint Apostle Paul wrote about that, *"Do not forget to entertain strangers, for by so doing some have unwittingly entertained angels"* (*Hebrews 13:2*).

Abraham's guests were the three angels that represent the Holy Trinity in Andrei Rublev's famous icon.

We may see in the person who comes and begs at our door his protecting angel who addresses our soul. The blessed Mother Theresa lived for love for the poor, the diseased, the addicted and the needy, because through them she felt God's presence. Do you find it sometimes annoying that someone calls or enters your office when you are very busy, and he puts you under pressure about something that he thinks should be done that very moment? Or, while concentrating on your silent prayer, the neighbor starts his extremely noisy lawnmower, chainsaw, or motorcycle? How should we receive all these intruders? We should do it with love, seeing in them Abraham's three visiting angels.

We read in the Epistles, *"Therefore receive one another, just as Christ also received us, to the glory of God"* (*Romans 15:7*). How much I would like to have this love, this interior impulse to welcome others! The beggars are our guests, even if they are annoying, harassing, arrogant, repulsive, or ungrateful. Someone recounted that, one day, walking with the famous German poet Rainer Maria Rilke, they passed by a poor woman. The poet checked his pockets and, because he did not find any alms to give, he offered her a rose, with much respect and condescendence. She was very touched. It was his way of praising human dignity, even the dignity of a woman who was feeling great misery. Rilke's gesture was like the beautiful and unforgettable gesture of rich bounty given to the priest who was robbed in Victor Hugo's novel "Les Miserables," which restored the human uprightness in the savage soul of Jean Valjean. By contrast, the rich man from a parable in the Gospel ignored Lazarus, the man full of sores who was sharing the food of dogs at the gates of that rich man's house.

We might ask a legitimate question: should I give money to all the beggars, without any discernment? To the aggressive gypsies that cover as in a spider web the main tourist places in Europe? I think it is not a matter of racism if we ignore them when they fake a handicap, or when they ask us for a little change in the offensive way that makes the job of their pick-pocketing fellows easier. What about the drug addicted or drunkards? They ask for money in order to pursue a vice. As a friend of mine argued, the drug or alcohol addicted people are trapped in a deep suffering. They are tortured by a tragic need that burns their poisoned body like a consuming fire. If my friend had spare time and resources, he would take them to a center of substance-abuse rehabilitation, and help them change their lives. Or at least he would give them food because their addiction prevents them from eating. Nevertheless, because he often does not have the time, money, and resources to help them in a substantial manner, he prefers to give them the little change they ask for, to extinguish the fire caused by their chemical dependence at that very moment, and to pray for them. He leaves with the promise in his heart that he will try to do more. If he meets them again he will try to direct them toward a life with faith in God.

LORD CARES FOR US. All of us know the Savior's teachings about worries (*Luke 12: 22-29*). The ravens *"neither sow nor reap"* but are fed by God. The lilies *"neither toil nor spin"* but their beauty is superior to the glorious robes of Solomon. We should not worry about tomorrow because, if we trust God, He will take care of us. Nevertheless, we have to think about tomorrow and plan to prevent our body from becoming lazy and multiplying its sins. Otherwise, the soul will be burdened, will lose all cleanness, and will collapse. *"Be anxious for nothing, but in everything by prayer and* *supplication, with thanksgiving, let your requests be made known to God; and the peace of God, which surpasses all understanding, will guard your hearts and minds through Christ Jesus. Finally, brethren, whatever things are true, whatever things are noble, whatever things are just, whatever things are pure, whatever things are lovely, whatever things are of good report, if there is any virtue and if there is anything praiseworthy – meditate on these things"* (*Philippians 4: 6-8*).

We wake up early in the morning and we do not know what the day will be like. We pray to God to help us to understand His will and give us strength to go through all He decided for us for that particular day without damaging our soul. After our prayer, we dive with courage into the cold water of the morning, with alert mind and senses, to labor at the maximum level of our abilities. The Lord will not let us lose our battle with the day despite all difficulties. Saint Paul wrote to the Corinthians, *"No temptation has overtaken you except such as is common to man; but God is faithful, Who will not allow you to be tempted beyond you are able, but with the temptation will also make the way to escape, that you may be able to bear it"* (*1 Corinthians 10: 13*).

We might be punished. Therefore, our day might be harsh, but the punishment will work to our benefit, for improvement, purification, and wisdom, as it was when we were children and were punished by our parents who were responsible for our education. The punishment can make us sad but eventually will induce joy through the fruits of our spirit (*Hebrews 12: 9-11*). Let us then arm ourselves with patience and attention.

A little story tells about a man who complained that his cross was too heavy and too painful to endure. The Lord took him into a big room and invited him to choose a cross from a great number of all kinds of crosses: of iron, of cement, and of wood, heavy and light, adorned and simple. After a long search, the man found, to his great relief, a tiny cross, very light, hidden in a dark corner. "This one, Lord," he cried, "this would suit me." And the Lord replied: "You are entirely right. It suits you. It is the very cross that you carried all the time."

THE TROUBLE, THE DEADLOCK, THE NUISANCE, AND THE SORROW. The Lord told Moses, "*My presence will go with you, and I will give you rest*" (*Exodus 33:14*). As Charles Spurgeon noticed, it happens often that, when we finally feel at ease in a certain place, we are called to another, entirely unfamiliar place. Nevertheless, if we believe that the Lord Himself will be our companion in all the strange places we will be sent, our worries should disappear. As the psalmist said, "*The Lord is my shepherd*" (*Psalm 22/23:1*).

Is it not true that the moment we finally succeed in setting up a kind of harmonious relationship with our society and environment, God humiliates us, imposing on us a new test and trial from His large store? Yes, He does not allow us to rust in a careless laziness that gives room to pride and vanity, thinking that the bright situation we achieved is entirely due to our own efforts and abilities. Even more, quite often when we irradiate enthusiasm and are fertile in our plans and efficient in our actions, God stops us abruptly with illness that keeps us temporarily in bed or prepares us for an approaching death. Let us not despair. Let us search and discover *His presence* that, as Moses was told, would watch over us with tender love everywhere and at all times.

A prayer designated for birthdays by the church asks God: "Please do not let the worldly worries bend me with their burden, nor the evil overload me as I age. Please persist and increase Your attentive love and, when the time comes for You to call me to You, receive me into eternal happiness."

REAL HAPPINESS. A Nobel prize-winning author, Gabriel Garcia Marquez, wrote in his essay "If God would give me another piece of life," that he learned in his life that all people believe happiness dwells on the top of the mountain. They ignore the fact that happiness is actually in the climbing itself. My own accomplishments during my existence were neither great nor spectacular, despite the fact that I made great and consistent physical and intellectual efforts and I exploited my talents to exhaustion. Even the magnificent accomplishments of the very few people who marked the history of humanity making an outstanding scientific discovery, building a castle, composing a symphony, or hosting an important social event are not sufficient to create constant happiness. An example of the lack of constant happiness is provided in the case of Marquez's novel "A Hundred Years of Solitude." Everything is temporary. The author of a masterpiece cannot actually control anything in this world, not even the destiny of his or her masterpiece.

Nevertheless, I could say, like Marquez, I learned that happiness is found in the work itself – a work done with complete devotion, sacrifice, and noble spirit. This is our way to feel God's benevolence and to multiply within us the love for our neighbor. A difficult and conscientious work was the only reasonable solution offered to the first man, Adam, after the mistake of his impatience in acquiring knowledge at any price. The Lord told him, *"In the sweat of your face you shall eat bread till you return to the ground"* (*Genesis 3:19*). Labor becomes a source of happiness, despite the fact that it blends sweetness with bitterness, as we accept car~·- our suffering and follow Christ's call.

REALITY OF LIFE. Is the life on earth suffering? Theoretically yes, as a consequenc sin (see *Genesis 3:17-19*), which caused illness, aging, and death. However, the beneficial elements of God's marvelous creation did not disappear. Following Christ's teachings, we aspire to restore our lost true human being, built by the Lord according to His image and resemblance. Salvation comes from the work of the Son of God. *"Salvation is of the Lord, and Your blessing is upon Your people"* (*Psalm 3:9*). By living in faith and listening to Our Lord's commands, we will reach a state of special joy and peace in the midst of suffering and tribulation, and we will be able to resist the damaging trials of our life with a serene soul. Tears will flow from our eyes but they will cease to be tears of pain and despair. They will be tears of gladness, fed by an abiding love for God and His creation. They will be tears of compassion fed by a deep love for our neighbor.

Forgiven and liberated from the entanglement of sins, our soul will walk toward light and this will strengthen us in the difficult times of our life. Therefore, faith was the supreme target the bestial prison torturers (so-called "tortionaries") tried to destroy by breaking the spirit of the political detainees in the communist prison of Pitesti (Romania). They tried to empty the people of any love and respect for friends, family, and God, leaving instead a cold nothingness, confusion, and obedience in doing evil. Using the harsh methods of the infamous Russian pedagogue Makarenko, they beat the victims with incredible violence and applied tremendous psychological pressure on them. Their goal was to ruin completely any *"manifestation of the Spirit given to each for the profit of all"* (*1 Corinthians 12:7*), to eliminate the last source of resistance in a human being, and to accomplish a complete washing of brain and heart. Reduced to a robot level, the victims were forced to beat in their turn other inmates, and this way the isons became an inferno, the seed of emptiness being spread more and more in the alienated captive souls. Fortunately, as Father George Calciu confessed in his book (Calciu, 1997), the faith never disappeared from the tortured detainees. Moreover, they regained power, because the Lord does not allow the evil to hurt the inner being of His chosen ones (see the Book of Job).

THE LIGHT THAT DIRECT US. I entered a basement with partial dividers and without any interior corridor, full of pipes at all levels and in all places, with electrical fixtures everywhere, tools, construction materials, shelves with paints, solvents and chemicals. I left the door to the stairs open to have a little light in order to see and find the electric switch in the basement. Unfortunately, the draft slammed the door and I remained in *absolute darkness*, in a perfect maze whose key I completely ignored. I was terrified because I realized that I could wander in that small basement several hours with the great risk of knocking my forehead on a pipe, or of hurting my legs by stepping on tools and into buckets, of being burnt by chemicals, of suffering an electric shock, or of having something fall on my head. I would have been happy to see at least *a thread of light* under the outside door to figure the way out. Fortunately, I managed eventually to get out without any damage. I will never forget that experience.

The blind man from Jericho (*Luke 18: 35-43*), who was immersed in an *absolute darkness*, felt the same terror fearing the potentially damaging Unknown, regardless that sometimes the arm of a compassionate person helped him. This state was extremely devastating because, before becoming blind, he managed without any problem to walk in the surrounding environment. He was in a far better position than the poor blind man we read about in Saint John's chapter 9, a man who was born without any sight, living in deep darkness from the very beginning of his life. The blind man from Jericho had known what light is. Therefore, covered by an impenetrable darkness, he feared the maze through which he had to move. He cried to the Lord with great perseverance, hoping for that *little light* I had needed so desperately for orientation in the strange and dark house basement. The Lord Jesus heard the blind man's shouting and His word healed the blind man's sight. The light suddenly invaded the man's eyes and the darkness dissipated. He could see in that *sea of light* a big crowd and, in the midst of them, the Son of God.

Our soul needs this thread of light. Without the help of the unseen presence of God in our difficult moments, we are the prey of an unlimited fear. After our physical death, we enter an existential darkness and our only hope is that, there, beyond the borders of this world, we will benefit from the protecting arm of the guardian angel and from the thread of light offered by the Savior, a beam of light that will lead us towards the sea of light of eternal life. The American psychiatrist Raymond A. Moody's book "Life after life" was very popular in the '70s. The book's subject was the great light that the people brought back to life from a clinic death said they had seen while being beyond this world. However, Father Seraphim Rose found in the Holy Fathers' writings many frightening things about the aerial tollhouses the soul has to go through after its departure from the earthly world (Rose, 1980). Fortunately, Christ's presence next to us gives us courage, strengthens us, and guides us on our trail through the dense, black darkness populated by spirits.

FEAR OF SECOND DEATH. The thing we should fear is not the first death that is the physical one, but *the second death* that can follow the Last Judgment. It is not the separation of the soul from the cocoon-like body that should we worry about, but the final separation from God of our soul, sentenced to separation that will last forever. "*He who has an ear, let him hear what the Spirit says to the churches. He who overcomes shall not be hurt by the second death*" (*Revelation 2:11*). These words refer to the necessary preparation done here on earth for the future eternal life with God. The second death can be the entrance into the hopeless everlasting darkness of suffering.

1.3. Should We Live in Faith?

THE IDEA OF A RELIGIOUS LIFE. Blaise Pascal used strong words in his book "Pensées." He wrote, "People despise religion; they hate it and are afraid that it might be real." Concerning those who deny religion, Saint John Chrysostom said, "It is extremely easy to deny the sun's existence. If you close your eyes there will be no sun, but darkness." Others are tolerant of religion, considering that it is a matter of personal choice. Father Anthony Coniaris wrote that, at the TV talk show of Dick Cavett, the Archbishop of Canterbury mentioned that Jesus is God's Son, as everybody knows. Jane Fonda immediately replied something like "Maybe this is true for you, but not for me." The Archbishop said that either He actually *is* or He *is not*, He cannot be both. He cannot be for me and not be for you at the same time. After hearing these words it seems that the actress changed her mind (see Coniaris, 2001).

A friend considered that religion is like communism: it makes you suffer deeply but promises a very happy future. The working class has to sacrifice itself in order to build a happy society, the Marxists said. A priest told us that he brought a young free thinker to faith in God, by convincing him that there is another life after this one and it is a deep tragedy if he should be unprepared before entering that life which is eternal. I think faith in God begins with the need for His helpful presence here, on earth. God has created us and called us to life. The eternal life begins here on earth, with our birth. Whether we believe in God or not, we cannot avoid the tribulations of the earthly life, and we cannot avoid the fear of death. The Christian achieves an inside power that helps him to pass more easily through all the difficulties of his existence, without losing his peace of mind and purity of spirit. Faith is a solid support for him even if he did not accomplish what he planned to do in his life and did not solve all problems he thought should be solved.

As the Romanian Father Arseny Papacioc said, a wall borders the road toward the Kingdom of God on each side. On one side the wall is the fear of God. On the other side the wall is the fear of death. The Christian's path, down the center of the road, leads straight to the Kingdom of God.

The Christians use to say that faith has no value if it is only accepted but not lived. The real understanding of the Lord's teachings and the authentic faith can be achieved only by living. The Russian theologian Vladimir Lossky wrote that Christianity is not a school of philosophy debating abstract concepts but, first of all, is a communion with the living God (Lossky, 1997). One can find the same opinion in the writings of the Elder Silouan from Mount Athos who avoided recommending people to spend their time with philosophy, even with a mystical philosophy.

RECEIVING GOD'S MESSAGE. It is true that a road in faith is not an easy one. Rarely the message of His reply to our efforts and prayers is obviously defined but what our mind hesitates to perceive our heart can fully understand. This is partially because God respects the free will of man and the latter has to open the gates of acceptance for what is vital for his soul.

During His short earthly existence, Our Lord Jesus was often asked by the people if He was Christ. He did not give a clear enough answer to their limited capacity of understanding: *"I told you and you do not believe. The works that I do in my Father's name, they bear witness to me; but you do not believe, because you are not of My sheep"* (*John 10:25-26*).

Neither did Our Lord, as Father Thomas Hopko noticed, answer directly the question of the disciples of the imprisoned Saint John the Baptist. Even the last prophet of the Old Testament, the Forerunner of Christ, had fallen prey to doubts, despite the fact that he had witnessed the descent of the Holy Spirit in the form of a dove and had heard the Father's voice at Christ's baptism. John's disciples asked, *"Are You the Coming One, or do we look for another?"* Here is what Our Lord gave them as an answer: *"Go and tell John the things which you hear and see: the blind see and the lame walk; the lepers are cleansed and the deaf hear; the dead are raised up and the poor have the gospel preached to them. And blessed is he who is not offended because of Me"* (*Matthew 11:3-6*). This is the "darkness" of God, His "silence." The Lord appeals to faith, not to logic. However, there is a moment in the Gospel when Lord Jesus declared unambiguously that He is the Messiah. It is the moment when He was in conversation with the Samaritan woman at the well. He said, *"I who speak to you am He"* (*John 4:26*). This Gospel episode, together with that of the miraculous healing of the man blind from his birth (*John 9*), is the most philosophical one in the New Testament. We still can notice that, despite Our Lord's indisputable answer, the woman kept her own doubts for a while: *"Could this be the Christ?"* (*John 4:29*).

Actually, the whole Gospel of Saint John is mainly about two things that Our Lord worked for: to make people to understand that He is the Son of God incarnated and to teach them the way to the God's Kingdom. *"These are written that you may believe that Jesus is the Christ, the Son of God, and that believing you may have life in His name"* (*John 20:31*), and cease to be servants but friends of Our Lord as He said to His disciples, *"for all things that I heard from My Father I have made known to you"* (*John 15:15*). He promised that despite of His Ascension He will be with us until the end of the world and He is so, through the Eucharist celebrated at every Divine Liturgy. As the disciples had the challenge to believe that their Teacher is the Son of God, so we have the challenge to believe that the Holy Bread and Wine are truly the Flesh and Blood of our Savior. This belief will open to us the way to the gates of God's Kingdom.

A ROAD OF TRIBULATIONS. Our Lord said to His disciples, *"In the world you will have tribulation; but be of good cheer, I have overcome the world"* (*John 16:33*). Certainly, Christians are not monsters. They can live in the earthly world, unnoticed in humbleness, with their soul rich with a deep understanding of the sacred world, with their minds and hearts in unceasing labor full of fervor. They sanctify the place where they live and affect the people around them without knowing it. Each of us is given a road leading to God and we have to make it entirely our own. The journey on this road is not void of trials and tribulations, and only the Creator knows if it will be long or short, full of excitement or boredom. What we have to do is <u>to find the goal of our life</u>, i.e. the sense of our earthly journey, and to strive to live accordingly with our limited abilities and with the help given from above for as many years as are given to us. People around us teach us how to make life a great success. They talk about the steadfastness of competition, and the tireless efforts for earning and securing a little fortune, for tasting the delight of glory, and for not missing the pleasant comfort of power. However, *"what will be the profit of the man, if he gains the whole world but loses his soul?"* What really counts is climbing the steps toward the Lord, no matter how far we succeed in going.

FAITH UNDER OPPRESSION. *"Do not fear those who kill the body but cannot kill the soul"* (*Matthew 10:28*). Hundreds of thousands of Russian priests were deported from Siberia in the first decades of the Soviets' regime. After that, without priests, with the majority of churches demolished, closed, or transformed into warehouses, theatres, stables, and public restrooms, many people forgot the main prayers but they did not lose the faith. For the East-European countries under the control of the Soviet Union it was somewhat easier, but in the '50's and 60's the believers did not dare to confess their profound belief openly, due to the intransigent atheism imposed by the communist regime.

We did not want to lose our jobs and, despite the fact that the Romanian churches, except those demolished by the President Ceaușescu's mad rage, have not been closed, we were afraid to frequent them. At home, we taught our children to keep the secret that we were praying together in the evenings. Thousands of Romanian priests and many more Christian lay-people were arrested in Romania and sentenced to many years of political prison because of their faith in God. Father George Calciu remembered how they prayed in the darkness of the prisons. They prayed at night while the others were sleeping. Each prayed for a quarter of an hour and then knocked the wall of the neighboring cell for the others to continue the prayer. After a while, the chain closed back to the first who started another cycle. The whole prison was praying hidden in the silent darkness of the cells, and God was present everywhere among them.

Nicodemus *"came to Jesus by night and said to Him 'Rabbi, we know that you are a teacher come from God'"* (*John 3:1*). Even suppressed daily at work and in the community, and forgetting how to pray, the spirit remains thirsty for God. A copied-by-hand manuscript, increasing its size gradually as another witness added a new story, circulated in Russia, in a secret "samizdat" manner. The Russian dissident Vladimir Bukovsky's definition of *samizdat* was, "I myself create it, edit it, censor it, publish it, distribute it, and get imprisoned for it." The manuscript related the miraculous life of Father Arseny Streltzoff who had spent twenty years in a gulag.

"Joseph of Arimathea, a prominent council member, who was also himself waiting for the kingdom of God, coming and taking courage, went in to Pilate and asked for the body of Jesus" (*Mark 15:43*). He was joined by Nicodemus who was *"a ruler of the Jews"* (*John 3:1*) and *"one of them"* (*John 7:50*) and who, by fearing the Pharisees, had visited Jesus to talk about his doubts in the darkness of the night (see *John 19:39*). All this time the others preferred to stay aside, watching from their hiding place, and leaving Our Lord's body prey to the anger of the crowds and to happenstance. According to the tradition of the Church, both Nicodemus and Joseph eventually had the courage to reveal the truth and their lives ended in martyrdom.

The communist gulags have brought forth many examples of strong Christian belief, unalterable by torture and other physical punishments and secretly kept inside, under a humble, kind appearance. Costache Oprisan was one of these. Mightily sick of tuberculosis, but without complaining, he helped the others with love and humility. The prison inmate Father George Calciu wrote about his inspiring life and death in the chapter "The message of a living martyr" in his book (Calciu, 1997). The legendary Father Arseny Streltzoff's life in Siberia's gulags was another deeply touching and inspiring example.

Unfortunately, under the atheist communist regime, there were people who preferred to deny formally their faith, because they were eager to grab the social advantages cunningly offered by the government. *"Nevertheless even among the rulers many believed in Him, but because of the Pharisees they did not confess Him, lest they should be put out of the synagogue: for they loved the praise of men more than the praise of God"* (*John 12:42-43*).

TRUST IN GOD. As soon as we decided to follow Christ we have to fully rely on Him, to trust His decisions. The Lord asked Abraham to leave his father's land and to go into Canaan (*Genesis 12:1*). Abraham obeyed, abandoned everything, and left. The Lord promised numerous progeny to Abraham. He said, *"I will make your seed as the dust of the earth; that if a man could number the dust of the earth, then your seed also could be numbered"* (*Genesis 13:16*). Later, after many events, trials and hardship, the Lord appeared in Abraham's dream, encouraged him and made new promises, *"Do not be afraid, Abram. I am your shield and will be your exceedingly great reward"* (*Genesis 15:1*). Abraham asked the Lord, *"Lord, what will You give me, seeing I go childless, and the heir of my house is Eliezer of Damascus?"* The Lord answered, *"Look now toward heaven, and count the stars if you are able to number them...so shall your seed be"* (*Genesis 15:1-2, 5*). Abraham trusted God, and God considered this as a sign of the purity of his soul.

98

God's words proved to be true. Eventually, Isaac was born. However, a number of years passed and the Lord told Abraham, *"Take now your beloved son, Isaac, whom you love and go to the land of Moriah, and offer him there as a whole burnt offering on one of the mountains I tell you"* (*Genesis 22:2*). Abraham went where he was ordered and took out the knife to kill his son but... an Angel stopped him, and truly, Abraham's descendants were as numerous as God had promised him a long time before! The same happened with God's promise about the land for Abraham's descendants.

So much faith Abraham had! So consistent was his patience of waiting for the fulfillment of Lord's promise! Doubt did not trouble his spirit. Why should we lose our faith during our life's journey, going through the fire of our trials and feeling that God does not listen to the voice of our supplications? We might say, "All right, but when will God make me a promise as He did with Abraham?" He made it the very moment we were born. When we came into this world, He promised us the gift of life. We do not know if our earthly life will be long or short but the fact that *it is life* means a promise. Let us not despair and let us continue walking the road of our life with patience, courage, and hope.

WE ARE HELPED. We are given an unseen angel at the time of baptism in order to protect us at every occurrence. I realized it with goose bumps after coming safely through several dramatic events of my life. The Morning Prayer calls him the "Christ's Angel" because our baptism carries a hidden Christic meaning and because he will defend us on our way to salvation. He will be with us after death. He will accompany us through the scary and severe aerial Tollhouses. He will plead on our behalf at the Last Judgment. The angels are always next to us. When I was a little child, my mother advised me, by using words originating from the Romanian folk wisdom that also express parents' care for keeping their children safe: "Hold the knife with its pointed end down. You might hurt your guard angel."

"Then all nations of the earth shall see you are called by the name of the Lord, and they shall be afraid of you" (*Deuteronomy 28:10*). This is how one of the blessings, given to Israel by Moses from the Mount Gerizim, sounds. The name is the mark and the skin of our soul and was sealed up forever by baptism. The name's power is very strong. Our Lord's Name is the core of our secret and intimate prayer to Jesus. At baptism, our name becomes the name upon which the Lord will make all His accountings.

Some parents take care that their little ones carry names of saints. Because the saints are already people fully loved by God and their soul mirrors God, the power of the saints' names will be transmitted to those who carry the saints' names, together with the saints' protection and intercession. Very often, when I meet someone whose name does not have a Christian correspondent like Roxanne, April, Nadia, Argentina or Serena, I think of Vittoria Lipan, the feminine character of a popular novel of the Romanian writer Mihai Sadoveanu. She knew the secret name of her husband, different from that the world knew, and in their intimate conversations, soul to soul, or in her prayers for him, she used it. This name was the name of a saint. For the person without a specific Christian correspondent name, we might look at the Church calendar for a secret personal name, proper to God's hidden universe. The name of the saint for that person's birthday might be used in our prayers instead of the worldly name.

LIVING IN FAITH IS A LEARNING PROCESS. As the Christians use to say, faith has no value if it is only accepted but not lived. The real understanding of the Lord's teachings and the authentic faith can be achieved only by living. The Russian theologian Vladimir Lossky wrote that Christianity is not a school of philosophy debating abstract concepts but, first of all, is a communion with the living God (Lossky, 1997). One can find the same opinion in the writings of the Elder Silouan from Mount Athos who avoided recommending people to spend their time with philosophy, even with a mystical philosophy.

Christians are disciples like the Apostles. Their Teacher is the wisdom of Christ's Church that is inspired by the Holy Ghost. They learn principles and rules, assimilate the experience resulted from various trials of their own life, practice the virtues, fast and pray, but there is a lot that they do not understand yet. However, when the Lord decides, they suddenly have the revelation of faith. *"He who has ears to hear, let him hear"* (*Matthew 11:15 and 13:9*). Everything becomes clear at that moment, the meanings tie together, and a mysteriously peaceful joy fills their soul. This is due to the revelatory descent of the grace of the Holy Spirit in the Christian's heart as, a long time ago, the Holy Spirit descended at Pentecost on Our Lord's disciples as tongues of fire. The sudden revelation is followed by an ardent living faith, which will support the spiritual work of the long and never finished process of deification (theosis). From now on, the journey toward God will consist of three phases, according to the Romanian theologian Dumitru Staniloae (Staniloae, 2002). The initial active phase, with the goal of dispassion and proficiency in virtues, will be followed by the phase of the contemplation of the created nature, which is a moral philosophy that explains the Lord's action in His creation. The third phase is the theological phase of the mystical contemplation of God Himself, which is a state of pure prayer. The youth Timothy was the son of a Greek (Gentile) father and a devout Jewish mother, and he had the privilege of gaining Saint Paul's attention. The Apostle gave him advice such as the following: *"Evil men and impostors will grow worse and worse, deceiving and being deceived. But you must continue in the things which you have learned and been assured of, knowing from whom you have learned them, and that from childhood you have known the Holy Scriptures, which are able to make you wise for salvation through faith which is in Christ Jesus. All Scripture is given by inspiration of God, and is profitable for doctrine, for reproof, for correction, for instruction in righteousness, that the man of God may be complete, thoroughly equipped for every good work"* (*2 Timothy 3:13-17*).

The Christian builds his life by working secretly inwardly, without ostentation and without falling prey to worldly temptations. "The wind carries very far, on its wings, both the scent of Sandalwood and the stink of carcasses, but it does not blend one into the other because it is only a vehicle. The same way the soul liberated from passion and directed toward God lives her life in the world she passes through [and observes all the world's pleasant and unpleasant aspects], but does not blend into the world" (Ramakrishna, 1936).

To live a Christian life is a continuous learning process involving mind, heart, and spirit. We are born in a world that, even when it cultivates moral truth, denies many Christian principles. *"I have given them Your word; and the world has hated them because they are not of the world, just as I am not of the world,"* Our Lord Jesus Christ said in His prayer to God the Father (*John 17:14*). The first Christians hid from the Roman world. They gathered in catacombs where the Romans were afraid to enter, because the catacombs to the Romans were equivalent to the darkness of death. After the world became Christian, the people who burned with the fire of faith and remained truly devoted to God, ran away from the world, hiding themselves in the desert. Then, along through the centuries, the truly faithful people, devoting their entire life to God, found another way of solitude, far from the real world, by living in remote places in monasteries, hermitages, and sketes, or as completely unknown simple ascetics in the depths of the wilderness. Today, as Paul Evdokimov noted (Evdokimov, 1977), Christians achieve anchorite reclusion in the midst of the crowds, the hidden, hardly accessible skete being their own heart.

ODOR OF SINS. Father Ambrosius was canonized as a saint after a long delay because of the Revolution in 1917. He died after very long hard suffering. He predicted the day of his death and even the way he would depart from this life. That day and hour, the monk who finished reading the Canon of the Theotokos, next to Father Ambrossius' bed, made a cross over the body of the ill elder. The dying Father, with closed eyes, slowly raised his right arm to cross himself. He succeeded touching the forehead, the chest, and the right shoulder. He lost the last bit of energy, so his hand landed hard on his left shoulder as a result of his superhuman effort. Then he sighed three times and died.

His face looked wonderful and bright, with the expression of a warm welcome greeting. Nevertheless, later on, as his body was surrounded by numerous burning candles, droplets of sweat started to cover his forehead and a heavy stench spread in the whole chapel. The monks remembered that, when Father Ambrosius fell ill, he asked the others to read for him, from the book of Job, the details about how all the family ran away from his place due to the unbearable stink: *"I am repulsive to my wife, loathsome to the sons of my own mother..."* (*Job 19:17*). The elder considered that he deserved all this misery because during his life he had accepted many undeserved honors from others.

But before long, despite the fact that the air in the chapel became extremely hot due to the crowds arriving to see him, the body began to spread a sweet fragrance that remained all the rest of the days until after the funeral. Dostoyevsky described very accurately this "smell of corruption" in the above-mentioned novel, when he wrote about the death of his literary character, father Zosima. It is very astonishing that the writer had finished his book ten years before the actual death of Father Ambrosius.

THE FIRE OF HEART. The mind perceives quickly the call to faith but the fire kindled in the mind is like a fire of straw. Fortunately, its blaze, powerful and immediate, kindles the heart and the fire of the heart is then stable. The heart is the only part of us that believes intensely and powerfully. Therefore, Orthodoxy refuses to use the tools of logic to dissect all the details regarding Lord's teachings, like for instance the mysteries of the Holy Trinity, the two natures of Christ's Person, or the afterlife. I remember the story written by the Russian scholar and theologian Paul Florensky about the humble monk Isidor (Florensky, 1987). The brilliant intellectual highly respected and admired this gentle monk for his lofty but simple spirituality. The elder Isidor wisely avoided discussing complicated theological problems that, as he humbly said, was the task of the more knowledgeable people who received more of God's grace. However, this way of thinking did not diminish the great sanctity of monk Isidor's person.

We can read in Patericon about Abba Lot who visited Abba Joseph to ask for advice to improve his spiritual struggle (Patericul, 1999a). Abba Lot began by telling Abba Joseph what he had been doing so far: fasting, praying, meditating, living in peace, and striving to purify his thoughts. He wondered what else he should do in addition to all these. Abba Joseph raised his arms up toward heaven and prayed. Tongues of fire came out of each of his fingers. He said to Abba Lot,"If you will, you can be all fire!" Our heart must burn longing for God's Person. *"For our God is a consuming fire,"* as Saint Paul said (*Hebrews 12:29*). The Holy Spirit descended on the Apostles' heads in tongues of fire (*Acts 2:3*).

Let us remember the conversation of Moses with God on Mount Sinai. *"The sight of the Lord's glory was like a burning fire on the top of the mountain"* (*Exodus 24:17*). And that fire was kindled in Moses. *"The skin of his face shone because he had been talking with God"* (*Exodus 34:29*, Revised Standard Version). An old icon refers to those moments. It is called the "Burning Bush Never Consumed" and does not represent Moses but the Theotokos with the Holy Child in the middle of a star of fire surrounded by angels. The Theotokos is the symbol of the fire of prayer - a fire that is unceasingly burning, without harm, and takes us up toward the heavens. The iconographer has painted a ladder on the Theotokos' chest – the ladder of ascension toward the Lord. In the years 1945-1958 the Romanian spiritual movement "The Burning Bush" from the Monastery Antim gathered together monks and priests with writers, composers, scientists, and many other laymen. They venerated this icon with a special Akathist Hymn, as a complex symbol of the Jesus Prayer, which is the Prayer of Heart that sets the spirit in flames and fills the whole human being with the infinite peace and happiness of the Lord's presence.

FOUR SUPREME CHRISTIAN FEATURES. On the 17th of September the Orthodox Church remembers three martyred maidens, Pistis ("faith" in Greek), Elpis ("hope") and Agapi ("love"), and their mother Sophia ("wisdom"), who were tortured and killed in the year 137 under the Roman emperor Hadrian. What a wonderful chain of supreme virtues! Faith, hope, love, and wisdom! However, love is above everything. As Saint Paul said, *"Though I speak with the tongues of men and of angels, but have not love I have become sounding brass or a clanging cymbal... And now abide faith, hope, love, these three; but the greatest of these is love"* (*1 Corinthians 13:1, 4-7, 13*).

Suffering becomes endurable by faith and transfigured by hope and love. A life spent that way is rich and fruitful. Mark Twain's saying sounds unforgettably great: "Wrinkles should merely indicate where the smiles have been."

"Love one another; as I have loved you, that you also love one another," said the Lord (*John 13:34*). *"Bear one another's burdens, and so fulfill the law of Christ,"* wrote Saint Paul, His Apostle (*Galatians 6:2*). The life of a Christian follows a long road leading from virtue to virtue, toward the state of full love. Saint Peter advised his disciples with words like these: *"Add to your faith virtue, to virtue knowledge, to knowledge self-control, to self-control perseverance, to perseverance godliness, to godliness brotherly kindness, to brotherly kindness love"* (*2 Peter 1:5-7*). The whole evolution process ends with the stage of Love that is actually the unit of measure of our closeness to God.

Many people have heard the saying: "Lord, give me serenity to accept the things that I cannot change, courage to change those that I can change, and wisdom to understand the difference between them."

We have to keep our aspirations at a moderate level and to live life according to certain balanced and compens; but we need to pursue one or two ardent goals wit passionate fire of our being. The effort and the achieve these human goals will justify our existen' good tennis players, others poets, surveyors, antiquaries, violinmakers, locksmiths, carpenters, philosophers or persistent searchers of an idea. The passionate fire that animates and justifies the Christian life is Faith. Faith helps Christians to serve God and follow Him during their entire existence.

There is no person without a certain gift or talent. We have to use and multiply our talents whether they be five, two, or one that we were given when we came into this world (*Matthew 25: 14-31*). Let us do it with diligence and devotion. *"Having then gifts differing according to the grace that is given to us, let us use them: if prophecy, let us prophesy in proportion to our faith; or ministry, let us use it in our ministering; he who teaches, in teaching; he who exhorts, in exhortation; he who gives, with liberality; he who leads, with diligence; he who shows mercy, with cheerfulness"* (*Romans 12: 6-8*).

VIRTUE OF HUMILITY. A friend once said that, in order to learn how to love his neighbor, he has first to learn knowing and loving himself. His thought began with the interpretation several European philosophers gave to Our Lord Jesus Christ's advice, *"You shall love your neighbor as yourself"* (*Matthew 22:39*). Unfortunately, the most influential modern philosophers like very often to play with words in a brilliant, but very confusing, manner. I think that the Lord talked so because He addressed the Jews who at that time were living according to the principles of law and not according to the attributes of love. They used to reply to their neighbor by the rule "an eye for an eye." We read in the Old Testament: *"If any harm follows, then you shall give life for life, eye for eye, tooth for tooth, hand for hand, foot for foot, burn for burn, wound for wound, stripe for stripe"* (*Exodus 21:23-25*, Revised Standard Version).

The temptation that is the hardest to fight against is pride. We live with it from our early childhood. It becomes an actual passion, with deep and strong roots in the flesh of our soul. The misunderstood term of "self-esteem," the pleasure of our ego, the love of ourselves, comes with a long queue of things: thinking highly of our person, loving glory and praise, being ambitious, being stubborn, jealous, and envious, feeling offended, judging others, feeling anger, hatred, quarreling, and competing, returning evil for evil, gossiping, mocking, being ironic and spiteful, and showing disrespect. Our Lord Jesus' birth is an overwhelming example of deep humility. We do not have to "love" ourselves. Humility is not a weakness, but a virtue. It gives us the strength to avoid the subjectivity of our ego and to avoid missing our goal. It is the opportunity to become closer to the blessed shadow of God.

Maybe, while waiting at the stoplight, you have tried to read the stickers glued on the trunk of the car in front of you. One of them says, "Love me as I am." It sounds very correct from the Christian standpoint regarding the way others should approach me. But what about me? Is there any reciprocity? Maybe I simply want to deliver the message, "This is me. I do not need to control myself and to correct my way of being. Good or bad, take it as it is and please love me." If I am not wrong, Jean Paul Sartre used to affirm, "Hell is others." Actually, my inferno is in me and, knowingly or unknowingly, with or without my will, I destroy what is good within me, all that I have received from my likeness to God. The Scripture said, *"God made man; in the image of God He made him"* (*Genesis 1:27*). The ego that overcomes me and makes me feel so proud; the ego that I am filled with is like a thick layer of mud that covers the mysterious kernel planted in me by God from the very beginning of my existence. That kernel is my real, unique being.

Yes, our duty is to love *ourselves*, not our ego. We have to love *our being*. We love it as something resulting from God's loving hands which made us (*Isaiah 64:8*), and from His life-giving breath. It is the very "something" we find scattered abroad in all the people who surround us. Father Thomas Hopko told us one day about an old monk who was talking with children. They were very fascinated and caught up by what he was saying about God's presence in his life. Therefore full of excitement they asked him, "Say, Father, did you see God? What is He like?" And the monk answered them, in a soft and loving voice, pointing to all the children present, one by one: "He is like you, and you, and you, and you..." Our Lord Jesus said, *"You shall love your neighbor as yourself."* We do not want to harm the pure and sublime being deep in us, mirroring God's image. We do not want to harm that image in our neighbor, either. No "an eye for an eye" rule should be applied in our relationship with the others.

LOVE FOR OUR NEIGHBOR. *"Love does no harm to a neighbor; therefore love is the fulfillment of the law"* (*Romans 13:10*). Society established a law for protecting the people. All the restrictions that the Jews' old law imposes, including those concerning adultery, murder, robbery, covetousness and all the other commandments, are contained in the commandment of love (*Romans 13:9*). Love transfigures all the law's restrictions elaborated by a cold judicious mind and makes the law acceptable to the heart. The Lord Jesus did not come to abolish the law and the prophets but to fulfill them (*Matthew 5:17*). By loving, the followers of Christ achieve a certain likeness to God Who is Total Love. By praying sincerely for the good of our neighbors who have harmed us, we finally love them.

Braham, the son of the bishop Dehqani-Tafti of the iscopal Church in Iran, was murdered in 1979. After the murder of their son, his parents paid more attention to their son's life and, as a result, their love for him increased. Bahram's blood multiplied the fruits of the Spirit in the dust of his parents' hearts. Since that time, the bishop's prayers asked God's forgiveness not only for Bahram but also for his murderers (see Every et al., 1984). Let us think of that prayer when we read so often how the newspaper, radio and TV reporters insist on stirring up the spirit of the victims' families so that they feel intense hatred and desire capital punishment for the guilty men!

Love for our neighbor is actually a gift from God, even when it comes from physical attraction, chemistry, good communication, and strong similarity of thoughts and feelings, or from close cooperation during a laborious process or a dangerous and precarious situation. We cannot acquire this love alone, with only our abilities. If we achieve something, it is unilateral, fragile, or temporary. The love God gives to us is solid, intense and for all neighbors including our enemies and it comes as a reward of an intense effort of mind, heart, and spirit. The main components of this effort are assiduous prayer and constant humility. How our heart's fire for others is ignited only God knows because the fire comes by grace. Therefore, the Holy Fathers say that the supreme measure of the strength of our faith and spiritual progress at the end of our spiritual struggle in suffering pain and privation, consists in the degree of love for our neighbor. This love is a real love because it is a total devotion to doing good for others, while we completely forget our own person. The goal of Christians, Saint Seraphim of Sarov said, is to receive the grace of the Holy Spirit. We feel that grace by the dimensions of our love.

THE GOOD DEEDS. Every time my mother mentioned someone who, full of gratitude, helped his benefactor many years after the fact, she concluded with a Romanian saying: "Do something good and toss it in the sea. Someday it will come back and it will reward you." After I grew up, I discovered that my mother spoke in the spirit of the Scripture: *"Cast your bread upon the face of the water, for you will find it after many days"* (*Ecclesiastes 11:1*). We might add what Our Lord taught us, *"When you do a charitable deed, do not let your left hand know what your right hand is doing, that your charitable deed may be in secret; and your Father who sees in secret will Himself reward you openly"* (*Matthew 6:3-4*). And also: *"You shall give to him freely, and your heart shall not be grudging when you give to him; because for this the Lord your God will bless you in all your work and in all you undertake"* (*Deuteronomy 15:10*, Revised Standard Version). Ananias and his wife Sapphira approached Peter in terms of business, with thoughts of a secret negotiation. They lied in the manner some politicians do today (*Acts 5: 1-11*). Saint Peter reproved them because no one forced them to tell the untruth that they sold the property and, in order to emphasize their devotion, they pretended that they brought to the community all the money they had earned. He said, *"After it was sold, was it not in your own control? Why have you conceived this thing in your heart? You have not lied to men but to God."* (*Acts 5:4*). And God punished them. Both of them died, to the astonishment of all the people there present.

We have to be patient in doing good for others and to carry the responsibility of sowing the seeds of love, letting God complete the rest of the process. God will make our gift yield fruits and, when He thinks it appropriate, He will return to us an overflowing bucket. *"Give, and it will be given to you: good measure, pressed down, shaken together, and running over, will be put into your bosom. For with the same measure that you use, it will be measured back to you"* (*Luke 6: 38*). We will receive at *least* the amount we gave but very often, we will be given manifold back. Was not Our Lord Jesus very generous when He converted six stone jars of water into wine, more than the people needed for the wedding dinner at the Cana of Galilee (*John 2: 1-11*)?

The archbishop Joseph Raya said that if we give a little it costs much, if we give much it costs little, and if we give all, it costs us nothing. The Romanian essayist Octavian Paler wrote that we are rich indeed, when we are happy with little. If we learn to share, we will lose the bite of greed, avidity, and covetousness, and we will finish by being happy with little.

Yes, there is a chance that the bread cast on the waters comes back to us or to someone we love. It is worthwhile not to miss this chance, even if it comes at the least expected time. But let us assume that we will never benefit from our good deed. Even then, our charitable deed is worthwhile because by it, we will make the world a better place for humankind to live in, and our own life will benefit from having done the good deed.

"MARK YOUR DAY" are the words that a friend of mine used to tell his sons. Do that for no days are alike. Actually, without doing anything special, we can mark the uniqueness of every day if we pay careful attention to the specific load of it because everyone's life is a succession of singular events.

Every liturgical day commemorates a saint whose story is always very inspiring. In the dining room of the monasteries, called refectory or trapeza, a monk reads about the life of the saint of the day while the others sit and eat. The flow of these days and great feasts can be the metronome of our spiritual life. Many people start their day by reading a fragment from the Gospel or a Psalm. My sister told me that the very few Bible verses that she had read in the morning inspired her words of love addressed to the old women she was nursing during the day. Every holiday, civilian or religious, should fill our heart with joy and we should live it fully. Thanksgiving Day has a tradition started in the New World by the colonists in Plymouth in 1621 in gratitude for the agricultural yields obtained with much hard work. The Archpriest Grigori Petrov wrote an Akathist of Thanksgiving in a Siberian prison camp in 1940, not long before dying. He was inspired by the words of Saint John Chrysostom "Glory to God for all things" that the latter said on his deathbed. The Akathist is read in many American Orthodox churches every Thursday morning of Thanksgiving. The British composer Sir John Tavener, who joined the Russian Orthodox Church in 1977, composed a highly expressive music for this Akathist in 1987.

The text of the Thanksgiving Akathist addresses the "Unchangeable Master of all times" with gratitude for all the good things, known or unknown by us, which He did and continues to do for our earthly and heavenly life. The Akathist prays for the Lord to hold us in His Mercy now and ever. Despite suffering the injustice, torture, hatred, and violence of this world, the writer of the Akathist praises the beauty of the creation: the delicate fragrance of the breeze, the majesty of the mountains joining the sky, the crystal waters mirroring the life-giving light of the sun, etc. The Akathist witnesses the joy of communication with the Lord and it prays to Him for resuscitating us and endowing our spirit with strong wings. It expresses gratitude to the Creator Who floods our soul with peace in times of suffering and hardship.

By listening to the words of Father Petrov's Akathist, we can realize the state of his spirit in facing death every day. He very often saw the reflection of God's Beauty on the silent visage of the dead. The author's steadfast hope made him stand with an intimation of eternity unshaken and without fear of facing imminent death. This hope was expressed in words like:

"Glory be to the Lord Who has covered with immortality all that is good and sublime, Who has promised us that we will eventually be able to unite with all our loved ones who have died." The Akathist is deeply inspiring and encouraging to our weak but thirsty hearts: "Make my hearing more sensitive to be able to perceive unceasingly Your mysterious whispers. We have the confidence that the Lord Who can raise back to light the consciences that started to alter and decay, will restore the soul of all who have lost it hopelessly, and bring it to its original unclouded beauty." (English translation by Marina Cheremetieff)

So let us be, on Thanksgiving Day and on every other day, grateful to all parents, relatives, teachers, supporters, and friends who touched our life with beneficial remarks. Let us especially thank God to Whom we owe everything, and let us understand that even the tragic events we had to go through were actually for the good of our eternal spirit. Let us learn to count all the moments of small joy that are spread over 24 hours. We might spend the whole day in bad moods but that is because we do not know to discern the numerous small blessings that surround us. At the Morning Prayer inherited from Metropolitan Philaret of Moscow, we say, "Teach me to treat all that comes to me throughout the day with peace of soul and with firm conviction that Thy will governs all" (see Ware, 1987). We need patience, kindness, wisdom and trust in God's work. We have "to act firmly and wisely, without embittering and embarrassing others".

Rudyard Kipling, in his great poem "If," encouraged the youth to fill the unforgiving minute with sixty sec them lived fully. Those who have practiced the and have achieved the status of an almost unc could mark every second with a word addr Learning to feel the continuous presence of th us, we succeed in giving a unique face to each portion of our day. This way, life will not be monotonous, but will be rich in meanings and will bring fortifying peace to our soul that longs for eternity.

ROLE OF PRAYER. We have to reach the stage of truly living with God, of feeling Him every moment, with every breath of ours. Saint Paul who wrote to Thessalonians, "*Rejoice always*" (*1 Thessalonians 5:16*), suggested them immediately the key of joy: "*Pray without ceasing*" (*1 Thessalonians 5:17*). The prayer is the expression of our dialogue with the Lord. This is what the Russian pilgrim wanted the most and this is why he finally succeeded in learning the Jesus Prayer, called also the Prayer of the Heart. Its short formula enables the monks to blend it with their own breath.

Father Thomas Hopko pointed out the fact that even the language of communication among the persons of the Holy Trinity is a prayer. Prayer is definitely the means of our communication with God. We end our Morning Prayer with the words, "Direct my will, teach me to pray, pray Thou Thyself in me. Amen" (see Ware, 1987). So can also be the Jesus Prayer, said in the silence of our mind, everywhere and at all times. We should say it when we are tired, when we are in danger, when we are assaulted by temptations, when we are afraid. We should say it when we are flooded with joy, when we are happy. We should say it when we go to bed, when we start the day or our work, when we watch our children, when we hear something wrong about our neighbor. The prayer makes our heart sense the Lord's warm, ubiquitous, and permanent presence and care.

Father Arseny Streltzoff, who lived twenty years in the Soviet death camps, was a living example of love and sacrifice for his neighbor. Regardless of what he had to do in obeying the guards' orders, he prayed unceasingly. Many detainees around him despised him and became angry assaulting him when they noticed the continuous movement of his silent lips, because they realized that he was deep in an unceasing interior prayer.

OUR WORK FOR EXISTENCE. In all our work, we have to do our best. The German painter Albrecht Dürer wrote in his diary that we should work not for our glory but for that of God. Yes, we have to aim high, to perfection, since Our Lord is perfect. We have to work diligently, with dedication, forcing every minute to bring forth fruits. Our conscience knows that if our boss is not always with us to put pressure on us, God is. *"But be strong and do not let your hands be weak, for there is a reward for your work"* (*2 Chronicles /2 Paraleipomenon 15:7*).

We can approach the notion of work from a theological perspective, *as a command* that was given to the first man after he was cast from Eden. Adam was given the command to work as *his sole remaining alternative* as a method to achieve the spiritual maturity that enabled him to properly use the knowledge of good and evil that he had acquired too early. If we follow the command to work to bring forth fruits, we can understand the noble principle that stands behind our honest and hard work, done with total dedication of our mind, heart, and body.

We actually work for the Lord and His Kingdom. It is a principle that applies not only to our daily work to earn our bread but also to our spiritual work: the steady prayer, the growth of virtues, and the commitment to good deeds. All of them are part of our Christian existence. *"Therefore, whether you eat or drink, or whatever you do, do all to the glory of God"* (*1 Corinthians 10:31*). Saint Paul also wrote, *"If anyone will not work, neither shall he eat"* (*2 Thessalonians 3:10*). The Creator told the first man, *"In the sweat of your face you shall eat bread till you return to the ground from which you were taken"* (*Genesis 3:19*). Is this a curse coming from anger or a punishment coming from an educational need? Neither one. This is part of the process of opening our mind, heart, and spirit to understand the reason for our existence. It is part of our mission as a human being in the created universe. Surely, if Adam had not chosen to take a bite of the tempting apple, the way of maturation would have been different and very likely it would have taken place in Paradise. In conclusion, because of our fallen condition, the work is our only chance to redeem ourselves.

We do not work to attract praise. We do not even expect to be acknowledged for our efforts. The Lord knows that we accomplished our duty well, with all our mind and heart, and this suffices. *"Whatever you do, do it heartily, as to the Lord and not to men"* (*Colossians 3:23*). If we want a little prestige, a prize, and recognition, we risk the weakening of our virtue of humility, and we need this virtue in the process of achieving a stronger faith and a deep love for God and our brothers.

We operate in concordance with the talent that we were invested with, at the top level of our capacities. *"Having the gifts, differing according to the grace that is given to us, let us use them"* (*Romans 12:6*). Thus, we become helpful to the others and we increase the Christian love in our heart. *"As each one has received a gift, minister it to one another, as good stewards of the manifold grace of God"* (*1 Peter 4:10*). There is no one in this world without an aptitude for something. Our duty is to discover this aptitude and to put it to work, respecting the specific aptitudes of others. *"And let the brightness of the Lord our God be upon us, and prosper for us the works of our hands"* (*Psalm 89/90:17*).

Before expelling Adam and telling him how harsh his labor will be to earn his bread *"in toil"* all the days of his life (*Genesis 3:17*), *"the Lord God took the man and put him in the garden of Eden to till it and keep it"* (*Genesis 2:15*, Revised Standard Version). The idea of the important task given to man in Paradise should be comforting and encouraging us toward a proper understanding of the real sense of work. As we see, the work itself does not necessarily mean toil and crushing labor but can be a pursuit that brings joy and peace as it was in Eden.

At the same time, it is scary to read Our Lords's words about the relationship between master and servant: *"Does he thank that servant because he did the things that were commanded him? I think not. So likewise you, when you have done all those things which you are commanded, say, 'We are unprofitable servants. We have done what was our duty to do '"* (*Luke 17:9-10*).

We have to comprehend that the burden of life is as it is, regardless of our feelings and opinion. If we must carry it then, let us do it with peace and all the serenity we can find in our faith. The Lord, our Master, will help us. *"I saw the Lord always before me; because He is at my right hand, that I may not be shaken"* (*Psalm 15/16:8*). He will take care of me and will make my load lighter.

VALUE OF WORK. There are several examples concerning the value of work in Patericon (Patericul, 1999a). A very pious elder full of grace had an apprentice in whose cell the evil spirits did not dare to enter. The elder wanted to know why. Therefore, one day, the elder visited the young brother and inquired about his daily activities, including the danger of laziness. The young apprentice pointed to some stones and said, "I build a wall with these and after I finish it I demolish and start again. This way I do not know what laziness is."

Another example is that of a monk who had his shack next to a pond with reeds. All day he was extremely busy making baskets out of them. After he finished the baskets, he tossed them in the river that was not far away. He did not weave the baskets for a gain of money or food but for the necessity of a labor "that induced fatigue and peace." These things accord with what Deacon Seraphim Bartneck told us he heard when he visited the monks from Mount Sinai Monastery.

It seems that work, besides generating a source of means for living, may play an important direct role in the work ethic: to prevent the laziness of the body and indirectly, to prevent the laziness of the spirit. We learn in our life that, despite the satisfaction of an accomplishment obtained with much diligence by using our top capacities, we can live without expecting praise or without even laudatory professional recognition for activities well done, because we did everything for God's glory and not for man's glory. But how should we react when our work does not reach the goal expected, when it does not lead to a real accomplishment? We try very hard to exceed our own abilities and we struggle with huge efforts to reach the target and, when we are almost to the point of seeing the accomplishment at the end of the tunnel, God destroys what we have done and we have to restart from scratch. Let us even in this case react with joy and patience and not with bitterness.

Our efforts are acknowledged in the Lord's eyes anyway. If He decided not to let us finish, it might be because he knew our weaknesses. He wants to keep the value of our endeavor hidden from the people and to help us, in this way, to keep our virtue of humility unaltered. In addition, as shown in the above paragraph, by preventing our accomplishment, God keeps us far from the laziness that gives birth to demons and exposes the spirit to temptations.

I remember that, in the summer, many villagers used to come to the Monastery Sihăstria in the Neamţ Mountains to make hay for the sheep flock at the Monastery. The men mowed the grass on the hills with scythes and the women raked and gathered the hay in stacks. Their work was very hard, in the coolness of the morning and evening and in the heat of the day. They never asked to be paid; they slept somewhere outside next to the monastery walls and ate modestly at the refectory. Despite the 10-12 hour-long workdays, the women crowded the small church at vespers, forgetting the fatigue and staying on their knees the entire service, absorbing with piety all the words of the hymns. Afterwards, under the star spangled sky they waited until midnight in line at the cell of Father Cleopa for confession. Where did that outstanding extra energy come from, after the exhausting work of the day? Why did the tired body not extinguish the great thirst of the soul of these simple and humble women?

KEEP GOD IN MIND EVERY MOMENT. Saint Gregory of Nazianz advised us to remember the Lord more often than we breathe. At every moment, He comes down to us. He knocks at our door with the desire to stay with us. It is important to welcome Him with the same frequency. We do that in a very significant way when we have communion with the Sacraments, with the bread and wine that are His Body and Blood. We prepare our soul for it, as a good host prepares the house for a very important guest, and we accomplish it by prayer, fasting, and confession. Some people say, "The communion is a simple formality; the most important is to confess your sins in order to be forgiven." Others say, "Why should I tell my sins to the priest who is also a sinner? I can confess my sins directly to God in my prayers." All of these people forget that our Christian goal is to follow Christ, to be with Him, to try to merge with His presence. We achieve that by the Sacrament of Communion. Nevertheless, we cannot be worthy of it if we do not first purify our spirit and body by confession and by living by the canon given after confession. The High Priest is Christ Himself (*Hebrews 5: 5-6*), and the priests of today act by the power given to the Apostles by the very Lord Jesus Christ.

As already mentioned, Saint Paul's words produced a shock of revelation in Saint Augustine's soul: "*Let us walk properly, as in the day, not in revelry and drunkenness, not in lewdness and lust, not in strife and envy. But put on the Lord Jesus Christ, and make no provision for the flesh, to fulfill its lusts*" (*Romans 13: 13-14*). Under the effect of these words, the young pagan intellectual Augustine, who enjoyed his concubine with his body and the Manichean thinking with his mind, began to live a different life – one marked by repentance, cleanness, and faith.

"*Agree with God, and be at peace; thereby good will come to you... If you return to the Almighty and humble yourself, if you remove unrighteousness far from your tents*" (*Job 22: 21, 23*, Revised Standard Version). Maybe the sin brought us to ruin. Maybe the struggle with poverty or other great difficulties wrecked our spirit. We have to turn to the Lord in repentance and faith. God will rebuild us. Our task is *to return*, and His is *to repair*, as in the parable of the prodigal son (*Luke 15:11-31*). As Father Anthony Mary said in a sermon, "we never find any punitive in God; remedial yes, not reprisal."

"*Their soul shall be like a fruitful tree, and they shall hunger no more*" (*Jeremiah 38:12*). The food will come from inside out, from the yield provided by a faithful soul. The same verses are translated in the Revised Standard Version as follows: "*Their life shall be like a watered garden, and they*

shall languish no more" (*Jeremiah 31:12*). It will be a garden
of God, separated from the wilderness, fenced with grace,
planted with wisdom, tilled with heaven's discipline and order,
and guarded by the Almighty's power. The separation
provided by this sacred garden does not mean forgetting the
others. Saint Seraphim of Sarov said, "Acquire the peace of
soul and thousands of people around you will find their
salvation." Living with God has an indirect beneficial
influence on our neighbors.

THE JOY TO BE WITH GOD. During our life, we have to
endure many damaging or tragic events decided by God. In
addition to that, our Church requires respecting four fasting
periods in a year, besides many fasting Wednesdays and
Fridays. We have to deprive ourselves from the "best" food
and drinks and from other pleasures of life for almost 50
percent of the year. Should the life on this earth actually be
only frustration, pain and suffering?

It is true that the tribulations are an element necessary to
our soul's maturation process. It is true that God allows
temptations to strengthen our faith. It is true that fasting helps
our efforts to grow in virtue. However, after we are brought by
the Lord from not being to being, the life on this earth,
representing the first part of our soul's eternal life, contains a
hidden joy that should continue after our departure from this
world.

This is the joy that enabled the Russian priest Grigori
Petrov, while being in a Siberian camp of death, to author his
beautiful Thanksgiving Akathist Hymn, praising the benefits
of life and the beauty of nature. The Patericon and the other
related writings say more about the exterior aspects of the
monks' ascetic struggle and less about their intimate thoughts,
but I believe a great part of their strength also comes from the

deep, peaceful joy of their soul. The love for Lord and neighbor includes *the love for life*, the love for the essence of the Creation.

What about the love for ephemeral things like the taste of a bottle of wine or a big chocolate cake? Eaten with moderation and joy in God, they might still be bliss. *"Man has nothing better to do under the sun than to eat, drink, and be merry,"* King Solomon said (*Ecclesiastes 8:15*), and, in his wisdom, he advised, *"Go eat your bread with merriment, and drink your wine with a happy heart; for now God is well pleased with your work"* (*Ecclesiastes 9:7*). However, this should be done with care and consideration, because many times *"sorrow does not mingle with gladness, but, in the end, this joy turns to sorrow"* (*Proverbs 14:13*).

Saint Apostle Paul told his young disciple, *"No longer drink only water, but use a little wine for your stomach's sake and your frequent infirmities"* (*1 Timothy 5:23*) but he advised his disciples, *"Do not be drunk with wine, in which is dissipation, but be filled with the Spirit"* (*Ephesians 5:18*).

Saint Paul also warned his followers, *"neither fornicators, nor idolaters, nor adulterers, nor homosexuals, nor sodomites, nor thieves, nor covetous, nor drunkards, nor revilers, nor extortioners will inherit the Kingdom of God"* (*1 Corinthians 6:9-10*).

The example of Job's life should encourage our heart. We read in the Holy Fathers' writings that the banquets in the rich men's houses might show love and friendship when the glasses are emptied one after the other for the health of this and that person. Nevertheless, these apparent kind gestures hide evil tides underneath, as the psalmist wrote, *"Let their dwelling place be laid waste, and let no one live in their tents. For they pursued closely the one You slew, and they added to the pain of my wounds"* (*Psalm 68/69:26-27*).

THE FINAL REWARD. Sometimes we need advice from people with deep knowledge of God. Their reliable words are for our life's journey like the North Star's guidance. We read in the Patericon that the young Zechariah saw his teacher, Abba Silouan, deep in prayer, with arms raised to the sky for several hours (Patericul, 1999a). As soon as Abba finished his prayer and relaxed, the young disciple, eager to learn as much as possible, asked him how he felt. The old monk, in self-defense, dismissed the monk's concern and simply said, "Son, I was sick today." The disciple did not give up. He kneeled at the elder's feet and begged, "I will not leave you until you tell me what you have seen with your soul." Then the old man took a deep breath and, with a sigh, said, "I was taken into heaven. I have seen the glory of God and I stayed there a long time. I came back a few moments ago." This sounds like the episode that Saint Paul mentioned in one of his epistles (*2 Corinthians 12:2-6*).

Inspired by the Saints' words and lives, we might make major spiritual discoveries, as the Romanian poet Sandu Tudor experienced, when he visited Mount Athos. He decided to renounce any intellectual adventure and to obey completely a humble old monk who led him from monastery to monastery, and from skete to skete. The monk crossed himself and made three prostrations in front of each icon. The poet did the same. After a while, the mechanical prostrations begun to warm up his heart, his spirit opened like a flower and the poet became receptive to the very holiness of the place. All this happened without words, without philosophical theories, without poetic adornments – just by simple veneration, respect, and short prayers. A process of spiritual transformation started in his soul, a process that was going to continue the whole rest of his life. Later, he became the hieromonk Daniel and he died in 1962 as a martyr for the faith in a communist prison.

The peaceful joy man experiences in his soul when God reveals to him deep meanings, is sometimes so great that it can cause the need and even the responsibility to share these precious thoughts and feelings with others. Saint Paul wrote, *"For if I preach the Gospel, I have nothing to boast of, for necessity is laid upon me; yes, woe is me if I do not preach the gospel!" (1 Corinthians 9:16).* It is like a big river that overflows the shores and fertilizes the neighboring land.

With his faith triggered on Mount Athos, the poet Sandu Tudor initiated later the well-known spiritual movement "The Burning Bush" at Antim Monastery in Bucharest. In that environment highly blessed with intense religious fervor, he wrote *The Burning Bush Akathist Hymn* dedicated to the Theotokos.

Fifty years later, when the communist regime was abolished and religious freedom was reestablished, the Akathist Hymn could be freely accessed by the multitude of churchgoers who began to love it and use it in their regular prayers. This fact was a big surprise for many, because the author included in the Akathist many rare and uncommon words, in order to express deep sacred mysteries. Despite that, simple uneducated workers and villagers, illumined by the Holy Spirit of their own faith, achieved naturally a full understanding of the verses overly rich in symbols.

This is a part of the miracles that occur in a heart longing for God, Who is the Protector, the Comforter and the Savior. *"I lifted my eyes to the mountains. From where shall my help come? My help comes from the Lord, who made heaven and earth"* *(Psalm 120/121:1-2).*

"A king is not saved by his large army; and a giant shall not be saved by his immense strength; a horse is a false hope for salvation, and it shall not be saved by its enormous power. Behold, the eyes of the Lord are on those who fear Him, on those who hope in His mercy, to deliver their souls from death, and to keep them alive in famine" (*Psalm 32/33:16-19*).

2. Living a Christian Life.

As soon as we have accepted the idea of God's existence and we have decided to live in faith, the key words that explain and guide our new manner of living are "The soul is eternal." In other words, there is life beyond the physical death and this life has no end. This is why the incarnation of the Son of God took place and why Our Lord Jesus Christ stayed a short while among us: to warn us of the perpetual life we were brought into when we were born. He called our attention to the fact that the earthly existence is a present but also our only chance to make our future eternity a happy state instead of an unbearable burden. Even if we ignore it, we *are* and *we will be* with God *all the time.* Therefore, it is for our good to learn to live conscious of His presence and to aspire to be closer to His own nature. We understand now the deep meaning of our earthly life and, from now on, we will look in a different way at the surrounding world. Thus, we will enjoy what was given to us. We will also approach the difficulties, tribulations, suffering, and illness with another attitude. Saint Dimitry, the Metropolitan of Rostov, noted that without bread for the body and without the thought of death for the soul, man becomes very weak.

2.1. The goal of a Christian life

WE HAVE TO PREPARE OURSELVES FOR ETERNAL LIFE because it *exists*. The state our body and soul are in when we start our earthly life does not fit the requirements for a happy everlasting life. *"For behold I was conceived in trans-*

gressions, and in sins my mother bore me." (*Psalm 50/51:7*). We have to transform ourselves. It seems impossible. Nevertheless, we receive much help if we decide to start the process of repentance ("metanoia" in Greek), of identifying the wrong sides of our being, of purifying it, and of changing ourselves. We are told that initially our human nature was different, as was that of the first man in Eden, and that we were made in *the image and likeness of God*, and it is the <u>likeness</u> that we have to regain. Fortunately, we did not lose the likeness completely. It is still in us but it is buried deep underneath all the layers of wrong doings and feelings. We have to rediscover it. We are helped in this process by the baptism that we receive in Church and by following Christ, the Son of God. It is only for us to start the hard work to trigger the process of deification. This is the reason of our life on earth. Preparing ourselves for eternity, we will be able to achieve the state man was created for: to live in the shadow of the Lord and to enjoy the order and beauty of the Creation.

"For indeed, the kingdom of God is within you," said Our Lord (*Luke 17:21*). The kingdom of God is a spiritual reality inside each believer. Unfortunately, I stain it every day with my sin. I crucify Christ with my transgressions. Does that not make my heart bleed?

THREE THINGS ARE IMPORTANT FOR A MAN during his life: to believe in God, to be conscious that His presence is with him every second, and to be aware of the Last Judgment. Everything else is a consequence of these three things. From the first, we receive understanding of the structure of the world, confidence in the power of life, hope, tolerance for the others and, eventually, love for God and neighbors. From the second we benefit from the feeling that we are not alone and abandoned, and we receive the needed support for our actions, the power of prayer, the blessings in the mornings and the promise of rest in the evenings. From the third, we discover the sense of duty and responsibility, the need of a vigilant watch for any evil temptations, the need for the strength of the virtues and the certitude of eternity for our soul and finally peace beyond all the turmoil. Well, where is the joy of life in all these? The joy results from the three strengths mentioned above that prepare the ground for the Sacrament of Confession, followed by the Communion with God, the incessant source of peace, power, and touch of eternity, raising us above the annoying traps and burdens of daily life.

The man who is restless in God, he is for God. The man who is resting in God, he is for God. However, the latter is better. Therefore, Saint Augustine wrote, "Martha is who we are. Mary is who we hope to be" (*see Luke 10:38-42*).

Father Thomas Hopko's mother asked her young son to firmly respect three rules, regardless of what he was doing: to say his prayers in his small room, to go to church and to keep the Lord in his mind and heart at every moment. These rules gradually will be marked by an extraordinary tension produced by the awareness of the gravity of our sins but, at the same time, by a never extinguishable love for God. In a morning prayer we say, "Our Lord Jesus Christ, the true Light, who sanctifies and enlightens every man that comes into this world, let the Light of Your Face shine upon us to enable us to see Thine Unapproachable Light."

RESPONDING TO GOD'S CALL. God sanctified us from the very moment we were created, from the instant we were conceived in our mother's womb. Even more, we continuously receive help in our spiritual life, because, due to His love for man, God the Father sent His Son to incarnate Himself, to live *among us*, to teach us, and to defeat Death (see *John 3:16*). He did that to lead us on the way to escape from the burden of sins and, by His sacrifice, He defeated the original sin, that is deeply planted in ourselves and is extremely damaging.

I hear in our city the siren of ambulances almost every half-hour. The ambulance crews are very prompt in responding to calls, ignoring their own needs, ready to help with courage and high professionalism, and driving fast to arrive where a body lies in extreme pain and cannot wait. I could think of an ambulance as God and the person seriously injured, lying on the street or on a bed of suffering, as myself, as the parable of the Good Samaritan (*Luke 10:30-37*) often is interpreted. On the other hand, the paramedics' rush back to the hospital should be the rush of my soul to be saved, especially because the place where my soul runs to with the flashing lights and sirens on, there is Someone Who truly heals, helping us to become a new person.

"*So the Lord God called Adam and said to him, "Adam where are you?*" (*Genesis 3:9*), but the man who had sinned was hiding. God looks for us all the time. Every sin hides us from His sight. Nevertheless, He does not cease to look for us in order to save, to heal, and to make us able to walk on the right path. A very common picture represents Our Lord Jesus knocking at the door. I hung it on the wall opposite my bed to be able to see it before falling asleep and after waking up, and to keep my conscience alert. I was afraid of missing His knock, due to all my daily worries and desires. "*Behold, I stand at the door and knock. If anyone hears My voice and opens the door, I will come in to him and dine with him, and he with Me*" (*Revelation 3:20*). The few pictures with the Savior at the door, which the orthodox tradition knows, show a door without knob. The knob is inside and therefore it totally depends on us whether Christ will enter the intimate room of our soul.

My heart has to be sensitive and open to guests as was

Abraham's heart when he saw the three travelers who actually represented the Holy Trinity (*Genesis 18:2*). As God manifested Himself through the three human travelers, Our Lord Jesus could be felt in each of our neighbors. *"I was a stranger and you did not take Me in"* (*Matthew 25:43*). Let us think of Leo Tolstoy's story about the shoemaker who learned to see the Lord Jesus in everyone who was appealing to his conscience for help. We will be judged for our lack of a positive response to the solicitors and we do not know when the time of Judgment will come. The Judge will take us by surprise like lightning (*Mathew 24:27*) or like a thief in the night (*1 Thessalonians 5:2*). The people who watch, waiting for the Master's knock at the door, are fortunate because *"He will gird himself and have them sit down to eat, and will come and serve them"* (*Luke 12:35-40*). Let us pay attention to how beneficial our watch will then be. After being accepted, in His reciprocity and His respect for our freedom of choice, Our Lord will not be the Master anymore. He will treat us with love like a servant (*Luke 12:35-40*) or like the Teacher Who washed His disciples' feet (*John 13:5*).

There is also another side of the story regarding the knock on the door. One day, chased by the shadows, storms and tragedies of my life, I might knock on Our Lord's door to ask for help or for shelter, and I am afraid the Master of the house will not open the door (*Luke 13:25*).

THE GOAL AND THE ESSENCE OF ORTHODOXY is *deification* – uniting with God through His energies. The Romanian philosopher Mircea Vulcănescu noticed that the Law for a catholic is a natural law ("what it is, it is so"), for a protestant the law is a moral law ("what it is, it must be so"), and for an orthodox is a law of deification ("what it is, it should be so"). In other words, the law "it is not so" i.e. from

2. LIVING A CHRISTIAN LIFE | 131

this created world, "it is not a must be so." It is not so due to
the personal efforts of man, but "it should be so" because it is
from the Kingdom of God, as it is revealed to us while we
advance on our path to deification. Continuing to speak in
Vulcănescu's terms, if the Catholic and Protestant Churches
consider the Christian's soul a limited object – an actual one,
the Orthodox Church considers it an unlimited object – a
virtual one (Vulcănescu, 2004).

WE ASK FOR GOD. When we say the prayer "Our Father,"
that we have learned from Our Lord Jesus Christ, we
pronounce the words "Thy Kingdom come." By repeating the
Lord's Prayer at home in the morning, at meals, in the evening,
and at church, these words become part of us and of the
rhythm of our life. They become our continuous aspiration.
During the deification process we walk toward God and, in
reciprocity, His Kingdom comes towards us. As Mother
Cassiana from Lake George Monastery noticed, the verse "Thy
Kingdom come" is heard before the verse "Give us this day our
daily bread," which means we ask first for the food of our soul
and only second for the food of our body. The Romanian
Hieromonk Raphael Noica underlined the ancient Romanian
translation of the request for bread, "Pâinea noastră cea spre
fiinţă dă-ne-o nouă astăzi" (i.e. not simply "Give us this day
our daily bread" but "Give us this day our bread for being").
This clause expresses the continuous need for feeding the very
essence of our being, of our human nature, of our spiritual
growth, and of our deification process, with a divine food.

GOD'S PARTICIPATION. Regarding the Savior's person,
Saint Apostle Peter wrote, "His divine power has given to us
all things that pertain to life and godliness, through the
knowledge of Him who called us by glory and virtue, by which

have been given to us exceedingly great and precious promises, that through these you may be <u>partakers of the divine nature</u>, having escaped the corruption that is in the world through lust" (*2 Peter 1:3-4*). As we will discuss this teaching in the following chapter, we will learn that we are not called to be partakers of God's nature itself, because God's nature is not cognizable; rather we are called to partake of the divine manifestation of God through His energies. These energies are working in the created world but they are not part of creation. They belong entirely to God alone and therefore are named <u>uncreated energies</u>. Saint Gregory Palamas wrote about them. According to what we learn from Vladimir Lossky's important book about the mystical theology of the Eastern Church, we can know only that part of the Lord's will that is expressed in His connection with the created world. This Lord's will is the contact point between finite and infinite.

OUR PARTICIPATION. As Father Kallistos underlined, the deification "is not something reserved for a few select initiates, but something intended for all alike" (Ware, 1987). "Deification always presupposes a continued act of repentance." If someone asks what one must follow in order to be deified, "The answer is simple: go to church, receive the sacraments regularly, pray to God 'in spirit and in truth', read the Gospels, follow the commandments" (Ware, 1987). "Deification is not a solitary but a 'social' process," because as the Holy Trinity dwells in each other, a man must dwell with his fellow men. We have to love God and our neighbor. Abba Anthony of Egypt said that from our neighbor is life, and from our neighbor is death (see Sayings of the Desert Fathers, 1975). In other words, our eternal life depends on our love for others. Deification also requires good deeds because as Father Kallistos wrote, "love of God and of other men must be practical." Deification "presupposes life in the Church, life in the sacraments." Only so can man "acquire the sanctifying Spirit and be transformed into divine likeness," a likeness that man lost with the first sin (see Ware, 1987). Saint John Chrysostom wrote that when we are at the Last Judgment, all the people that we helped will cry out to support and defend us in front of the Great Judge.

STAGES OF DEIFICATION. We strive for a complete unification with the Lord by focusing on two planes: action (purifying our heart) and contemplation (meditating on grace). Saint Isaac the Syrian, quoted by Lossky (Lossky, 1997), considered three stages in our struggle for unification with God: repentance (change of will), purification (dispassion), and perfection (acquiring the fullness of love). The repentance, according to Saint John Climacus, is a renewal of baptism - a thirst for the fruit of grace that we received at baptism together with a guardian angel. Repentance is, according to Saint Isaac the Syrian, a strong shaking to awaken our soul in front of heaven's gate. As Vladimir Lossky emphasized, we will not be condemned for not having done miracles, but we will be judged for not having mourned for our sins.

Mircea Vulcănescu distinguished the following six stages in the inner transformation of a Christian: humility that leads to an understanding of human weaknesses, resignation that adds strength of endurance, repentance that ignites the decision to improve, expiation that adds the bitter mature reminder of suffering, redemption that opens the heart for receiving God's grace, and finally salvation (Vulcănescu, 2004). I think that if a distance reasonably <u>measured in human units</u> separates the former four mentioned stages from each other, a distance inspirationally <u>measured in the Lord's terms</u> separates the latter two stages. The efforts made in the first four stages are very worthy regardless of the response from heaven. Very likely, the complete achievement of supreme virtues such as love and humility will be the sign of the moment when the expiation stage ends and the beneficial divine touch begins.

Father Dumitru Staniloae distinguished three great stages in a Christian's life along his way of deification (Staniloae, 2002). They are: (1) the active stage, when man labors for dispassion and growth of virtue, (2) the contemplative stage, when man contemplates the created world and (3) the theological stage, when man contemplates God's world. The bridge between the two first stages is provided by the spiritual love that comes after the purification from passions.

The second stage, that of contemplating the material creation, is concluded by acquiring the knowledge of the corporal world.

The third stage contains (a) the sub-stage of contemplating the bodiless beings such as the Angels that leads to the knowledge of the non-corporal world, and (b) the sub-stage of contemplating God that leads to the knowledge of the Holy Trinity, expressed by an ecstasy of love brought on by dedicated concentration on the Lord.

Philokalia is a collection of Holy Fathers' teachings about living with the presence of God, based on the Prayer of Heart (Jesus Prayer). Philokalia traces its name to the term *Love of Beauty*, because as the Russian theologian Nicolai Arseniev said, "Beauty helps the soul to prepare for the meeting with the Lord." According to Father Coniaris (Coniaris, 1998), Philokalia talks about ten important subjects, arranged spiritually in an ascending order. They are: (1) dispassion, (2) purification of heart, (3) humility, (4) watching out for temptations, (5) Jesus Prayer (the most efficient weapon in our battle), (6) guarding the thoughts while praying, (7) attention, (8) prayer, (9) unification with Christ in love, and (10) real wisdom, when the heart enjoys the profound peace of the depths and heights of true knowledge. Those who reached this last stage bring the Lord's light on all the people around them. "Acquire a peaceful spirit, and around you thousands will be saved," Saint Seraphim of Sarov said.

AWARE OF SIN. Mircea Vulcănescu wrote that although Christians start their spiritual work with the discovery that they live in a sinful world and that they have their own sins, Christianity does not consist of a feeling of guilt but rather consists of the road exiting the dark sinful state and leading toward God's perpetual light. Let us think of the Savior's first words when He began His spiritual activity in the human world: *"The time is fulfilled and the kingdom of God is at hand. Repent and believe in the gospel"* (*Mark 1:15*).

We hear every year the Gospel reading about the healing of the paralytic (*Matthew 9:1-8*). Before accomplishing the miraculous physical healing of the paralytic, the Savior forgave the sick man's sins, and the scribes considered this a blasphemy. Did we ever stop to pay deeper attention to Our Lord's words? He asked, *"Which is easier, to say, 'Your sins are forgiven', or to say, 'Arise and walk?'"* In other words, it is actually harder to forgive the sins than to miraculously heal an illness! This is a really FRIGHTENING discovery!

It is good to start our spiritual introspection with the intense emotion of this striking discovery. Father Dane Popovich said that Adam's sin was much greater and more damaging than ours because his nature was pure, without sin, while we are born in an already sinning world, as the psalmist David said in *Psalm 50/51:7*. However, we have to deal with our denatured structure, prone to sin, and to try to improve it.

A monk asked an elder why many worries come to his mind while he is praying. The elder replied that the evil spirit, who out of his pride refused to obey God, the Master of the Universe, and estranged himself from the heavens, wants to make us endure his present misery and therefore tries to pull us away from our connection with God (Patericul, 1999a).

THE REAL HUMAN NATURE IS GOOD. I firmly believe that, because man was built according to God's image, only the fallen angel is truly evil. What is not good in man is the sin, and the sin is the consequence of lack of opposition to the assault of the temptations. The road of the sinful through life is wide. It is very easy to walk on it, and it seems to be much shorter. By contrast, the road that requires a continuous cleaning of soul and body is strenuous, narrow, and long.

Father Constantine Galeriu said that the origin of evil is not in matter, as Plato thought, but in the pride and vainglory of the soul. He also says that evil is not human but inhuman, because it existed before man was created. Evil is everything that does not possess a creative ability and leads to destruction – pleasure, desire, addiction.

Some Western Christian Churches say that the human nature became sinful as a result of Adam's fall and it is enough to believe in the Lord Jesus Christ in order to be saved, as we read in *Acts 16:30*. We, the Orthodox, think that man did not lose the image of God because the human being was created with a superior nature to that of the angels. However, man has to restore his likeness with God. Human nature in its profound essence was not and is not sinful but is weak in the absence of God. It can surrender in the battle against temptations and consequently can commit sins. We are born again by God's grace, we are forgiven by Christ's gift as a response to our spiritual efforts, and we are sanctified, freed from sin, by the Holy Spirit's work.

DEIFICATION IS A VERY LONG PROCESS and it is delayed because of the impurities caused by the sins. Therefore, it is not true that salvation comes at once, the very moment you believe in Christ, as the Protestants affirm. The paralytic from Bethesda (*John 5:2-9*) and the old woman who was bent over (*Luke 13:10-13*) were healed at once. Nevertheless, we know that no physical healing comes without the spiritual healing that is the forgiveness of sins (see for instance *Matthew 9:1-8* and *John 5:1-16*). These two people had been suffering for long time – the old woman for 18 years, the paralytic for 38 years. The long periods of suffering generated a harsh battle in their heart and, very probably, they obtained the spiritual victory that God liked. This is why Our Lord Jesus decided to heal them. It only appeared that they were saved at once. Their salvation was in fact prepared in time during their struggle and life in faith.

ARE THERE CHOSEN PEOPLE? We might wonder, based on some of Saint Augustine's precepts, why the Creator privileges some people and grants them good conditions of spiritual growth while He abandons and exposes others to the irresistible evil influences. I think there is no predestination. We all are given opportunities to mature spiritually and, whether some do not succeed while others are more or less successful, depends first on their own will, and only second, on the force of their calling. However, there are still a few that are chosen from the very beginning, before they make any effort to approach God. These are the saints that the Creator plants in the world to help us with their powerful prayers and to stimulate the positive work of our soul. They do not need, like the rest of us, to experience the challenges of an entire life in order to understand the truth and to believe in it. They are saints since their childhood, as Abba Silouan noted. They are never happy to live on our world's terms. They prefer to live on the terms of the Heavenly Kingdom and many end in dying as a martyr.

NOBODY IS PREDESTINED. In a prayer of the hours of the day that the Church inherited from Saint John Chrysostom we say, "Lord, I know that You do as You wish; so let Your will also be with me, the sinner, that You are praised forever." Does God's will decide our life ahead of time? What about the liberty of decision that God gave man?

People are not designed good or evil persons at their birth. The temptations are the same for all people, only the number and the severity of the temptations differ according to the strength of everyone's spirit. God never gives anyone tribulations that overwhelm and destroy them. God never makes the "not chosen ones" evil persons who will perish.

Judas had many opportunities to change his mind. These opportunities are mentioned in the services of Holy Wednesday and Thursday. Judas was not "chosen" to do evil. The betrayal of Judas was not necessary for the divine plan of salvation of mankind, with the incarnate Son of God's work on the Cross and in the Resurrection. We do not know God's thoughts and plans. We know only what happened.

Judas would not have accomplished his abominable deed if he had thought differently. Our Lord warned him (*Matthew 26:24-25*; *Luke 22:22*; *Luke 22:48*; *Luke 21:34*). We hear the choir singing at the Matins of Holy Thursday: "Your life, O lawless Judas, is filled with deceit. Sick with avarice, you gained the contempt of all men. If you desired wealth, why did you follow Him who taught poverty? If you loved the priceless One, why did you sell Him?" And also: "Without conscience Judas accepted the Body that cleanses from sin and the Blood that was shed for the world. But he was not ashamed of drinking what he had sold for a price. He was not offended at evil, and knew not how to cry: Praise the Lord, all works of the Lord!" Saint John Chrysostom commented on the Evangelist's words about Jesus at the Last Supper, *"He was troubled in spirit, and testified and said, 'Most assuredly, I say to you, one of you will betray Me'"* (*John 13:21*). Our Lord was troubled, saddened, heavyhearted, seeing that Judas sank into the darkness of destruction, despite the often-repeated teachings and frequent advice and despite the long-suffering patience and love of his Lord.

Judas could have repented as Saint Apostle Peter did after denying Christ three times before the rooster crowed. Our Lord called Judas "friend" in the very moment of the hypocritical kiss of the latter, so He loved and forgave him (*Matthew 26:50*). Nevertheless, Judas did not repent. He went and hanged himself. Let us remember the people in Nineveh who repented and, consequently, neither was their city overthrown, nor they did perish (*Jonah 3*). The mission of the Son of God on earth might have taken another way if the free decision of man had been different.

No man is born with a predefined life, a life to be condemned. However, God can see ahead of time the man's decision. The words of King David about the betrayer, recorded in the Old Testament, were just a premonition through the Holy Spirit (*Acts 1:16*). Some Saints benefited from the gift of premonition, which was received from the Holy Spirit. If the gift of foresight comes from Evil, it will be abolished. Saint Paul exorcized the woman from Philippi who brought profit to her masters by fortune telling (*Acts 16:15*). We, as Christians, are not allowed to listen to fortune-tellers.

It is known that the Holy Scripture is a harmonious unit and the Old Testament is tied closely to the New Testament. These links are continuous: the New Testament is connected further to the unwritten events of Christian life. The fact that the empress Helen found Christ's cross with the help of a local man named Judas might very likely not be a simple coincidence. This man knew from the old people's stories that all three crosses that she found were hidden in a hole that had been dug in a cliff. According to the Church's tradition, Judas was later baptized with the name Cyriacus. He became the Patriarch of Jerusalem and died as a martyr in the year 363, as a victim of the rage of the emperor Julian the Apostate. So, a Judas sold the Lord to be put on the cross and another Judas found the Cross and helped the faithful elevate it for veneration. This is not very far from the deep sense of the orthodox faith, which is firm faith in the love of God, the power of repentance, and the hope of forgiveness and salvation.

2.2. The Interior Labor. Dispassion.

THE INTERIOR LABOR, the battle of the soul, the unseen warfare, that is necessary in order to advance on the deification road, starts with the purification (the dispassion), repentance and replacing the weaknesses and vices with virtues, and continues with the vigil and the struggle against temptations through which the evil spirit tries to bring us back to passions. The permanent support in this unseen warfare is fasting and, most important, prayer.

SOURCE OF PASSIONS. We read in Saint John Climacus' writing "The Ladder of the Divine Ascent" that God did neither cause nor create Evil. Therefore, all those who consider that the passions come naturally into the soul are entirely wrong. It is we who take the natural attributes of our human nature and convert them into passions. We exacerbate the seed that we have within us for conceiving children into voluptuous pleasures. We are naturally armed with anger to act against the snake of temptation but we use it against our neighbor. We have a natural persistence in us to stand in virtue but we use it in persevering to do evil. Our ego leads us to look for praise and glory from the neighbors and we forget that glory is meant for God. We possess a natural appetite for food in order to maintain our body but we become gluttonous.

Vladimir Lossky wrote that the heart is the center of the human being and is like a vase that contains God, the Angels, the Life, the Kingdom, the Light, the Apostles, the treasures of Grace, and the passions (Lossky, 1997). Grace enters the human entity through the heart. While the heart is always on fire, the mind has to remain cold since the mind watches over the heart. The mind is man's contemplative capacity, the most personal part of man, represented by his conscience and freedom, and the means by which he aspires to God. The Holy Fathers often identified the mind with God's image in the human being. The mind is that which merges into the grace received at baptism and brings it into the heart. The heart is the core of the human being that has to undergo the deification process. The mind is powerless without the heart that is the center of everything but the heart is blind and confused without the mind that gives directions.

There is an opinion that the Evil Angel longs for God from Whose Kingdom he fell. Nevertheless, pride, rebellion, and negativism make him continue to oppose God. Without any chance of winning when he faces the overwhelming power of the Lord, he seeks to defeat the human soul, because man was made in the image and likeness of God. He tries to destroy man by frightening or seducing man's spirit. If man falls into the trap, the Evil Angel is happy because, enslaved by passion, man will be further and further from God, diminishing his original divine likeness.

We see how carefully Saint Mary of Egypt tried to avoid temptation even after forty-seven years of spiritual battle in the desert. Saint Mary acquired the gift of discernment. She could immediately detect any small hidden sin. We, the ordinary people, say "God have mercy" in our prayers twelve or forty times for being absolved of all the sins that we have committed without willing or knowing, due to our human limits. Usually we are mindful of the big sins that are very clearly emphasized by the Ten Commandments and their derivatives. But these sins have numerous fine nuances that remain ignored. When we look at the roots of a tree we see the big woody roots, and we barely notice the many thousands of tiny roots that are actually the active points of absorption of soil nutrients. It is very hard to be aware of the enormous multitude of pores the temptations try to sneak through into our body, as it is very difficult to avoid the many sins we commit by falling into traps set up at every moment. When Our Lord Jesus Christ asked the demon-possessed man to say his name, the answer was, "Legions," because many unnoticed demons (temptations) had entered the mad man (*Luke 8:30*).

Let us not forget Kierkegaard's thought: prayer does not change God, but changes the person who is praying. Prayers and steadfastness in practicing the virtues will finally open the eyes of our mind and we will discover, with the grace of the Lord, the myriad of aspects under which a serious sin that we thought we had purged, can still hide in us. This is the case of the greatest sin of all – pride, our vainglory. The virtue that rescues us from all hardly perceptible aspects of pride is humility – a virtue that is not very easy to understand or to acquire.

The Akathist Hymn to Saint Demetrios from Basarabi, whose sacred relics have been in the Romanian Patriarchal Church since 1774, contains the following words of praise:

"The Angels in heaven wondered seeing how you, Father Demetrios, <u>like an earthly angel, limited in your body, have defeated the bodiless demons</u>." Maybe the greatest difficulty we experience in our podvig is that we live wrapped in the weaknesses of a body but we have to combat a bodiless tempter. It is the battle of an unseen war, and we do not have equal weapons with the tempter who uses numerous barely perceptible strategies in hunting us down and putting us in captivity.

NECESSITY OF DISPASSION. The joy in this world is measured in moments, but the joy in the Lord is measured in eternity's units. Saint Innocent of Alaska noticed that every thing that we desire is interesting to us only for a short time because it becomes boring not long after we acquire it. Thus, we can never reach a real and perfect happiness and prosperity.

In order to feel that long lasting joy we have to detach ourselves from the ephemeral pleasures. The priest in the altar prays at the Divine Liturgy with a thrill of awe and fear while the choir sings the Cherubic Hymn. He says, "No one, who is bound with the desires and pleasures of the flesh, is worthy to approach or draw near or to serve Thee, O King of Glory; for to minister to Thee is great and awesome even to the heavenly powers." Therefore, a purification of our mind, heart, and body is necessary.

"You shall be perfect, just as your Father in heaven is perfect," said Our Lord Jesus Christ (*Matthew 5:48*). Unfortunately, no one can be perfect except God. Neither are the Saints perfect.

Saint John the Evangelist wrote, *"If we say that we have not sinned, we make Him a liar and His word is not in us"* (*1 John 1:10*). Therefore the nuanced meaning in the Savior's words probably is: <u>tend to perfection</u>, try to be spotless and unflawed, and work hard for that. In our attempt to walk toward God, we have to begin with dispassion.

THE BODY IS THE TEMPLE in which the soul worships God. Therefore, we have to take care of it - to keep it clean. When we are anointed with blessed myrrh after Liturgy or Service of Holy Unction, we receive communion with the Holy Spirit through our body. We use our body when we venerate God: we make the sign of the cross and we kiss the icons with awe. But what about our soul? Is our soul also a temple? Yes, the soul is the temple of God (*1 Corinthians 3:16*). The soul meets the love of God in order to be filled with His fullness (*Ephesians 3:19*). How should our heart not be shaken when we hear Our Lord Jesus Christ's prayer in the garden of Gethsemane, read on Holy Thursday? *"The glory which You gave me I have given them, that they may be one just as We are one. I in them and You in Me, that they may be made perfect in one..."* (*John 17:22-23*). Our Lord Jesus reminded the Jews how the law calls those *"to whom the word of God came"* (*John 10:34-35*), referring to the verses of the psalm of Asaph, *"I said, 'You are gods, and you are sons of the Most High'"* (*Psalm 81/82:6*).

Then, if the soul is the Temple of God, how can it stay in a dingy, murky, smirched body? The body is fragile, breaks like a vase, but it is illumined by the inner light of the soul that listens to the word of God and not to its own will. *"But we have this treasure in earthen vessels, that the excellence of the power may be of God and not of us,"* Saint Paul wrote (*2 Corinthians 4:7*). In relation to the importance of the body, let us not forget that Our Lord Jesus ascended to the heavens in a human body (*Acts 1: 9-11*). How the Son of God will keep this body, as a new feature acquired by incarnation, is a mystery. We can read about the unity between the purity of soul and that of the body in a note found in the Orthodox Fathers' writings by the Russian thinker Sergei Fudel, who suffered great tribulations in the Siberian gulags and whose father was a priest (Fudel, 1989). A special grace was given to the Holy Martyrs, in order to make them strong and resistant to the abominable torture they were exposed to, and this grace was given not only to the spirit but also to the body. Sergei Fudel also commented that several Holy Fathers, including Saint Irenaeus of Lyons, taught us that our soul, after death, maintains somewhat the image of the body, accurately enough to be recognized (Fudel, 1989). The reason is because the human soul loves the body, as its temple, with a divine love.

Father Cleopa Ilie often gave beautiful advice to his visitors. He said that we should be worthy with your body like Martha and with your spirit like Mary. Benjamin Franklin considered that a good clean conscience is like a continuous Christmas feast. The conscience is the word of God planted deep in us. It is the guardian of our soul and helps us keep the commandments. If our conscience is clean, the good of the world remains open to us and, more than that, we can look up at the Lord with joy and full trust. *"If our heart does not condemn us, we have confidence toward God"* (*1 John 3:21*).

Consequently, our soul will be blessed because it did the good work and yielded abundantly. *"The fruit of the Spirit is love, joy, peace, longsuffering, kindness, goodness, faithfulness, gentleness, self-control"* (*Galatians 5:22-23*). All these fill the soul that, in its turn, transfigures the body, when the latter is clean of passions. Did you ever see people who have been born with ugly marks like a big nose, swollen lips, drooping ears or frog eyes, and whose faces cease to look ugly when their good heart embellishes them with a great light coming from inside, attenuating the sharp edges and smoothing the wrinkles?

DISPASSION IS A CROSS. In order to perform outstandingly as he does and to enjoy it unceasingly, Roger Federer, probably the greatest-ever tennis player, had to spent long hours and days of painful training. God, the master of perfection, created man in His image and after His likeness (*Genesis 1:26*). According to Saint John the Damascene, the image indicates rationality and freedom, while the likeness indicates assimilation of God through virtue (see Ware, 1987). In order to regain the lost likeness, this supreme state of happiness, man has to restore his nature in virtue. This is achieved here in this world by dispassion, by the spiritual death of our earthly being followed by the resurrection in a new spiritual being (see *John 3:3*). "*He who finds his life will lose it, and he who loses his life for My sake will find it,*" Our Lord said (*Matthew 10:39*). Losing the previous worldly life brings tears, dislocation, and much suffering. "*He who does not take his cross and follow after Me is not worthy of Me,*" said the incarnate Son of God, Who suffered for us on the cross (*Matthew 10:38*).

We hear in the prayers for Friday and in the Akathist Hymn of the Holy Cross the followings words: "How can we run away from the Cross when we see Christ on it? How can we complain of our torments when we see that our Master loves them, does not prevent them, but considers them a great honor?" We also pray saying, "Increase O Lord our labor, temptations and pain, but give us also patience and strength to endure everything that will happen to us." At the end of the Akathist Hymn of Our Lord Jesus Christ, we say the powerful Prayer of Saint Isaac the Syrian: "Heal my wounds with Your wounds, clean my blood with Your blood, and leave in my body the scent of Your body... Let Your head that you bowed on the cross raise my head slapped by the enemies." These words show the great support we receive from Our Lord in the midst of our battle with the temptations.

We have to be prepared for the end of our earthly life, the physical death, when our body will cease to function, any minute. That time the knock will not be at the door of our heart or of our consciousness, but at the door of our soul. We say in our morning prayers, "And give us a watchful and pure heart to depart from the night of this life. Teach us to wait for the bright and sacred day when Your Only Begotten Son, Our Savior Jesus Christ, will come to earth in glory to judge all and to pay to each according to his deeds. For we should not be found lying down and sleeping but standing up for His orders and ready to enter the room and into the joy of His Divine Glory, where there are those who sing praises with unceasing voices, who feel the sweetness of Your presence and see the marvelous beauty of Your eternal glory." This text is rich and covers all. We say "the night of this life" not because the earthly life might look like a dark tragedy, but look like a contrast to the bright light of God. After the Last Judgment, if we are forgiven, we can enter the Kingdom of God where voices sing a perpetual hymn of glory to the Lord, a hymn inspired by an unlimited joy, love, and freedom of spirit.

JOB'S SUFFERING. When our father died at a young age, our mother read to my sister and me from the Book of Job. I often wondered why God, Who loved Job, allowed the prince of evil to damage him so much for the sake of a simple test or bet. Why did God do such a thing? Is He not pure Love by definition?

Suffering is part of the underline. This is a Slavian word defining the Christian's hard sacrificial work for perfecting himself. It marks the death to the earthly things and the resurrection into the heavenly ones. This is how we understand the Book of Job's tragic suffering. The Lord loved Job because Job was "*true, blameless, righteous, and God-fearing, and he abstained from every evil thing*" (*Job 1:1*). He had many animals and numerous servants. "*His sons would visit one another and prepare a banquet every day, and invite their sisters to eat and drink with them*" (*Job 1:4*). "*When the days of the drinking were ended, Job sent and purified them, and he rose early in the morning and offered sacrifices for them according to their number*" (*Job 1:5*). However, the Lord decided on the school of suffering for His favorite servant, wishing to bring Job to spiritual perfection. The purity of his soul and his many virtues were not enough. He had to separate himself from the earthly things. "*Through many tribulations we must enter the kingdom of God*" (*Acts 14:22*).

After hearing of Job's tragic events, his friends Eliphaz the Temanite king, Bildad the Shuhite ruler, and Zophar the Naamathite king went to his place "*to visit and comfort him*" (*Job 2:11*). They were right when they said that this suffering was caused by his unknown sins. Obviously no one, including Job who was so beloved by the Lord, is sinless. They said, "*Shall a mortal man be pure in the Lord's sight?*" (*Job 4:17*). "*For who is the mortal that shall be blameless, or who is born of a woman that shall be righteous?*" (*Job 15:14*). "*Is not your vice plentiful, and are not your sins innumerable? For you have taken pledges from your brethren for no reason and taken away the clothing of the naked. Neither have you given the thirsty water to drink but have even withheld a morsel from the hungry*" (*Job 22:5-7*). They also suggested to Job a reason for cursing God. The Russian existentialist thinker Leo Chestov, who influenced the philosophy of several important writers like the French Albert Camus and the French Romanians Barbu Fundoianu (Benjamin Fondane) and Emil Cioran, commented on the Book of Job in his book "Speculation and Revelation." He saw the whole Book of Job as an endless debate between the painful shouts of the long-suffering Job and the cold thoughts of his rational friends. However, on one hand, the three Bible friends did not refer to Job's particular case but to *general principles of ethics.* On the other hand, Job wanted to confront God directly, with a deeply hurt but unshaken faithful spirit.

The Book of Job ends with Job's humility and repentance. In response to Job's behavior, *"the Lord restored Job's losses when he prayed for his friends, and He forgave their sin. But the Lord gave Job twice as much as he had before"* (*Job 42:10*). However, Chestov was right when he questioned about Job's sons. Did God give Job his same sons back? Certainly, the notion of sacrifice stands firmly in Job's story. In this sense, we might think that God decided a renewal of the family, a rebirth, and a clean restart, because Job's lost sons might have been sinful. The Scripture says that Job sacrificed every time *"one calf for the sins of their souls,"* for he said, *"lest my sons consider evil things in their mind against God"* (*Job 1:5*). In contrast to His pleasure in Job, the Lord was angry at Job's friends. He told Eliphaz, *"You have sinned, you and your two friends, for you have not spoken before Me what is true, as My servant Job has"* (*Job 42:7*). The three men were absolved only due to Job's prayers and to the offering of bulls and rams brought by them that Job burned. It is in a way an example of repentance and renewal (*metanoia*) for Job, but not for his friends who remained coldly critical thinkers.

In fact, Eliphaz, Bildad, and Zophar did not bring erroneous arguments to Job. Why then did God rebuke them? I think He did that because they denied the personal, intimate relationship every man has with the Creator, a relationship that is the essence of the Christian faith. It is true that they loved Job and had fear of God. They encouraged Job to pray for relief from torments, knowing that God is good and cares for the righteous people. Nevertheless, they skeptically said,

"What concern is it to the Lord if you are blameless in your works? Will He enter into judgment with you?" (*Job 22:2-4*). They talked to him in a cold discouraging tone saying, *"Since He does not trust His saints and heaven is not pure in His sight? Alas then, detestable and unclean is man who drinks wrongdoings like water!"* (*Job 15:15-16*). I think this is another point where they were wrong: they doubted that God gives respect to the human person. The mere fact that the Creator gave man the freedom of choice pleads to the contrary. Let us think of the extremely important fact that the Theotokos was asked if she wanted to be part of an overwhelming thing, as it was the process of incarnation of the Son of God. She had the right to choose to accept the Lord's will and she accepted it with all her heart. She told the Archangel, *"Behold the maidservant of the Lord! Let it be to me according to your word"* (*Luke 1:38*).

They, Job's friends, also emphasized the idea that God is always right and the punishment is immanent, saying, *"Is not your vice plentiful, and are not your sins innumerable?"* (*Job 22:5*). It is hard for man to know why he is punished because human knowledge is very limited and many aspects remain hidden to it. They asked, *"Will you find the traces of the Lord? Have you reached the outer extremities of what the almighty has made? Heaven is high, and what will you do?"* (*Job 11:7-8*). Despite the appearances, all three men were wrong for they underestimated the never extinguished fire of God's love for His creatures. As the Holy Fathers said, if God acted for reasons of Justice, and not for reasons of Love, no one would have a chance to be saved.

"The Lord raises up the gentle, but humbles sinners to the ground... The Lord is pleased with those who fear Him, and with those who hope in His mercy" (*Psalm 146/147: 6,11*). This principle is not accomplished *in general*, as Job's friends

were thinking, but *in each particular case*, because the Lord cares for each of us in an intimate relationship.

"*Lord, You test me and know me; You know my sitting down and my rising up; You understand my thoughts from afar; You search out my path and my portion, and You foresee all my ways*" (*Psalm 138/139:1-3*). *"The very hairs of your head are all numbered,*" said the Lord (*Matthew 10:30*). "*If a man has a hundred sheep, and one of them goes astray, does he not leave the ninety-nine and go to the mountain to seek the one that is straying?... Even so it is not the will of your Father who is in heaven that one of these little ones should perish,*" said the Savior (*Matthew 18: 12, 14*).

Job underwent his spiritual process of learning in a direct dialogue with God. The process apparently looked like a painful battle with the Divinity. It resembled the fight of Jacob with the Angel, after which Jacob was named Israel, i.e. "He who strives with God" (*Genesis 32:24-30*). However, the suffering yielded plenty of fruits because it ended in a deep inner humility and an authentic repentance. I might be mistaken, but here we might have to deal with the mystery of the direct touch between the Divine Person and the human person.

The theologian Vladimir Lossky underlined the difficulties in understanding the mystery of God and His hypostasis in the Holy Trinity that can be intimated not by the reasoning of the mind but by the faith of the heart. He wrote in the terms of the Eastern Church that the Trinity's dogma is a cross for human thinking, and that the apophatic ascendance of the spirit is climbing up the slopes of Golgotha. Therefore, I would believe that God was favorable to the faithful Job and not to his friends who acted as exterior judges of his tragedy.

By enduring his terrible torments, Job accomplished the ascent of Golgotha with the sacrifice of his own being.

WORKING ON PASSIONS. The advertisements and commercials are proud of the irresistible force of attraction the movies have today: passion, vice, adultery, seduction, nudity, language abuse, violence, homosexuality, horror, panic, disasters, dishonor, revenge, madness, ghosts, sorcery, and malefic supernatural.

The public of the present is excited to watch movies that advise viewer's discretion, as we were excited in the '50s to watch colored movies, with the idea that the color brings a superior quality to the story in comparison with black and white. *"Woe to those who draw sins to themselves as with a long rope and lawlessness as with the strap of a cow's yoke"* (*Isaiah 5:18*). It is sad that people use art, games and other entertainment means to produce such things. *"Woe to those who call evil good and good evil, who put darkness for light and light for darkness, who put bitter for sweet and sweet for bitter!"* (*Isaiah 5:20*).

It seems strange when persons of much decency and candor were invited to Jay Leno's talk show and, due to their inoffensive kindness to the host and to the joy of conversation, agreed to say foolish things or even showed some "spicy" pictures that made them blush.

The Holy Fathers consider that there are eight serious passions: gluttony, lack of chastity, avarice, anger, dejection, listlessness, self-esteem and pride (see Staniloae, 2002). Some of these passions belong to the heart's domain and are maintained by the body's passions. Others belong to the spirit's domain. If we tie together the two ends of the list of the above mentioned passions, the cooperation between gluttony and pride will generate all the others like a string of beads.

Gluttony and pride are caused by egocentrism, by selfishness.

We can learn from Saint Paisius' writing "Field Flowers" (St. Paisius Velichkovsky, 1994), how the chain of passions do build up. Forgetfulness, anger, and ignorance precede all the sins. They cause the insensitivity of the soul, weaken the faith, and strengthen the self-love (the egoism).

Self-love loses the feeling of mercy and friendship.

Mercilessness and love of money cause pride, and pride leads to love of glory.

Love of glory opens the gate to love of sensual pleasures (a never satisfied belly and a thirst for fornication).

Fornication directs the soul to anger because the heart becomes vulnerable and irascible.

Anger extinguishes the fire of love in the heart and ruins all the virtues. Anger can bring the remembrance of evil and the trend to blasphemy.

Blasphemy creates a feeling of loneliness and sorrow that cuts into the soul. The sadness grows despair and ruins the strength of the blessed human qualities. As a result, the fortress of the human soul remains without any defense like an empty backyard and all the other passions find free entrance into it.

As Saint Paisius from the Romanian Monastery of Neamț, who lived in 1722-1794, wrote, the body's desires might come from heat and comfort, from too much food and sleep, from the action of Evil, from absent-minded conversations, from the out-of-control sight or from loving the beauty of the body. Only fasting and prayers can eliminate the clouded thoughts and fantasies coming in the night sleep, in the carelessly spent daytime or during the excitement of the flesh. According to the teachings of other Holy Fathers, the prayer before going to bed closes the doors to the temptations that try to invade our conscience during sleep when the mind is relaxed and defenseless.

2.3. The Interior Labor. Repentance, Virtues.

REPENTANCE. After the baptism and the 40-day fasting in the desert, Our Lord Jesus Christ *"began to preach and to say, 'Repent, for the Kingdom of heaven is at hand'"* (*Matthew 4:17*). Remorse and change (*metanoia*) are necessary in our preparation for eternal life. Peter, who denied the Lord Jesus three times, repented and changed himself, while Judas, who sold the Savior, repented but because he did not change himself, he ended his life by hanging himself. All the Scriptures tell us about the changes that occurred in the righteous people. The cheater Jacob, who stole his elder brother's birthright and their father's blessing, becomes the just Patriarch of the people of Israel. The angry Moses, who killed an Egyptian, becomes a silent and patient wise man. The unstable Simon becomes Peter, who did not hesitate to be the herald of Jesus. The hostile unbelieving Saul becomes Paul who spreads the word of the Savior.

On our way toward the Kingdom of God, we err, realize the transgression, repent, and try to improve, in a process without end. A disciple of Saint Sisoes the Great despaired because of his continuous falls. Abba Sisoes, who was such a great Saint that his face shone like sun on his deathbed, encouraged his disciple in going unceasingly through the cycles of repentance and improvement. It is good if the end of our life catches us in repentance and not in sin.

THE BURDEN OF OUR SINS. A heavy sin, committed with the fervor of youth, might be easily forgotten; however, very often it springs up later with an obsessive power in the memory of the one who committed it. The tears of repentance at a mature age become bitterer and more painful because of the long delay. Such was the grief caused by the hammer-like fist of staretz Silouan that struck the chest of an aggressive cobbler when Silouan was a young villager. Fortunately, the cobbler lad did not die but struggled with death on his bed of suffering for long time.

However, many sins pass unnoticed by us because they are habitual, while the senses capable of discerning the sins are not watchful. We pray to God to receive the gift to see the sins we commit; we ask for help to escape from them through repentance, and to detect any hidden temptation. As far as we progress in our hard work of achieving dispassion, we learn the nature and the roots of the sin and we succeed smashing the snake's head before he bites.

However, there are still sins that escape our attention, despite our increased vigilance reached by the podvig process. We will pay for them at the last Judgment as well as for those of which we are aware. Therefore, we say with fear and worry in our prayer before receiving the communion, "Have mercy upon me and forgive my transgressions both voluntary and involuntary, of word and of deed, committed in knowledge or in ignorance." We do not wish that our communion with the holy Mysteries be to our judgment or condemnation. This is also why we say, "Lord, have mercy" twelve times and forty times – for the unknown sins.

BUILDING VIRTUES. The actual foundation of the virtues is provided by properly-used passions. Father Staniloae quoted Saint Maximus the Confessor who separated the passions in natural and unnatural ones (Staniloae, 2002). The natural passions are necessary and help to protect the nature of the human being. After man's fall from the perfect world of Paradise, the natural passions have lost their initial form. The appetite for spiritual things, for the Divine, was replaced by the desire for bodily satisfaction. The joy of the cooperation between mind and grace was replaced by a voluptuous pleasure of the flesh. The care to avoid the unhappiness caused by sin was replaced by fear and anguish. The repentance poised to hope was replaced with depression and despair.

The ascetic manner of living does not mean to exterminate the passions but to reestablish their natural characteristics. The efforts of the ascetics do not intend the mortification, as many erroneously consider, as a destruction of life but as a return to the initial harmony when everything was under the soul's control. I think that the joy we feel in our life (from contemplating beauty to tasting food and drinks, etc.) is authentic if it comes in a moderation of senses, in a balance needed by the soul, the real leader of the body. According to Father Staniloae, it seems that the human essence must be considered as a large unit of energy, equally distributed in all the structural zones of the human being.

When the passions become denatured in vices, the energy ceases to be uniformly spread in the body and concentrates only in some zones. Therefore, man has to work for a redistribution of his vital energy, in order to rebuild the *natural* spiritual energy by an appropriate relocation of the energies within the body. He has to reestablish the energies that, by serving only the body's supreme satisfaction and pleasures, have been transformed into *unnatural* (or anti-natural) energies.

I would speculate that controlling, redirecting and restructuring the energies according to the true needs of the soul and body of the man who strives to regain the original likeness to God might also succeed in eliminating any unnecessary extra amount of energy. Thus, the flesh will be protected from the excess of energies that carves it with wrong passions and vices. As a result, a certain mummification of the body might occur, conserving its cleanness. This could explain why the apparently fragile bodies of the reposed Saints miraculously do not decay but spread a pleasant fragrance, very different from the odor of putrefaction.

Father Staniloae mentioned the thought of Saint John of Damascus that the passions are the expression of the movement of the soul, induced by the wrong understanding of the idea of *good* and *evil* by the first man after eating the forbidden fruit in Paradise. The primary cause of the passions consists in man's sensitivity on one side and the tempting action of Evil on the other side. Because of their interactive process, the mind ends by being enslaved by the senses; the soul descends into the body, becomes covered by sensual pleasures and sadness, enters a deep darkness, and eventually is lost. Consequently, the balance, so much needed during life's journey, is not conferred anymore by the wisdom of the mind and spirit but by the dynamics of the fleshly pleasures. The pleasure, as soon as it is consumed, leaves a big vacuum within man's being. The body feels a great fatigue and the heart, which was on fire during the episode of pleasure, is invaded by a deep and painful sadness. The solution to escape from the burden of this state is to look for a new pleasure. Thus the cycle continues with a never satisfied heart that bleeds without stopping until it loses the breath of life. Without the beneficial leading of the spirit, the human being is ruined and everything begins a disastrous downfall. I know, to my bitter sorrow, a few people who eventually sink deeper and deeper in drugs or alcohol and are haunted by the thought of suicide because life starts to look completely useless.

We say in our morning prayer, "I confess to You, my Lord, Who are glorified in the Holy Trinity – Father, Son and Holy Spirit, my sins committed in all the days of my life until this hour, with the word, thoughts, sight, smell, taste, touch, and all my spiritual and body senses, which angered You, my Lord, and wounded my neighbor." The prayer lists all the things that Father Staniloae wrote about. The actions, the words, and the thoughts, that are a manifestation of the mind and spirit, are ranked first among them. The list ends with the lack of care for others, care that Saint Maximus the Confessor considered a priority.

THE VIRTUE OF HUMILITY, THE GREATEST VIRTUE. Father Staniloae wrote that, if man had the conscience of his unique nature, of his absolute spiritual loneliness and his perpetual standing in front of God, then pride could not exist. Pride is the result of the world's victory over man. Man compares himself with others; he is in a continuous competition and feels superior or inferior. He is jealous, frustrated, offended, "unfairly" regarded or misjudged. Pride is also a victory of the senses, a blindness of the mind that ceases to see God beyond the brambles and bushes of the earthly world. The energy required by God for our spiritual progress is transformed into energy for our pride's satisfaction, into the energy required by the pleasure of dominating others.

Mahatma Gandhi used to say that man has to be humble like the dust in order to become able to discover the truth.

Paul Evdokimov (Evdokimov, 1977) wrote that, because the will is the natural faculty that carries the desires, the asceticism starts, before anything else, by renouncing our own will, i.e. by growing the virtue of humility. There is a story in the Patericon about a young monk who was told by his superior to plant a dead stick in a vertical position in the sand of the desert, and to water it every day with a bucket (Patericul, 1999a). He did that worthless thing for three years. The fourth year the stick grew leaves. What was the goal of the task given to the young monk? Was it for learning the fruits of obedience or it was just for performing a miracle? Obviously, what was important for that monk was the school of obedience, since the miracles belong exclusively to the realm of God.

The Elder John of Valaam mentioned that all the obedience trials that he had to go through at Valaam (Valamo) Monastery were very unpleasant, seemingly unbearable at times. However, he tried to remain in peace and to avoid getting depressed. The obedience, he said, builds up humility and strengthens the will. The Holy Fathers very often considered that the monastic obedience is martyrdom (see Schema-Abbot John of Valaam in "The Orthodox Word", 1999b).

Father Nicolae Steinhardt, who converted from Judaism to Orthodoxy, and ended as a monk at Rohia in the Northern part of Transylvania, confessed that for him the most difficult thing in his monastic life, harder to accomplish than fasting, praying with prostrations, or staying awake in vigil hours, was the practice of patience and tolerance toward the other monks. Patience and tolerance are components of the virtue of love (*John 13: 34-35*). I would add another difficult test to the test of love: humility, including the coenobitic form of it which is obedience.

THE COURAGE OF HUMILITY. One of the great aspects of the virtue of humility is the courage and patience to endure what the Lord gives. This does not mean cowardice, resignation, or defection from the fire of the confrontation, but the strength to strive to keep what was established by One with a higher ranking, respected and beloved, and in Whose shade we continuously grow and mature. When we are in the midst of a trial we should not ask in a reproaching aggressive tone, "Why me?," or in a paralyzing concillatory tone, "That's it.

From now on, this is the end."

Humility means that we fight, trusting the One Who is watching there above and, because we have accepted the trial by obeying His will, He will help us when our strength weakens. Saint Ephrem the Syrian recommended to "be perfectly patient in the work that one has been called for." Let us remember the powerful prayer that he left to the Orthodox Church, which we say, with kneeling and prostrations, during the Great Lent period: "O Lord and Master of my life, take from me the spirit of sloth, despondency, lust for power and idle talk. But grant unto me, Thy servant, a spirit of chastity, humility, patience and love. Yea, O Lord and King, grant me to see mine own faults and not to judge my brother; for blessed art Thou unto the ages of ages. Amen."

In the period of the Old Testament, the people of Israel had a very restless existence, with numerous up-and-downs. When they were listening to the Lord and accomplishing what He said, they lived in peace and defeated their enemies. When they were protesting, rebelling, or ignoring Him, they were endangered with oppression and slavery. The people in the East-European communist empire had to suffer unimaginable tribulations. Due to the oppression, they rarely tried to exit their tragic condition by rebellion or by outside help. The end of the communist era resulted from a simple implosion of the political system and surprisingly, in the majority of the countries, was bloodless. "*If my people who are called by My name humble themselves, and pray and seek My face, and turn from their wicked ways, then I will hear from heaven, and will forgive their sin and heal their land*" (*2 Chronicles 7:14*).

THE HUMILITY OF CHRIST. Even the Son of God was incarnated and entered our world in a deeply humble manner. Every time we prepare ourselves to celebrate the great Feast of

Christmas we discover, with a contrite heart, a fact of exemplary humility: *"And she brought forth her firstborn Son, and wrapped Him in swaddling cloths, and laid Him in a manger, because there was no room for them in the inn"* (*Luke 2:7*).

According to Vladimir Lossky, the completion of our person is achieved when we try to respond to God's will instead of ours, as the Son of God after incarnation replaced His will with His Father's will, obeying it up to His death on the cross. The incarnation was the result of the Holy Trinity's work done by a triple will: the Father's will (the source of will), the Son's will (obedience) and the Holy Spirit's will (accomplishment). The earthly will of Christ manifested itself by an interrupted humility. Our Lord accepted hunger, thirst, fatigue, sufferance and death on cross.

OUR LORD LIFTS UP THE HUMBLE IN A SECRETE WAY.

"Humble yourselves in the sight of the Lord and He will lift you up" (*James 4:10*). *"The fear of the Lord is instruction in wisdom, and humility goes before honor"* (*Proverbs 15:33*, Revised Standard Version). *"All the works of the humble are evident before the Lord"* (*Proverbs 16:1*). Live your life *"with all lowliness and gentleness, with longsuffering, bearing with one another in love, endeavoring to keep the unity of the Spirit in the bond of peace"* (*Ephesians 4:2-3*).

It often seems that it is almost impossible to achieve a genuine love for our neighbor, when the person we address acts like an enemy, contradicts our actions and opinions, and opposes us, or when we have an aversion to that person. We hardly can work on the virtue of humility because the first obstacle in the way of our love is our own ego. This ego is very vulnerable, bleeds easily, is quick to take offense, and is quick to anger. The love for our neighbor is a gift from God that we receive through a consistent prayer for the others' good while we totally forget our own person. Saint John the Evangelist advised his disciples to love each other, as Christ urged us (*1 John 3:23*). Saint Maxim taught the faithful: if you cannot keep the commandment to love each other, at least do not hate each other.

We read in the Patericon that a woman was ill and went to Abba Longinus to ask him to pray for her healing (Patericul, 1999a). She had never met him before, so she did not know what he looked like. She saw him gathering firewood on the beach and asked, "Could you tell me please where Abba Longinus lives?" He replied, "What do you want from that cheater?" Then he made the sign of cross above her sick part of the body and sent her home, adding, "Go and the Lord will heal you, for Longinus cannot be of any help." The woman was healed on her way back home. When she described to others what that old man who sent her away looked like, she discovered that he was actually Abba Longinus. He did that because of his great humility and of his fear to be trapped into the temptation of pride.

WE DO NOT PRAY TO GOD TO HAVE OUR DESIRES FULFILLED. An American pastor urged the faithful people to plan ahead of time and to establish goals for a day, a week, a month, a year, and five years. This is excellent advice. We should not live our life as the wind blows. We should structure our short earthly time in a well-thought-out manner. However, "l'homme propose, Dieu dispose" (French: man suggests and God decides). We should always condition our accomplishments so as to allow for God's intervention. Therefore, we should not put our goals first, but try to understand God's will and to follow it. This is how we should pray: Lord you know my need, be it satisfied according to Thy will and to my good.

Surely, it is good to have a life set in order. It is our duty to do it. We received talents that we have to develop to the highest value possible. We confer a sense to our life by the abnegation of our work, and by setting everything under the Lord's sign. However, it is hard to know God's thoughts. Vladimir Lossky observed that we cannot meet God's will more than that which is expressed in His relationship to the created world (Lossky, 1997). This is why sometimes we have difficulties in making the right decision. We ought to pray and, after exposing all our needs and goals to Our Master, we should ask for His will to be done as it is for our good. This is also called humility.

IMPORTANCE OF OUR DAILY WORK. Some people have fun debating the commonplace question: do we work to live or live to work? If man should not need to work in order to earn his food, he would not work but he would unceasingly rest. He would become very lazy and would look for all kinds of pleasures in order to kill the boredom, pleasures that might lead to sins and destruction of his spiritual being. A large part of the progress of a civilization consists in a higher comfort level – not only in the domain of sofas and reclining love seats but also in that of transportation and work tools, because all these serve to generate a longer period of rest and a shorter period of work. It is true that work is given to us for making ends meet but, in parallel with the persistent hard effort required by it, we have to exercise our mind and heart to maintain the spirit in good shape.

The task of acquiring the right philosophy of the noble goal of work is part of the soul's maturation process that every man who came into this world after Adam has to undergo. It is a process proper to the world outside of Paradise. While the body suffers through its toil, the spirit reaches the serenity needed to understand the sense of the Creation. *"In the sweat of your face you shall eat bread,"* the Lord said to the first man (*Genesis 3:19*). The "bread" has here the meaning of <u>food for the body and the spirit</u>, exactly the same as the meaning of the "bread" in the "Our Father" prayer.

THE ROLE OF THE UNEXPECTED. The Lord does not omit moulding our spirit with unexpected events. He never lets us rust by living in a routine, in a certain relative comfort despite the often tiring requirements of our activities. Some events make us worry while others make us suffer. All of them feed the fear of the unpredictable – the fear of Almighty God (*"Let us cleanse ourselves from all filthiness of the flesh and spirit, perfecting holiness perfect <u>in the fear of</u> God,"* Saint Paul wrote (*2 Corinthians 7:1*). *"Work out your own salvation with <u>fear and trembling</u>"* (*Philippians 2:12*). This fear leads to humility, to paying more attention to God's will and to building up a strong desire to walk towards Him, with obedience and steadiness, through all the tribulations of life.

MANY OF US STRIVE FOR GLORY. Richard Wagner's example is well known: he planned (and prepared himself very carefully) to demolish the old music and to achieve fame and crowns of laurels. In the tennis world when the reporters talk about the great champions, they do not forget to mention their "killer instinct." Does that not sound like the intent to assassinate the opponent? Honoré de Balzac wrote, "La gloire est le soleil de la mort" (French: Glory is the sun of death). Saint Sophronius, the monk who narrated the story of Saint Mary of Egypt and Saint Zosima, wrote, "For what is done for the sake of gathering praises from people is not only useless to the one who does it, but can cause very harsh punishment." We Christians, should work neither for glory nor for being acknowledged. We should work hard and well, with all the strength of our mind and devotion of our heart, for God and not for people's laudations. An elder mentioned in Patericon said, "Regardless how little a man works if he does it right he will be rewarded by the Lord, provided that he works with the faith that all he does is as it ought to be." (Patericul, 1999a)

Vanity is so strong in us that even the most bizarre or childish compliments touch our sensitivity and flatter us, despite the fact that our mind realizes their ridiculous aspect. Politicians and social scientists know this human weakness and use it to manipulate the people.

Let us think of the reaction people in Lystra had when Saint Apostle Paul healed a man who had been crippled since his birth (*Acts 14:8-18*). *"When the crowds saw what Paul had done, they lifted up their voices, saying in Lycaonian, 'The gods have come down to us in the likeness of men!' Barnabas they called Zeus and Paul, because he was the chief speaker, they called Hermes"* (*Acts 14:11-12*). The priest wanted to bring bulls to offer sacrifice in the Apostles' honor. Then Barnabas and Paul tore their clothes and cried out that they were simple men like the others, but the time had come for them to believe in God who performs miracles through men as He pleases. This is a powerful example of what happens if one accepts the praises of men instead of addressing praises to God for all that surrounds us. The soul is in a frightful danger when it loses humility and slips away from the Lord.

PRIDE IS THE MAIN DANGER FOR OUR SOUL. We can read in the traditional Romanian Orthodox Book of Prologues (Proloagele, 1995) an interesting story. The layman brother of a hermit died and was survived by his little 3-year-old son. The hermit took the child with him into the desert. There the child grew up without seeing any other human person than the old hermit who fed him with a few vegetables. The child did not know what a village looked like; he did not see any woman, ate no bread, nor did he gain any knowledge of the life the sinful world lived. He spent eighteen years praying, fasting, and praising God. After he died, the old man buried him and prayed to God to show him in what group of saints the youth was taken to live for eternity. To his great surprise and deep sadness, the hermit learned that the pure youth, who had lived far from the evil things of human society, and had spent his virtuous life in prayer, was in the frightening kingdom of darkness. Seeing the old man crying bitterly for his nephew's fate, the Lord's Angel asked, "Why did you not teach him humility? Your disciple was very proud and self-satisfied in the depth of his heart. He thought he was a great Saint." The Angel added, "Every man who praises himself highly in his thoughts remains impure in the sight of God, as the prophets said." The old hermit came to himself and, until the end of his life, prayed with bitter tears for that child, hoping in the great mercy of God. *"For whoever exalts himself will be humbled, and he who humbles will be exalted,"* Our Lord Jesus said (*Luke 14:11*).

CONFIDENCE AND CERTITUDE. The enthusiasm of action and the joy of creativity combine naturally with man's confidence in his own forces and with the certitude that in the future he will reach his goals with ease. If we look more carefully into this reality, we notice that the last two, the confidence and the certitude, open a door to the probability of ignoring God. We reach a stage, still characterized by good ethics but limited exclusively to the human area, a stage that eliminates God from our existence. We are used to saying, "I am proud of you," every time we wanted to compliment our children for their success. The expression comes from a feeling of love and admiration but it actually hides a trap, because, against our expectations, the next possible step might consist of developing self-esteem and pride in the child, setting forth firm concepts of belonging and property, and thoughts of superiority and invasion into our neighbor's territory. God will become an intruder or even an enemy to one who thinks more of his status and his property than he thinks of God. How great is the enthusiasm shining in the eyes of youth, though! How sad we are when we have to reprove someone and see that he, wounded in his pride, listens in silence and accepts the blame with resignation (despite the fact that a defensive reaction might be the most positive solution possible!). Definitely, our confidence and certitude must be not in us but in God.

THOUGHTS OF UNFAIR TREATMENT. "Sometimes a thought bothers me," a friend said. "I feel that in my work place I am not treated in a fair manner, in a correct, objective, and impartial way. I have the impression that the superiors and my colleagues do injustice to me, oppress and humiliate me, are sarcastic or despotic, offend me, ignore my efforts and merits, force me to work long hours while they relax and rest, reduce me to the position of a slave, and deform the truth about me with malevolence and egoism." In America, the country of individualism, boldness, achievements and justice, the natural reaction and attitude in these cases is a vigorous and combative reply, within the limits required by decency, cooperation and common interest. If that is not enough, one goes to court with well-founded and judicious accusations (maybe this is why, in this country, one of the most common and popular jobs is that of a lawyer). I learned during my life that the human ego is so strong that all these confrontations, even done at a decent common-sense level, with a pure spirit, in an inoffensive tone, with calm and respect, are unwelcome. They harm and do not help the general interest of a team. Therefore, keeping in mind the natural sensitivity of the ego of the person we are criticizing, we should not quash his personality even when we are indubitably right. We always have to offer him a way of dignified escape, a chance to find excuses for his behavior, allowing him to retire from his defeat with an unhurt pride.

From a Christian point of view, all these conflicts and injustices are challenges given to us by God for strengthening our humility and increasing our love. We should not react in an aggressive way, except when something might endanger the faith or the church. Our ears, mind and heart should be unreceptive to any sound intended to harm our pride, because the latter simply does not exist if we are truly humble. Turn the other cheek if someone slaps your face (*Matthew 5:39*). This gesture does not mean weakness. The conclusion of the teaching is merely that there is no need for revenge, and that the desire to collaborate with the person we want to help is called love.

We should fight against anger, against the desire for violent confrontation, against the trend of conversing in a flaming mode with the person who opposes our thoughts and acts, and we should try to find the reasons that justify his apparently unfair actions. We should learn to see our opponent's qualities. We should pray. Above all, these challenging tests have to end in humility, reciprocal trust, peace, and love.

HUMILITY AS MEANS FOR COOPERATION. When two strong personalities have to work together, one of them might be *like a stone*, stubborn, and tough in defending his opinion, unreceptive of points of view other than his own, imperative and even authoritative. In this case, the other person should be *like water* – humble, going around the obstacle, flowing with the whole strength of his heart, respecting and hugging the boulder but keeping to the direction of the flow despite the detour. Finally, the hard, sharp cornered boulder will become smooth, with rounded edges and, together with the water, will create a gorge where the gravitational roaring will express, reverberating with magnitude, the force and enthusiasm of their cooperation. *"Let nothing be done through selfish ambition or conceit, but in lowliness of mind let each esteem others better than himself. Let each of you look out not only for his own interests, but also for the interests of others"* (*Philippians 2:3-4*).

HUMILITY OPENS THE DOOR OF THE SOUL to receive God. Our Lord Jesus praised the children (*Matthew 19: 13-15*) because their heart has the capacity to stay with enthusiasm with the person that speaks to them. They are not caught in the net of the mind's pride that brings on doubt, egoism, greed, jealousy, hostility, and enmity. I remember Father Vladimir Lecko saying that every time he gives communion to the children he enjoys looking in their eyes full of light and receptivity. Surely, the children can be scared and, in this case, they might refuse communion. But if they are interested in something - and they are usually largely open to learn something new - they do that wholly.

Let us not forget that the Son of God chose the way of humility in order to come closer to us, to teach and save us. He was born into very humble conditions. He totally abandoned Himself into the people's hands, giving them full freedom of will – and they crucified Him. Do we not feel that we ignore His sacrifice and we crucify Him again with every new sin we commit? The presence of the Savior seems to be fragile and vulnerable. This is not because the Divinity is perishable but because our unaltered pride makes us transform His presence inside us into a fragile and vulnerable one. Let us watch carefully - the instability of our mind can end in rejecting Him instead of receiving Him with a wide open heart as the children do. *"I thank You, Father, Lord of heaven and earth, that You have hidden these things from the wise and prudent, and revealed them to babes,"* said Our Lord Jesus (*Luke 10:21*).

Humility is the key to unlocking the gate of faith, but locking out pride and self-centeredness and letting love enter and dwell in their souls. For women, who acquire the same depth of knowledge in a more intuitive and less discursive mode, love is an intrinsic part of their being. Therefore women can feel much easier the fire of faith (whose essence is love as we read in *Luke 10:27*), despite the fact that they probably cannot theorize it as well as men.

HUMILITY PRECEDES THE LOVE FOR NEIGHBOR. Saint Basil's prayer, included in the Orthodox morning prayers, ends with the following request to the Lord: "Help us to be ready to enter with joy the space of Thy divine glory, where unceasing voices praise Thee and where the indescribable happiness of eternally seeing the ineffable beauty of Thy glory reigns, for Thou art the true light that illumines and sanctifies all, and everyone praises Thee forever. Amen."

We will be asked in the other world what good deeds we have done. *"Faith without work is dead"* (*James 2:20*). We should do as Our Lord Jesus said, *"I was hungry and you gave Me food, I was thirsty and you gave Me drink..."* (*Matthew 25: 31-46*). Father Kallistos told us the story of the old woman from Fyodor Dostoyevsky's novel *The Brothers Karamazov*. She was in Hades and was given a chance to be taken out of the stinky and suffocating swamp, if she remembered a good thing done in her earthly life. Yes, she remembered that she gave a beggar an onion from her garden! The angel held that onion in his hand and asked her to hang on it in order to pull her out. Everything looked promising but while she was getting out, some desperate people hung onto her, slowing the whole operation. She kicked them with her foot in hot anger and said, "Get away from here, this is my onion." At this word, the onion broke and all of them fell back into the swamp.

The Holy Fathers' writings offer us another instructive story. A monk had to do some work far from the monastery. On his way there, he met a beggar. The monk had nothing to give him but, because he noticed that the poor man's body was almost naked and blue of cold, he took out his coat and covered the man. The monk continued his walk, reached his destination, did the work he had planned to do, and on his way back home he saw the beggar without the coat and suffering again of cold. The man had sold the coat and resumed his begging. This made the monk very sad. After returning to his monastery cell, he prayed for a very long time. Later he had a vision: Our Lord Jesus, dressed with the monk's coat, said, "When you gave the coat to the beggar you gave it to Me." Leo Tolstoy wrote a similar story about a compassionate shoemaker.

WATCH THE WORDS ADDRESSED TO THE NEIGHBOR. *"Even so the tongue is a little member and boasts great things. See how great a forest a little fire kindles! And the tongue is a fire, a world of iniquity. The tongue is so set among our members that it defiles the whole body, and sets on fire the course of nature; and it is set on fire by hell. For every kind of beast and bird, of reptile and creature of sea, is tamed and has been tamed by mankind. But no man can tame the tongue. It is unruly evil, full of deadly poison. With it we bless our God and Father, and with it we curse men, who have been made in the similitude of God"* (*James 3:5-9*). This is a terrible truth. The wise men say that if we cannot control our mouth we cannot control our deeds.

"Surely you also are one of them, for your speech betrays you" (*Matthew 26:73*). This is what the servants told Peter, when he was in the yard of the High Priest's house where the Lord Jesus was taken for trial. The Galilean accent revealed Peter's real identity. Our intentions and hidden thoughts about our neighbor are disclosed by the finest nuance of our voice.

Among all the beings created by God, man is actually the only being that speaks. This characteristic can be a great beneficial gift but can also put us in great danger. *"I say to you that for every idle word men may speak, they will give account of it on the day of judgment. For by your words you will be justified, and by your words you will be condemned"* (*Matthew 12: 36-37*).

Unfortunately, our restraint from reproaching, arguing or replying angrily when we are offended and we defend ourselves in front of denigrators and malevolent people, will stress us so much that we will explode at some point. Our reaction of relief will cause only enmity and sadness in the others, while our soul will lose her peace. This is a huge temptation and only persevering in prayer, in tears, can rescue us from such a great deadlock. I cannot understand how spies are able to hide so well things that could betray them at any moment of the day or night. Very likely, the effort of keeping all the offenses and discontent inside us can end in changing us in an undesirable manner. The only solution for all the conflicts is to transform them into love, but this only God can do. He is our Savior. With parental care, severity, and perseverance, He gives us adequate temptations for "sweetening' us and building up our strength. As we learn from Saint Seraphim of Sarov, God puts men to the test, marking the limits of their work and helping them to the degree He decides. We received the grace of the Holy Spirit at our baptism by the Holy Unction and this grace will be our guide for the rest of our life's journey.

OUR COMMUNICATION WITH THE NEIGHBOR. A story in
Patericon speaks about a monk who was upset at one of his
brothers in the monastery (Patericul, 1999a). Full of remorse,
he decided under the pressure of his conscience, to go to that
one and humbly ask for forgiveness. He knocked at the other's
door but the other did not want to open it, persisting in anger
and bitterness. Returning deeply disappointed to his cell, the
monk seeking forgiveness stopped at an elder's cell for advice.

The elder said, "Son, check first your thoughts. They tell
you that you have no guilt and that all the evil is coming from
the other. You give justice to yourself while blaming the other.
Therefore, God did not encourage your brother to open the
door and receive you. God knew that you went there not in
repentance but in hypocrisy. Your heart should be convinced
that the mistake belongs to you. Absolve the other from any
guilt. God will take care to give him the humility for
reconciliation."

The monk prayed, repented, cleansed his soul, and went
again to the other's cell. The latter heard him from afar and ran
to the door with joy and understanding. There was no need to
knock when the monk arrived because the door was waiting
wide open.

The Hieromonk Damascene Christensen from the
Monastery of St. Herman of Alaska in Platina (California)
called our attention to the words of Saint Paul in his letter to
the *Ephesians* (*4:31*): *"Let all bitterness, wrath, anger, clamor
and evil speaking be put away from you, with all malice."* He
added that, if we want to correct our brother when he does
something wrong, first we have to remain calm. Otherwise, we
will end in being contaminated by the very illness we want to
heal in the other person. Sometimes a calm attitude can
infuriate our brother, but if the calm tone is accompanied by
kindness of the heart and lack of any self-pride, we have every

chance to succeed. This is another example of how humility works. The Romanian Father Justin Pârvu advised (see Irme, 2013), "When we see our brother making a mistake... we rather should first consider ourselves guilty of that mistake - and this is what it means to carry the weakness of our brother; thus he is relieved. This kind of sacrifice is greatly pleasing God... since the Lord said, '*Love the neighbor as thyself*' (*Matthew 22:39*; *Mark 12:31*)."

Reacting with anger in an argument with our neighbor and trying to crush him with the weight of our opinion leads to a double negative effect: we are invaded by bitter feelings that drive away the peace of our heart, and we make an enemy instead of a friend. Persisting to present the truth of our opinion with humility, patience, kindness, and love, the cause will be accepted after a longer while and will be beneficial for all.

Sometimes we might be the target of evil minds. We should not answer evil by doing evil. Maybe neither by doing good, because doing good might humiliate, hurt, irritate and anger the malefactor, and because at the same time, this might fill us with pride for our ethical "superiority." Again it is better to answer not in fear or despair but with humility and patience, even if the malefactor is tempted at that moment to continue to torture us, being excited and happy that he "defeated" us. I think this is the deep meaning of Our Lord' words: "*I tell you not to resist an evil person. But whoever slaps you on the right cheek, turn the other to him also*" (*Matthew 5:39*).

We learn from Patericon, the words of an experienced soul, Abba Nilus: "Everything you do in revenge against a brother who has harmed you will come back to your mind at the time of prayer", as a remorse of your conscience and also as a painful means of healing both souls and of restoring peace (see The Sayings of the Desert Fathers, 1975).

PRAISE YOUR NEIGHBOR, PRAISE GOD. We learn from everyday life that, if we praise our neighbor, he will welcome us in a favorable manner. This idea might sound like a matter of investment and gain, of giving and taking, but his welcome could also sound like a natural response to our devoted offering. When we sincerely compliment someone, we are *glad* for the talents of the other; consequently, the other responds with joy for the talents he sees in himself, realizing at the same time that these talents do not belong to him but to God Who gave them to him. Therefore, joy fills the hearts of both persons and unites their souls in praising the Lord.

I asked Father Thomas Hopko, "Did God create us to praise Him?" "No," he replied, "we praise him in gratitude for being brought to life and for all the joy that life offers us. God lives by Himself and does not need to be praised." I think there is more than a simple gratitude that makes the angels and us praise the Lord. The glory that we sing about comes from the fact that we are part of His creation and we aspire to become part of Himself, of the immensity of His Being. If we keep the conscience of our ego and the pride of our soul, while we sing Glory to God, it seems to be a kind of negotiation and not a true offering. When we offer something to someone, we do it out of our love, and in that very moment we feel like blending our heart with the heart of that person. We accomplish this offering in humility because only in this state we forget about ourselves, about the selfish demands of our ego. The Romanian Father Arsenie Papacioc said often, "You have to give what *you are*, not what *you have*", encouraging the self-sacrifice (see Eternity Hidden in the Moment, in The Orthodox Word, 281/2011). It is not about what alms you give to the poor from what you possess, but what you give *from you*, how much you sacrifice from your own being, how much love you give according to what your Christian heart is.

One can add that the voice of our prayer that contains praises and thanks in addition to requests is very close to the voice used for communication among the persons of the Holy Trinity. The praises are actually a joy of communication – a communication that is like a sharing of love. Our Lord Jesus summarized the ancient commandments of the Law in two commandments regarding love (*Matthew 22:37-39*).

2.4. The Interior Labor. Vigil, the Unseen War.

NECESSITY OF VIGIL. After the work of dispassion the vessel of the soul becomes empty. We have to act quickly and fill it with virtues because otherwise its void will absorb back the evil influence, as the vacuum avidly sucks the air and the black hole the light. The emptier the vessel, the bigger the suction power is. While building the virtues we have to keep a vigil, being alert to all the temptations, all the attempts of evil penetrations. The fight against temptations is hard but it strengthens the spirit and helps it to progress in its aspiration to God.

THE EXAMPLE OF OUR LORD JESUS CHRIST. After being baptized in the Jordan River, Jesus went into the desert where He fasted for 40 days. At the end of this period the fallen angel, the prince of the sinning world, subjected Him to the fire of temptations (*Matthew 4:1-11*, *Mark 1:12-13* and *Luke 4:1-13*). In a way, this happens to us, too. After we are baptized, we follow the road of our life through the desert of this world, where millions of temptations swarm. A morning prayer addressed to God the Father, considers the part of life spent in the desert, a period of darkness: "And give us strength to pass through the night of this life with a pure and alert heart and wait for the light of the Holy Day of Your Only-begotten

Son." It is important to understand that the Son of God Himself, by His human incarnation, let the servant of evil attack Him. He taught us a lesson about the ascetic labor and the fight with temptations. After forty days of fasting, Our Lord was weakened in His human body but stronger in spirit, as Moses was after wandering forty years in the desert when he was tested and humbled by God with hunger and thirst (*Deuteronomy 8:2-3*).

The first temptation of Our Lord Jesus refers to something that we always complain about: our "vital" needs generated by the desires and passions of the body in the world we live in. If these needs of the body, evenly balanced, clean and not vicious, keep our mind and soul occupied with them as top priority, we are lost. Yes, we might care for tomorrow but not worry. Lord said, *"Do not worry about tomorrow, for tomorrow will worry about its own things. Sufficient for the day is its own trouble"* (*Matthew 6:34*). *"Is not life more than food, and the body more than clothing?"* the Lord asked (*Matthew 6:25*). The man feeds not only on what the body hungers for, but also on what the soul hungers for. Our Lord was challenged to convert stones into bread in order to satisfy His body's hunger. He replied, *"Man shall not live by bread alone, but by every word that proceeds from the mouth of God"* (*Matthew 4:4, Deuteronomy 8:3*). As the Holy Fathers said, contemplating the word of God and praying are the breath and bread of our soul.

The second temptation went deeper. Our Lord was asked to jump from the roof of the temple to prove that the angels cared for Him. They would catch Him and He would not be hurt. This kind of temptation addresses the personal pride and self-esteem, the consciousness of man's power and talents that is always ready to show off, to feel superior, and to reject any denial of his value. Certainly, it was very easy for Jesus to accomplish what the fallen angel demanded. However, He refused because, very likely, He had something else in mind. Maybe that was also to have the Scriptures fulfilled, as Our Lord said when He was betrayed by Judas and was arrested in the garden of the Mount of Olives (*Matthew 26, 53-54*). Therefore, He answered to the evil tempter: "*It is written again, 'You shall not tempt the Lord your God*" (*Matthew 4:7, Deuteronomy 6:16*).

But what connections have all these with us? We will be surprised to find out that we also tempt our Lord. Maybe we sin and we know that we sin, but we do it because we hope that God will eventually forgive us. And maybe even more – we blame God for our problems and lack of success, for every suffering and sadness. We think that God treats us very unfairly. We say in our mind, "Why did that happened to me? I was good, I respected the Commandments, and now I have to suffer while my neighbor who did so many wrong and unethical things is so lucky and happy." We also say, "All my life is only struggle; the opportunities for rejoicing are rare and life is so short that we miss most of them. What is life then? Just infinite misery?" We even go further and listen to the people who dare to doubt the mystery of incarnation of the Son of God. "How can you believe Him," they say, "if He Himself cried out on the cross as any ordinary man, '*Eli, Eli, lama sabachthani, that is, My God, My God, why have You forsaken me?* '" (as we read in *Matthew 27:46*). We tempt the Savior with all these thoughts and feelings. As Father Cleopa said, quoting from Saint John of Damascus, the words of Our Lord on the cross were referring to our human status, He was talking on behalf of the sinful mankind for which He made the sacrifice. Christ could not be forsaken by God the Father because Christ was "true God from true God", "of one essence with the Father". I think God gave us, through the Gospel, the example of this second temptation in order to make us to understand that, in our battle with temptations and sins, it is not enough to know the Word of God, but <u>we have to live by it</u>, to fill our life with it. The word is like the good seed spread by the sower (*Luke 8:5-8*) and we have to be the fertile soil to grow it into a beautiful plant (*"others fell on good ground, sprang up, and yielded a crop a hundredfold"*). Jesus ended His story about the sower by saying: *"He who has ears to hear, let him hear!,"* which means, <u>receive the word and live by it</u>. "God gives the nuts but He does not crack them," an old German proverb says.

We have to go toward God, and to open our heart to Him. This is the actual joy of earthly life - a permanent joy that comes even in the middle of the worst suffering. We become conscious of this feeling through the comfort the love for others brings into our soul. We have to try not to tempt God by the way we think, feel, and act, but to receive Him and live with His presence every day, every hour.

The third temptation was the hardest to resist - the offer of *"all the kingdoms of the world and their glory"* (*Matthew 4:8*). This is a temptation addressed fully to our ego, to our glory, our vanity, our honor. We want our person not only to be protected from being hurt or judged by other people but we also want to be praised and rewarded. This is actually the background of man's striving for wealth and power. We are born with love for ourselves, with greed, covetousness, and desire to fight against others, in accordance with Darwin's theory of the survival of the species and the competition among individuals within a certain habitat. Since we were little children, we have said, "This is mine." Nevertheless, the Christian life has to be lived humbly and in peace with others. We have to forget our own ego and to replace the love for ourselves with the love for God. Our Lord Jesus said, *"For it is written, 'You shall worship the Lord your God, and Him only you shall serve" (Matthew 4:10).* This should be our only philosophy and our only worry.

THE BREAD OF GOD. *"Man shall not live by bread alone, but by every word that proceeds from the mouth of God,"* Our Lord said (*Matthew 4:4*). The Savior reminded us of this principle using similar words to those put in Moses' mouth by God the Father, when the people of Israel were fed with manna during their exhausting journey through the desert (*Deuteronomy 8:3*). The bread does not satiate man because the next day man hungers again, but the Word of God satiates him.

Christ said to the people gathered to listen to Him, *"Most assuredly, I say to you, Moses did not give you the bread from heaven, but My Father gives you the true bread from heaven. For the bread of God is He who comes down from heaven, and gives life to the world "* (*John 6:32-33*). The people, who were fed on the mountain by the miraculous multiplication of the loaves and fishes, replied in a single voice: *"Lord, give us this bread always"* (*John 6:34*). The Lord told them, *"I am the bread of life; he who comes to me shall not hunger, and he who believes in me shall never thirst"* (*John 6:34-35*). *"Do not labor for the food which perishes, but for the food which endures to everlasting life which the son of Man will give you, because God the Father has set His seal on Him"* (*John 6:27*). Unfortunately, the people did not believe. However, the woman of Samaria believed in Him when she heard about the water of life (*John 4:14*), and she passed from the need of her body for the daily water to the need of the soul for the eternal water that is God (*John 4:1-26*). The tradition of the Orthodox Church says that she died later, as a martyr, together with her sons, for faith in the Lord Jesus Christ.

CONSEQUENCES OF THE PRIMORDIAL MAN'S TEMPTATION. Making man according to the Lord's image and likeness, the Creator intended to have man beside Him to contemplate and enjoy the creation. Because man was endowed with the freedom of choice, first he had to go through a process of spiritual education, a process of deification, in order to reach in himself the mature understanding necessary to enjoy the creation fully. The fallen angel knew this truth but he also realized that by announcing very early the final stage of deification, he would interrupt the process and might take the opportunity to obstruct man's spiritual education. "You will be like gods," the snake whispered in the ears of the first two human beings and urged them to eat prematurely from the tree of the knowledge of good and evil. The Lord, in His supreme wisdom and love, avoided disasters in Paradise by punishing the tempter and expelling man out of the Garden of Eden, but giving man the alternative to continue the spiritual process of maturation in a more difficult way.

Responding to the temptation, man suffered three consequences.

(1) Listening to the snake's misleading words about becoming gods, and being impressed by the false belief that he (man) had deciphered the secret of the universe after gaining the knowledge of good and evil, man remained infatuated with pride, love of himself, and haughtiness like a master, who thinks he is equal to God and can compete with Him.

(2) Man entered the realm of disease and death, because he disrespected the natural laws of order and harmony. The Lord told man, *"You may not eat, for in whatever day that you eat from it you shall die by death"* (*Genesis 2:17*), which means that the minute man eats from the tree of knowledge of good and evil, he will become a mortal being. These words of the Lord were not judicial, threatening with a punishment for a

possible disobedience (like "I will kill you"). They sounded more like the words of a parent who cares for his children, worries and tries to avoid mishaps.

(3) Man also fell prey to disease and death because he opened himself to temptation and made himself vulnerable to sin. He continued to sin until the present day. *"Each one is tempted when he is drawn away by his own desires and enticed. Then, when desire has conceived, it gives birth to sin; and sin, when it is full-grown, brings forth death"* (*James 1:14-15*).

As soon as Adam and Eve sinned, they could not see the face of God without being hurt. Therefore, they had to take cover. *"Adam and his wife hid themselves within the tree in the middle of the garden from the presence of the Lord God"* (*Genesis 3:8*). They could only hear God's voice. This is why neither Moses nor Elijah could look at God. The sin had built a wall between man and God. Man became fragile and perishable. He burns at the sight of God. Only Theotokos was a burning bush never consumed. Her example illustrates the condition necessary to regain the capacity to see God, to reach the purity of Adam's heart at the time he was walking with God in the Garden of Eden, before the fall. Our Lord said, *"Blessed are the pure in heart, for they shall see God"* (*Matthew 5:8*).

WHERE ARE WE NOW? In a state in which we have to battle with the temptations targeting our passions, mainly with the most dangerous and destructive of them - pride and vanity. We have to go steadfastly through a process of denying the passions in order to reach the original state. This battle, made more difficult by sickness, toils, and the continuous threat of death, is hard but indispensable, and requires sacrifice. God gives man trials and diseases according to each one's strength, in order to help man in the process of ridding himself of his passions, cleansing himself and aspiring to the heights of the Spirit. Therefore, to learn how to confront the temptation which tests the degree of purification and strength of faith, becomes a priority. Intending to help man, God the Father sent His Son Who, incarnated, *"was in all points tempted as we are, yet without sin. Let us therefore come boldly to the throne of grace, that we may obtain mercy and find grace to help in time of need"* (*Hebrews 4:15-16*). We should not forget that the Son of God, The Word, entered a human body but "the divinity did not become humankind and neither did the humankind become divinity" (Lossky, 1997). Jesus Christ's nature was 100 percent divine and 100 percent human. As a Teacher and a Priest, He showed us the road to follow and as a Savior, He defeated the spiritual death that humankind has suffered since the first man's sin.

THE EDUCATIVE IMPORTANCE OF TEMPTATIONS. Abba Anthony the Great noted, "No one will be able to enter the Kingdom of Heavens without battling with the temptations. For it is said: take away the temptations and no one will be saved" (Patericul, 1999a). Like the contagious diseases in childhood – if one had them during that time and survived, he would have immunity for later ages.

Saint John Chrysostom wrote that a Christian must be a soldier, a navigator, a ploughman, and a fighter. As Saint Paul said, *"we do not wrestle against flesh and blood, but against principalities, against powers, against the rulers of the darkness of this age... therefore take up the whole armor of God, that you may be able to withstand in the evil day, and having done all, to stand"* (*Ephesians 6:12-13*). Saint Paul also confessed, *"Therefore I take pleasure in infirmities, in reproaches, in needs, in persecutions, in distresses, for Christ's sake. For when I am weak, then I am strong"* (*2 Corinthians 12:10*). As Saint Paisius Velichkovsky of Neamţ said, the warfare is extremely difficult because, despite our visible nature, we have to battle against an enemy whose nature is invisible. After the fall from Eden, the fight against temptations became an important part of man's deification process.

The hieromonk Ioan Guţu from Kolitsou Skete at Mount Athos, who died when he was 90 years old, at the very hour he had predicted two months before, said that we should start with the fear of God and finish with the love of God, since the latter is the crown of our good deeds. Prayer always precedes the good deeds. More prayer, more humility, and more love for God and neighbors would easier carry us toward the Kingdom of Heavens. He concluded, "However, we cannot be saved without temptations, patience and repentance." (see Nicodemus, 2001). Saint Paul wrote to his young disciple, *"For God has not given us a spirit of fear, but of power and of love and of a sound mind"* (*2 Timothy 1:7*). Here is how fear becomes power - power of the spirit, love, and wisdom.

DOES GOD HIMSELF TEMPT US? Sometimes the temptation is so seductive that we are frightened that we cannot resist anymore. Therefore, we say with despair in the prayer to Our Father, *"And lead us not into temptation."* Christ Himself has taught us this major prayer. However, something strikes us here. Our mind is unable to comprehend entirely the sense of this sentence. Can that be true? Does God Himself truly tempt us? Father Lev Gillet, the unsigned author of the popular book of Orthodox catechism, did not offer a direct answer to this question (The Living God, 1989). However, he mentioned that, actually, we should stress the word "but" in this whole saying: "*And lead us not into temptation but deliver us from evil.*" Yes, now we have a better understanding: these words are mere words of prayer for help, for protection against evil and the temptations that evil brings. "*Let no one say when he is tempted, 'I am tempted by God'; for God cannot be tempted by evil, nor does He Himself tempt anyone. But each person is tempted when he is drawn away by his own desires and enticed*" (*James 1:13-14*).

Actually, the meaning of the words "*And lead us not into temptation*" is, as the Patericon teaches us: "and let us not be swallowed by the temptation." (Patericul, 1999a). Temptation is like a beast. As long as we keep our distance or succeed in fighting temptation, we will be all right. As soon as the beast bites us, we will be poisoned and we will end in being totally enslaved by the temptation. In a way, the temptations are like insects: they come and go, have a short life, are innumerable and, by the power of their plurality and of their short-lived generations, they are capable of building resistance to our antidotes / insecticides and, consequently, to threaten to become an eternal torture for our soul.

GOD DOES NOT TEMPT US AND THE TEMPTATION IS NOT IN US. It is the Evil Spirit who brings the temptation. However, God allows the temptations in order to help us to learn, strengthen, and mature, and He checks our progress periodically. He educates us in order to protect us from the risk of a catastrophic mistake such as Adam made.

We say in our morning prayers to the Lord, Who is the Father and the Master of the universe, "O Lord who holds everything, Lord of all the powers and all the bodies, You dwell in the highest and look down on us, You *test* the hearts and the inner nature, and You fully know the secrets of man." Indeed the Lord does not *tempt* us. He does not lure us into corruption but He *tests* us and watches us to see how we respond to the challenges and how we undergo the hard times. Nothing remains unknown to Him: what we do, what we accomplish, or in what we fail. Definitely *"the lust of the flesh, the lust of the eyes, and the pride of life" are "not of the Father but of the world"* (*1 John 2:16*), i.e. of the evil prince of the world. However, God sometimes allows the evil spirit to tempt us. He does that for strengthening our spirit and for fortifying our virtues that our moral choices may be truly free to choose the Good as an alternative. Nevertheless, because we are weak, we ask God to spare us from temptations and He does that partially, as a good parent, allowing only temptations that we can bear without the danger to be lost and fall.

God let the Prince of Evil test Job, a man spoiled with wealth and a large united family. But the Lord said to the tempter, *"Behold, whatever he has I give into your hand, but do not touch him"* (*Job 1:12*), and later He said again, *"Behold, I give him over to you; only spare his life"* (*Job 2:6*). For *"God is faithful, who will not allow you to be tempted beyond what you are able, but with the temptation will also make the way of escape, that you may be able to bear it,"* Saint Apostle Paul wrote (*1 Corinthians 10:13*). Job found the strength to endure all the pain and toils due to his deep humility.

BE SOBER, BE VIGILANT. Saint Anthony the Great, who lived in the years 251-356, told Abba Pimen, "This is the most important work of man: to recognize his sin in front of God and to expect a new temptation until his last breath" (The Sayings of the Desert Fathers, 1975). Temptations surround man and challenge him during his entire life. Therefore, Saint Apostle Peter was totally right when he said, *"Be sober, be vigilant."* The evil adversary *"walks about like a roaring lion, seeking whom he may devour. Resist him, steadfast in the faith, knowing that the same sufferings are experienced by your brotherhood in the world"* (*1 Peter 5: 8-9*). When tempted, the Christian's goal is not to end in being trapped and lost to the great joy of the destructive Tempter, but to learn to resist and to grow in virtue. *"Do not love the world or the things in the world. If anyone loves the world, the love of the Father is not in him. For all that is in the world - the lust of the flesh, the lust of the eyes, and the pride of life - is not of the Father but is of the world. And the world is passing away, and the lust of it; but he who does the will of God abides forever"* (*1 John 2: 15-17*).

THE DEGREE OF TEMPTATIONS. We, the ordinary people, are full of sins of which we are not very aware. We are so weak and hesitant that the servants of Evil do not worry much - their small temptations suffice to keep us chained. By contrast, for the strong ones, for the people who actually battle and acquire purity of the soul, the evil spirits try all kinds of desperate means and therefore the temptations become strong and very frightening. The monks succeed in reaching a stage wherein God's presence becomes almost "material" in their being and ceases to be ethereal. They reach this stage through the practice of long prayers, fasting, repentance, and practice in the virtues, surpassing the degree to which we ordinary Christians feel God's Presence. For the strong ones, the most abstract temptations do not cause His almost material presence to disappear.

Father Cleopa Ilie narrated the terrible torment he endured during the time of his solitude in the middle of the dense remote woods in the mountains. One night, while he was reading his prayer book and saying the Akathist of Protection of the Theotokos, he heard a loud noise like a disastrous earthquake. With fear, he opened the door of his shack a bit and saw a big wheel as tall as the largest spruces around his shack. Hideous creatures with forks of fire were on each side of the wheel. They were crying, "This is the elder from Sihăstria Monastery! Let us hang him on the wheel!" Soon they put him on the turning wheel, ready to push and spike him with their forks when he slipped off it. The elder bravely threatened them with the Akathist book in his hand, yelling to them to go away, and, after a short while, they disappeared (see Balan, 2000).

I remember reading that many ascetics were found badly beaten and covered by blood by the evil spirits who became "material." Elder Cleopa said often that the Holy Fathers forbid the hermits to tell anyone about what they have to endure. Father Cleopa could confess that if we, the regular people, had been living as an ascetic in the wilderness and we had seen an evil spirit, even if we had been tied to a tree, we would have pulled it up by the roots and we would have run away with the tree on our back! The few who are very advanced in their spiritual growth, have the capacity of living in the space that is "not of this world." They can even feel God's Presence, Who is abstract because He is above everything, "ineffable, inconceivable, invisible, incomprehensible, ever-existing and eternally the same," as the priests says at the Divine Liturgy. Therefore, their temptations, so frightening, seem not veridical to us and therefore impossible to occur.

OUR BATTLE WITH TEMPTATIONS. We can react in two ways when temptations rise up to bite us: to run immediately far away from them or to face them and fight. We, the majority, are weak and are afraid that the temptations will bend us and destroy us. We pray to the Lord "not to lead us into temptations." The Lord said to Saint Apostle Paul, "*My grace* *is sufficient for you, for My strength is made perfect in weakness,"* and Saint Paul wrote in this sense about the importance of faith and trust in God, *"when I am weak, then I am strong"* (*2 Corinthians 12:9-10*). But the very few who are closer to perfection have gone further in their zeal. They pray to the Lord to help them follow Him in His passion, as Saint Francis of Assisi did and eventually he received the stigmata of the cross. *"You will drink my cup,"* Our Lord Jesus told His disciples, anticipating their suffering, and, yes, they were real fighters grabbing firmly the horns of temptations. *"Therefore I take pleasure in infirmities, in reproaches, in needs, in persecutions, in distresses, for Christ's sake"* (*2 Corinthians 12:10*).

When we battle temptations in unseen warfare, we do not battle against our flesh and blood but against the evil spirits (*Ephesians 6:12*). As we learn from the Holy Fathers, the action of the temptation develops itself in four stages: (1) the *impulse* that comes from all the things around us whether good or bad; (2) the *interaction* with the temptation, when we become aware of it and pay attention to it; (3) the *consent*, when we open the gates and our mind and senses start to be involved in the temptation; and (4) the *sin*, when we become full slaves of the evil desire. All these four stages can follow each other very fast if the spirit is not watchful.

Tito Colliander noted that the Holy Fathers taught us that we need humility, vigilance, will to resist, and prayers in order to have a chance to win our war (Colliander, 1985). With these weapons we will succeed in doing what the psalmist says - to *"dash against the rock"* the temptations as long as they are still little ones, *"infants"* (*Psalm 136/137:9*). The *"rock"* is Christ since He is our help and our strength. Some people, full of pride, ignoring the Church's teachings through Saint Augustine's writings, take erroneously *ad litteram* the words of this Psalm of exile. For instance, when the terrorist act of

September 11 happened, they said, "we have to kill the terrorists as the sons of Zion killed in anger the infants of Babylon, smashing them against the rock."

When we clean the land of our soul, we start with the large plants, like trees, and we cut them down. Then, according to our strength, we go to smaller and smaller plants, and we never finish cleaning. Therefore, we do not understand the terrible temptations that assault the few persons who succeed in reaching a complete cleansing. The stories about how the evil spirits torture them seem to us unreal, fictional, fantastic. The enemy of faith does not fiercely attack us with heavy artillery as they do to the spiritually advanced persons. We are so trapped in the evil spirit's fishnet that he can damage us even with small temptations, without worrying that he might lose us.

Nothing can be done without God's help (*John 15:5*). We read prayers of repentance in preparation for confession with the certitude that God's love will work in us and He will teach us what branches are sick and must be cut off (*John 15:2*).

The strong believers battle with temptation. We, the weak ones, learn to recognize it immediately as it comes, and we avoid it. A beautiful and famous poem of the American poet Portia Nelson, entitled "Autobiography in five short chapters," tells about "a deep hole in the sidewalk." She was walking along the sidewalk and fell into the hole. It was hard to get out. The next time she went for a walk, she pretended not to see it but fell into it again. Both times, she considered that it was not her fault but she learned how to get out the hole faster. The third time she walked on that sidewalk, she saw the hole very clearly, fell into it but she managed to get out immediately, because she realized that the fall was her fault. When she went for a walk the fourth time, she saw it and went around it and was able to continue her stroll on the street without any more damage. Finally, she concluded that it was preferable to avoid it completely by simply walking down another street.

TEMPTATIONS IN OUR RELATIONSHIPS. We notice sometimes that, while listening to the news our neighbor gives us about his family, our mind tries to anticipate in a negative way what we hear: the person the neighbor talks about is either sick or has suffered an accident, or died. After the neighbor finishes his story, if the news is good we are not sincerely glad, and if it is not good we do not worry, feel compassion or desire to help, as genuine love would react. We even rush to offer our neighbor explanations, to blame someone or to tell him *our* news, with a real indifference and deafness to his trouble and difficulties.

We are angry at the driver who cuts us off, who drives too slowly in front of us, who passes us, who does not yield, or who does not watch out for us in the parking lot. With such an attitude toward others, the result is that when we are close to sacred things (when we venerate an icon, we receive communion or we are anointed with holy oil), we feel a kind of hostility, repulsion, apathy, or coldness instead of being thrilled with awe, peace, love, and confidence.

All these situations reveal the sin that has handcuffed the spirit and does not allow the latter to fly free, to communicate, or to participate. We say in one of the morning prayers, "Therefore with humility I pray – forgive me Lord and *untie* me from all my sins, for You are good and love mankind."

There is a resistance in us every time we try to open ourselves to God. Our thirst for communication is not constant and intense. Even our prayer is often formal and cold, but we say it because we were taught to do it as a rule of life. Saint Paul wrote about this struggle in his epistle to the Romans. "*I see another law in my members, warring against the law of my*

192 | HORIA ION GROZA

mind, and bringing me into captivity to the law of sin which is in my members" (*Romans 7:23*), *"for the good that I want to do, I do not do; but the evil I will not to do, that I practice"* (*Romans 7:19*).

Therefore, the complete opening of the Virgin Mary's mind and heart at the time of the Annunciation was so extraordinary. She said to the Archangel Gabriel, *"Behold the maidservant of the Lord! Let it be to me according to your word"* (*Luke 1:38*). The door of her soul was largely open for the entrance of the Light of God, without any darkening shadow of resistance, doubt, hesitation, or indifference. Her heart's door was like the open Royal Doors of the Church's altar on Easter Sunday, and like the open gates of the prison where Paul and Silas were detained. *"But at midnight Paul and Silas were praying and singing hymns to God, and the prisoners were listening to them. Suddenly there was a great earthquake, so that the foundations of the prison were shaken; and immediately all the doors were opened and everyone's chains were loosed"* (*Acts 16:25-26*).

While the Saint of Transylvania, Father Arseny Boca, was in the Security Police's prison in Braşov in 1948, each night at midnight, when he was praying all the locks from the heavy doors and the heavy bar on the outside gate fell down and frightened the guards. This is how, during ardent communication with God all the ties of the soul are untied, and the hostile shadows disappear, allowing the Divine Light to enter the soul without any obstacle, like a sunbeam cutting a trail through the night of the soul.

Such an opening cannot be achieved by only the simple work of dispassion. We can pull up the weeds but we cannot find and gather the huge amount of hidden seeds of sin in the soil of our being. We are able to prepare ourselves by fasting, repentance, and prayer, but eliminating all the weed seeds comes by grace. Only then, our entrance door will not be slightly ajar as usual, but it will be wide open. Then all the nascent shadows inside our soul will become white, transfigured by Light.

This is the reason why, for us, the Theotokos is the "most pure." She was the only human being capable of containing the incarnation of the Son of God. She is the ladder to the heavens. She is our intercessor to God. We implore her to pray for us due to the power of her purity. She is the most venerated person after God.

There is a famous icon of Theotokos at Iviron Monastery in Mount Athos. The name of it is Portaitissa and it has a wonderful story. The tradition says that the icon was painted by Saint Evangelist Luke, the disciple of Saint Apostle Paul. The icon was lost in Palestine after this country was conquered by the Turks and water currents carried it miraculously across the sea to Mount Athos. A Georgian (Ivirian) hermit who bore the name of the messenger Archangel Gabriel and lived in a cave on the rocky shore, saw two little lights floating on the water while singing the evening akathysts. He ran to them, spotted the icon, and brought it out of the water into his cave. The monks from the Iviron Monastery heard about the mysterious icon and came to take it for the church. All of a sudden, the icon became so heavy that ten people were needed to carry it up to the Monastery. The following morning the icon disappeared and was found back in the cave of the old hermit. This happened several times, without any intervention from the elder. Out of respect for the icon (it seemingly did not want to leave the hermit's place), the monks decided to leave it in the cave. After the old hermit departed to the Lord, they found the icon hanging at the entrance of the Monastery. With utmost respect, veneration, and prayers, they installed it in the church. To their great surprise, the icon disappeared during the night and was found back at the gate of the Monastery. The monks then built a special little chapel at the gate, to shelter the icon. Since then, the icon bears the name Portaitissa and spawned many miracles. Today's visitor can see a little black spot, that smells of incense, on the Theotokos' depicted face. It is the mark left by the sword of an Arabian scoffer. Blood gushed instantly from that wound and scared the pagan who fell down on the ground and, mortified, prayed to the Mother of God for forgiveness. He entered the Monastery as a humble novice and, after a long life of prayer and repentance, became a saint. This wonderful icon is a perfect symbol of what the Holy Virgin Mary, the Mother of God, is for us: the gate to Heavenly Kingdom. Let us not forget that Theotokos is also depicted in the church above the altar, like a link between earth and heaven, as the supreme intercessor for us before her Son and God.

OUR WEAPON IS FAITH AND TRUST IN THE LORD. The Lord tested Abraham's faith when He asked him to sacrifice his own son (*Genesis 22:2*). Søren Kierkegaard elaborated greatly on this subject in "Fear and Trembling." The Danish philosopher considered that Abraham obeyed the Lord's request because he put his faith above all other values. In the same manner, Kierkegaard himself sacrificed his love to Regine Olsen in favor of a deeper faith in God. From an ethical standpoint, Abraham was not making a mistake when he was going to kill his son because he was simply accomplishing the Lord's will. Kierkegaard's comment is that Abraham's ethic remains "theologically in suspense." As Hegel thought, Abraham's drama is very intense because man does not possess a native conscience that allows him to envision with clarity God's will all the way up to the happy end. To be honest, nothing in the human sphere could have convinced Abraham that he was right in his obedience to the command to sacrifice Isaac.

Kierkegaard believed that something hidden – an inexpressible mystery – lies in the depth of our soul and therefore the inner man with its mystery is superior to the physical person. This is why Abraham was silent – he did not feel the need to express himself in the outside world. However, I think that the old patriarch had taken his son to the place of sacrifice not only with the feeling of obedience but with the faith that what he was going to do was for his good. Man knows that God's will brings good to him but man with his own logic cannot know exactly what God's will is and what the consequences of His will are. I also think that the strength of Abraham's faith consisted in his trust in God's promise that his descendants would be innumerable (*Genesis 13:16* and *18:18*). God had repeated that promise many times (*Genesis 15:4-5*). Even more – God had pointed out very clearly this thought after Isaac's birth: "*For in Isaac your seed shall be called*" (*Genesis 21:12*).

Saint Paul's comments brought up another aspect: "*by faith Abraham, when he was tested, offered up Isaac, and he who had received the promises offered up his only begotten son... concluding that God was able to raise him up, even from the dead, from which he also received him in a figurative sense*" (*Hebrews 11: 17-19*). Let us remember the exact words of the Scripture: "*So Abraham took the firewood of the whole burnt offering, and laid it on Isaac his son. Then he took the fire in his hand, and the knife, and the two of them went together*" (*Genesis 22:6*). That burning wood, that fire, was his ardent faith.

In his silence, mentioned by Kierkegaard, and in his meditation, Abraham looked toward the ground the whole time during their three-day journey. "*Then on the third day Abraham lifted his eyes and saw the place afar off*" (*Genesis 22:4*). I would dare to believe that all this time the old patriarch was confident that an extraordinary thing would happen and the sacrifice would not be allowed. He might have been praying unceasingly, "Lord Thy will be done. Lord have mercy." Isaac asked his father, *"where is the sheep for a whole burnt offering?"* Abraham answered, *"My son, God will provide for Himself the sheep"* (*Genesis 22:7-8*). As we read in *Genesis 22:14*, after everything was done and Abraham sacrificed the lamb brought by the angel, Abraham called that place *"Jehova-jireh"* (King James Version), which means *"The-Lord-Has-Appeared"* (SAAS Version) or "*The Lord will provide*" (Revised Standard Version).

In conclusion, as the French Father Lev Gillet commented on the text from *1 Corinthians 10:13*: "If God let a temptation hit the man He also had prepared the way out of it in order to make the man capable of endurance" (The Living God, 1989). "*Do not be afraid; only believe*" (*Mark 5:36*).

"*For with his heart one believes unto righteousness, and with the mouth confession is made unto salvation*" (*Romans 10:10*). But watch out! Man with his own power does not acquire this justification but receives it by grace from the Lord, after a long and laborious process of humility, cleansing and prayer. *"They have a zeal for God, but not according to knowledge. For they being ignorant of God's righteousness, and seeking to establish their own righteousness, have not submitted to the righteousness of God"* (*Romans 10:2-3*).

I heard someone say, "You are what you love not what loves you." God loves us but we are not what His love gives us. We are what passion we offer, and we are the response to God's love.

DISCERNMENT IS THE OTHER WEAPON, and we ask its wisdom from the Lord. Sister Luke (played by Audrey Hepburn), the main character of "The Nun's Story" movie made in 1959, was the daughter of a well-respected doctor, and wanted to go to Congo to serve as a nurse, sacrificing her life in order to help the sick people in a population struggling with poverty and epidemics. She chose to be a nun and to devote herself to the love of the poor neighbors, full of fervor as a servant of God and desiring that her talent for medicine might yield fruit. The monastic discipline was very strict, the main emphasis being on the monastic prayer and work and only secondly on her work as an unsalaried nurse. She underwent many harshly disciplinary trials such as isolation, long periods of silence, continuously trying to erase all the memories of her previous life, and cutting off all contacts with her family.

Unfortunately, she failed in her struggle to become accustomed to the main monastic rule, which was obedience. Directing her passion into doing good to the sick and suffering, and working long hours ignoring her exhaustion, she entered into conflict several times with her monastic superiors in the order, those who emphasized other things. She kept God always in her mind and heart, responding with fervor and sacrifice to His commandment of love, but she could not adapt herself to the strict discipline of obedience, which hindered her work as nurse. She was called away for monastic activities even when she was in the middle of a surgical operation or while she was responding to the acute need of a patient.

Realizing eventually that she could not advance further in her deification work in the form required by the Monastery's rules, she resigned and asked to be released back to the world. Far from being a humanistic attack on the faith and church philosophy, the movie presents some important spiritual problems of Christian laypeople.

We see here a continuous battle with the ego. One accepts, grows virtues such as humility, love, and patience, and keeps the rule of prayer. Nevertheless, a question arises: does humility mean forgetting our personal characteristics? Does the fact that we have in mind our strengths and we want to develop them with a noble goal mean that we are still attached to our ego? Is that pride?

The Christian people who live in the world outside the monasteries have their physical body's limits. They cannot pray all the time. While they practice their profession they have to be a hundred percent focused on all the specific details, and their mind and heart have no time for prayer. The laymen have to devote that time to thinking wholly of the demands of their job and at the same time be noetically reciting the interior prayers (usually the *Jesus Prayer*). It is true that they can compensate for ignoring their prayers while focusing on their work by feeling the presence of God everywhere and at all times and by dedicating to God the quality of their accomplishments. However, is this enough?

How compatible with the will of God is the dedication to work? We pray to learn God's will and to acquire the strength to accomplish it, because we know that God's will is for our good even when we do not comprehend it. We deal here not with selfishness because we do not put our desire first and ask the Lord to help us satisfy it. We fear God, we love Him, and we want to obey His will. However, there are times when we do not know which way we should choose. For instance, we apply for a job; we are interviewed trying to do our best, but we pray, "Lord, let it be as you will and it will be good for me, because I do not know if this is the right job for me."

In other cases we use the education received in Church that tells us what is good, and we make decisions and direct our efforts accordingly, trying to live a life in harmony with the Christian principles. It happens sometimes that, despite all our hard work, God denies us success or even upsets our plans. We let it go, we ask God to do whatever is good for us, and then everything comes to a happy-ending. Nevertheless, there are times when new difficulties are added, one after the other, and our very trust and confidence in God is in danger of being damaged. We do not see any end to our suffering, and we are overwhelmed. Then the only thought that can save us from confusion and despair is the thought of Job's steadfastness. When his wife said, *"How long will you hold out?... Say a word against the Lord and die!,"* Job replied, *"If we accepted good things from the Lord's hand, shall we not endure evil things?"* (*Job, 2:9, 14, 15*). We can think also of Abraham's hope while obediently on his way to kill his only son Isaac.

WHAT WORRIES OUR ENEMY THE MOST. The enemy does not worry about losing us if the passions are still part of us, whether or not they become vices. We still cannot resist eating a good dessert. Our imagination is on fire when we hear an erotic story. We do not help the people in need, with the excuse that we are not greedy but we have good "healthy" economic reasons not to intervene. We fall into despair if we have no luck when we are gambling. A bitter anger stirs our heart when we think that our partner was not fair to us and we want to punish him in a manner he will remember, and so on.

Nevertheless, the enemy starts to worry when we succeed in dampening our passions through our own efforts and with God's help. If we reach the more advanced stage at which we pull out not only the weeds of the passions but discard even their seeds and destroy all chances to have them germinate, the enemy fights furiously to regain territory and strikes hard in *our* weakest moments. Such a terrible battle Saint Mary of Egypt had to endure forty-seven years, in pain and tears, with the fear that she could have missed a seed that might germinate again. Fortunately, while our mind and soul is awake, continuously watching, God smoothes our life and enables our feet to walk on water as Our Lord Jesus walked on the sea "*in the fourth watch of the night*" (*Matthew 14:25*), and as Saint Mary of Egypt walked on the Jordan River.

All of us have spiritually betrayed or almost betrayed God with each sin we have committed. By sinning, we have ignored, disobeyed, or denied Him. A prayer before the Communion at the Holy Liturgy says: "Of the Mystical Supper, accept me today as a communicant; for I will not speak of Thy mystery to Thine enemies, neither like Judas will I give Thee a kiss but like the thief I will confess Thee: Remember me, O Lord, into Thy Kingdom." By sinning after communion, we accept again the Tempter's game, we ignore temporarily the Lord's teachings and, which is worse, we interrupt our efforts to achieve dispassion, our purification. It is like unveiling to the Tempter our Christian status and efforts. In other words, we "speak" to the Tempter, who is the enemy of God and of ours, about the mysteries of God, about His Body and Blood that have been given us as a token of the Lord's participation in our deification process.

DEEP CONTROL OF BODY. If we read about the life on Mount Athos, we might find the story of an old Russian monk, Tikhon, in "Athonite Fathers and Athonica" (1993) who departed into the Lord's Kingdom in 1964. He had reached such a high spiritual level that, while his mind was continuously praying to God, his body was not at all sensitive to anything from outside. He was plagued by many flies, mosquitoes and fleas. His body was marked with numerous bites and stings, and bloodstains covered his clothes. One monk said that even if someone had extracted his blood with a syringe the old ascetic would have not felt anything. All kinds of creatures were moving freely in his cells, from insects to rats. I remember another example when the body's challenges were defeated by the spirit and the person did not notice anything. Father Arhimandrite Ioanichie Bălan from Sihăstria Monastery (Bălan, 1996) wrote the story about old George, a saintly villager who was sleeping in the winter directly on the cold cement of an ancient fortress tower in Piatra Neamț and who walked barefoot regardless how deep and cold the snow layer was.

THE FOOLS-FOR-CHRIST are the humble believers who try to be ignored and want to be considered mentally retarded. They prefer to be despised by the world, instead of being sympathized with or pitied, in order to acquire the peace needed for a complete and secret dedication to a life of sacrifice and faith (the reason for this strange manner of life might be given in Saint Apostle Paul's epistles (*1 Corinthians 1:18-24, 2:14, 3:18-19*). An example of a fool in Christ is Saint Blessed Andrew, who saw The Holy Virgin Mary surrounded by angels and saints, above the crowds at Vespers in Blachernae Church in Constantinople, in year 911, on a day which became the Feast of Pokrov (The Protection of Our Most Holy Lady Theotokos and Ever-Virgin Mary). Another example is Saint Blessed Xenia of Petersburg (1730-1803) who lived 45 years on the streets, wearing the military uniform of her deceased husband, a colonel.

I think that how these authentic God pleasing persons are considered by the Christian people around them, can characterize very well four possible stages of living in faith and understanding God.

(1) Living for accepting the idea of God. The people in this stage follow a set of humanistic ethical rules in their lives and strive to develop several important virtues. They respect the principle "do not harm others in order to avoid any harm from them," expressing a moderate selfishness and self-esteem. They maintain a certain balance between the worldly

pleasures and the requirements of a decent Christian life, observing the religious holidays, having icons in the house, going for confession and communion once a year. They lack the capacity to distinguish the real *fools-for-Christ* from the religious fanatics (those pseudo-fools in Christ who are socially active and always in danger of losing the initial flame of faith and its authenticity).

(2) Living with the idea of God. The people in this stage change the humanistic ethical way of living for a true Christian one, become steadfast in virtue, are eager to know more about the Church's teachings, read the Bible, and are active in the Church. The selfishness is diminished in favor of a more frequent charitable giving to others, helping others etc. They are able to notice the real *fools for Christ* and respect them despite the fact they do a lot of odd things, apparently without any reason.

(3) Living for God. In this stage the social position and welfare does not count anymore. Such people are in podvig, in a continuous battle of dispassion. Their repentance is sincere and profound and, as it is said, they are living "with the soul in Hades" or "with the acute thought of the Last Judgment." The supreme principle of their ascetic life of prayer and fasting is a deep love for God and for their neighbor. Humility is a stable and powerful virtue. The people in this stage understand fully the and perceive exactly the amount of their holiness.

(4) Living in God. This is only for the Saints. Their perception of the *fools-for-Christ* goes beyond the limits of our mind.

2.5. The Interior Labor. Fasting, Prayer.

SINCERITY IS NOT ENOUGH. The protestant denomination members are very sincere in their faith. Their zeal often exceeds that of the parishioners of the traditional churches. They have a clean life, do not smoke, do not drink liquor, and do not fall prey to fornication. They are honest people, living in harmony with the surrounding world, despite the fact that their virtues contrast so much with the habits of others. However, their spiritual progress stops there. The very impressive moral austerity they reached does not help much. For them the Orthodox Christian's problem of continuous dispassion, of searching the deep roots of sin, does not exist. They do not recognize the Saints; for them all people are the same - just honest believers. The Protestants do not consider that vigil is important and that they have to chase every thought or feeling that might answer a temptation. For them the fasting is not a way of purification on the ascendant way of deification. In their mind and soul, Saint Mary of Egypt is not possible. As Father Kallistos Ware said, they will be asked, when they will face God after repose, how they used the symbols and sacraments, taught by the Savior and His Apostles.

IMPORTANCE OF FASTING. By fasting, the spirit is freed from the tyranny of the body. Our soul becomes more skillful in the perception of the most sophisticated temptations and more accurate in comprehending the danger of transgressions. Saint Mary of Egypt acquired that strength by struggling in the desert seventeen years with heat, cold, hunger, thirst, and her passions, before living another thirty years with God in peace and holiness. While she was telling Abba Zosima the story of her previous worldly life, she suffered when she had to refer to her sins and her struggle for dispassion, because she had eliminated them, not only like pulling weeds from the prepared soil of her soul for the Lord's word, but also like discarding the whole reserve of the weed seeds. The fasting periods of the religious year are not merely a chance to refresh our resources through abstinence nor simply a way to prepare for the holidays they precede, but also a cumulative process in rising to follow our soul's continuous aspiration for unity with our Creator (*"Therefore we do not lose heart. Even though our outward man is perishing, yet the inward man is being renewed day by day"* – 2 Corinthians 4:16).

"This kind can come out by nothing but prayer and fasting", Our Lord Jesus Christ said (*Mark 9:29*). "Fasting and prayer somehow constitute our boldness before God. With these you can rise to heaven" said Father Justin Pârvu, one of the greatest spiritual elders of rhe Romanian monastic world (see Irme, 2013). Father Cleopa Ilie said that prayer, confession and humility have to accompany the prayer, adding the words of Holy John Chrysostom that fast strengthens the body fragility, retrains the gluttonous retrains the ardent desires and purifies the spirit, filling it with light and elevating it (see Elder Cleopa of Romania, 2000).

BUT ABOVE ALL IS THE PRAYER. When we pray, we are with God. Saint Paisius of Neamţ (Velichkovsky) wrote in the "Field Flowers" that Prayer is merely the border between the visible and invisible worlds (St. Paisius Velichkovsky, 1994). Father Kallistos Ware thinks that Prayer is our entrance into the community of Saints. The role of prayer is to keep us always with God, as the Russian priest George Florovsky said. Saint John Climacus noted that as fire tests gold so prayer tests the zeal of the monk and his love for God (St. John Climacus, 1982).

Prayer is the clean breath of the spirit, its health, and its strength. We learn from Father Thomas Hopko that the intimate communication within the Holy Trinity is done in the form of a prayer. The voice of the angels who unceasingly praise the Lord is also a voiced prayer. *"I have prayed for you, that your faith should not fail; and when you have returned to Me, strengthen your brethren,"* said Our Lord to Peter when the tempter was close to him (*Luke 22:31-32*). The evangelists tell us that the Son of God prayed to God the Father many times: in the wilderness, on the mountain where He multiplied the bread and fishes, on Mount Tabor, in Gethsemane. Prayer is the intimate way in which the spirit communicates.

A prayer of Cyril of Constantinople, included in Apanthisma, says, "You are the Master of my soul and you carefully protect me not to return into non-being." (St. Nicodim Agioritos, 1996). This is another role of the prayer to the Lord: it keeps us in the frame of a mystical being because prayer does not mean only a complete focus of the heart and mind. The Apostle said, *"I will pray with the spirit, and I will also pray with the understanding"* (*1 Corinthians 14:15*).

"Prayer is the seed of gentleness and the absence of anger. Prayer is a remedy against grief and depression", as we can read the words of Abba Nilus recorded in Patericon (see The Sayings of the Desert Fathers, *1975*).

PRAYER HAS TREMENDOUS POWER. We read in the Patericon about an old monk from Sinai who visited an Abba and complained about the lack of rain despite all the prayers and litanies (Patericul, 1999a). The Abba said, "This is because you do not pray truly." Then he raised his arms to the heaven, prayed and immediately it started to rain abundantly. The old monk was very frightened, fell down in front of the Abba, and praised him. But the Abba rushed away in order to avoid any pride. Man has the liberty of his decisions. If he chooses by his own will to believe in God and follow him, he will be able, by the Lord's grace, to do things that are considered impossible for humans. The Savior told us that a little faith, as minuscule as a mustard grain, can move the mountains (*Matthew 17:20*).

Prayer brought a shelter to Jonah in the belly of the deep-sea monster and got him out (*Jonah 2*). Prayer brought Hezekiah back to life from his deadly sickness (*2 Chronicles/2 Paralipomenon 32:24*). Prayer changed the frightening flames of the furnace into refreshing dew for Daniel's young companions of Babylon, Shadrach, Meshach, and Abednego (*Daniel 3:49-50*). Elijah's prayer caused the fire that burnt the offering and humiliated Baal's prophets (3 Kingdoms/1 Kings 18:38). His prayer opened the sky and an abundant rain poured down after a three-year drought (*3 Kingdoms/1 Kings 18:42-45*).

My heart was deeply touched by a prayer heard in America: "Lord Thou knowest my cares and my fears. Help me to turn them all over to Thee, Who hast promised to give rest to our souls." Paul Evdokimov wrote, "God works and man sweats."

Saint Maxim the Confessor said that, "for flying up to heaven, man needs two wings: liberty and grace." God confers Grace after the reciprocal consent of action (*fiat*) by both persons – from God (Who by the word *Fiat* created the Universe) and from man (who by the word *Fiat*, pronounced by the Holy Virgin Mary, mediated the incarnation of the Son of God). Every Christian aspires to reach the state wherein the Savior becomes an intimate part of his soul, as the Mother of God had the Savior incarnated within her. An eloquent personification of the necessary preparation for spiritual ascension is the monk. As Paul Evdokimov would say, the monk does not diminish his being by his extreme asceticism, but he enlarges it in order to contain in his existence a part of the image of the Divine Existence. The main element of man's action consists in prayer, followed by virtues, purification, and good deeds (Evdokimov, 1977).

"Pray. There is immeasurable power in it," Jackson Brown *Jr* very pragmatically suggested to his son on the brink of leaving his parents' house to enter College life. It is not rare for a community of Christians to notice with a thrill of joy the effect of the prayers they said for the healing and help of one of the members (Jackson Brown Jr., 1993). The united voices of souls and the services in Church are clearly heard and welcomed by the Lord.

WHAT DO WE PRAY FOR? As Father Cleopa Ilie says, the prayers contains three main things in the following order: praise, thanksgiving and request. The request is for forgiveness of sins and for our and our neighbor's needs. An elder, mentioned by the Patericon commented that "Prayer is the defense of the guilty, the comfort of the grieving, and the joy of the happy people." (Patericul 1999a). In our prayers we do not want to disobey God's will because He is the Master of the Universe and He knows what is really good for us. We only submit our request to Him and we pray for His decision according to His judgment and to our good. *"My counsels are not as your counsels, neither are your ways My ways,"* said the Lord (*Isaiah 55:8*).

The more ardent believers ask the Lord to teach them His will, to give them the wisdom to perceive it and the ability to accomplish it. Father Thomas Hopko expanded this kind of thinking and affirmed that the simple request of mercy, without any specified details, suffices, because the Lord knows our intimate desires in addition to our real needs and leads the events in the direction that may truly help us. Despite the fact that a short formula of prayer like "Lord have mercy" apparently simplifies and reduces our efforts, we should not stop saying the traditional prayers that the Church advises us to say. Certainly, no one can oblige us to pray. The Lord cannot ignore our freedom of choice. However, only if we call for God's help, will

He respond. Father Kallistos called our attention to the fact that, because we Christians represent the faith incarnated in this world, Orthodoxy does not make any distinction between sacred and secular matters. Therefore every detail of man's life and work is blessed by the Church under the protection of divine grace. Man asks for help from the Lord in all he does. The prayer books contain prayers for sewing, for wine making, for blessing the tractor or the fishing nets, for the children who learn to read or for the college students before exams, for healing the sick cows or sheep, for getting rid of insomnia, for controlling the damage of caterpillars to the crops and even for eliminating dead rats at the bottom of the water wells.

We pray for the dead (a more correct term is "for those fallen asleep" because we believe in eternal life). In our prayers, we also ask forgiveness for those who committed suicide, even though the Church does not offer services for them. However, once a year, the Vespers for Pentecost include a prayer of Saint Basil for those enchained in unceasing harsh affliction in Hades (including those who killed themselves), asking the Lord to give them hope and relief from their suffering. It is written somewhere in the Patericon that an elder, in his humble sanctity, even prayed for the forgiveness of the Prince of Evil, the Fallen Angel (Patericul 1999a).

We pray for those fallen asleep because from the moment a person is brought to life by God in this earthly world, the soul of that person becomes eternal and is called to a process of deification. The people fallen asleep continue to pray after leaving this earthly life. That is why we pray to the Saints, asking them to intervene for us. Our prayers and theirs are a united fire, like the smoke of sacrifice rising to the sky. Those departed from us still have a chance to be forgiven before the time of the Last Judgment. The Orthodox Christians do not believe in the existence of Purgatory. This intermediate stage of purification was artificially introduced by the cataphatic nature of the Catholic Church. However, the exact status of the departed remains a deep mystery that only God knows truly and entirely.

NUMBER FORTY. We pray for forgiveness, for the sins we know and we do not know. A friend told me about the deep thrill he feels when he says forty times "Lord have mercy" during the morning prayers. This repeated formula is referring, as we know, to the sins we have committed without knowing, the sins we have forgotten, and the sins for which we did not realize their actual nature. When he utters the words slowly and counts the times with his fingers pressing lightly one by one on his heart place, he feels like a cleansing shower washes through his entire being.

The Church advises us to say forty times "Lord have mercy" because this number echoes deep in the Scripture's meanings. There is a certain length of time given to people to experience and a certain length of time necessary to reach maturity. Forty years David reigned over Israel (*1 Chronicles 29:26*) and his son, Solomon, reigned for the same number of years (*2 Chronicles 9:30*). Forty years Moses lived as a shepherd in Midian until the Angel of the Lord appeared to him as a burning bush (*Acts 7:29-30*), and forty years Moses and his followers wandered in the desert (*Exodus 16:35*; *Numbers 14:33*; *Deuteronomy 8:2*).

There is a certain length of time for purification, for washing the sins away. The flood lasted forty days (*Genesis 7:17*). Moses abode forty days in the mountain without drinking or eating before receiving the tables of stone (*Deuteronomy 9:9*). There is also a certain length for preparing to meet God. Forty days Our Lord Jesus Christ fasted, in a sinless body, in the wilderness, before starting to preach (*Matthew 4:2*).

HOW SHOULD WE PRAY TO GOD? "Take off your shoes," Father Anthony Coniaris wrote. *"Take your sandals off your feet, for the place where you stand is holy ground,"* (Coniaris, 1998) the Lord told Moses who was watching the Burning Bush on Mount Sinai (*Exodus 3:5*). The place where we pray should be considered as such, regardless where it is – in our room, in the church, in the forest, in the plane or in our car - because this is the condition in which we are able to say the words of our prayer, with love, fear, piety and awe. We may do it in secret even if we are in the midst of a crowd, because we keep it deep in us, in the private "room" of our heart. *"But you, when you pray, go into your room, and when you have shut your door, pray to your Father who is in the secret place; and your Father who sees in secret will reward you openly"* (*Matthew 6:6*).

How ought we to address God? In a personal manner. Father Anthony Bloom considered that a relationship becomes personal and real the very moment we start to distinguish a person from the rest of the crowd (Bloom, 1970). As long as we speak about a person as "he/she," we are not actually attached to that person because another person from the crowd can replace him/her anytime. The relationship remains functional but it is far from being personal. I think this is why the Lord praised Job and reproved his friends – they did not look at the relationship man-God as at an intimate, personal link.

We, the Christians, are linked with each other through the Holy Person of Christ. Another interconnection is between the people sharing the same baptism name that corresponds to the name of a certain Saint. On the other hand, we carry a particular name, proper only to us, a name that we do not know, a name that is known only by God. The name that He used when, with one word, He created us, as He created the world. This name was the specific word spoken by God to bring us from non-being, and it defines our absolute and unrepeatable uniqueness. The name is marked in heaven on a unique white stone, and *"no one knows it except him who receives it."* (*Revelation 2:17*).

We say the Lord's Prayer kneeling in awe and fear. "And make us worthy, O Master, that with boldness and without condemnation we may dare to call on Thee, the heavenly God, as Father," the priest says at the Divine Liturgy before the Lord's Prayer. Only we, the Christians, are allowed to say this prayer. Therefore, the Lord's Prayer is in the third part of the Liturgy - the Liturgy of the Eucharist or the Liturgy of the Faithful. The catechumens, may stay only for the second part, the Liturgy of the Word that contains the Gospel readings, but they have to leave before the third part begins. Only we, the faithful, the baptized, are allowed to call the Almighty God, *Our Father*, because through Our Lord Jesus Christ we become children of God the Father. Saint Paul wrote to his disciples, *"For you did not receive the spirit of bondage again to fear, but you received the Spirit of adoption by whom we cry out, 'Abba, Father'"* (*Romans 8:15-16*). *"And because you are sons, God has sent forth the Spirit of His Son into your hearts, crying out, 'Abba, Father!'"* (*Galatians 4:6*).

The Romanian Father Theodore Gîrlonţa used to warn us that our request for forgiveness for our sins might turn against us, bringing condemnation, because we say in this important Prayer, *"And forgive us our trespasses as we forgive those who trespassed against us."* If we do not forgive, we will not be forgiven but sentenced (cf. *John 20:23, Luke 6:37, Mark 11:25-26*).

It is good to read and eventually learn by heart prayers from the Orthodox Book of Prayer. We have to pay attention to all the words. We do it with our focused mind and also with our heart if the latter is in a receptive mood (however we keep praying even if our heart is "cold", as Father Thomas Hopko said). While we pray, we do not have to hurry. Otherwise, we will miss the chance to perceive with our mind the whole load that every word hides in the silence behind it, and we will not let the power of the divine space penetrate our heart. The silence behind each word is as important as the pauses in a musical composition or the white spaces in a watercolor drawing. Every sound of a church bell carries a silence on its back, a piece of infinity. We need those pauses for the awe of our soul.

PRAYER AND IMAGINATION. Einstein adamantly encouraged his students to develop the power of imagination as a means of inventiveness in technology and of progress in science. The imagination helps us visualize the phenomena and predict the manifestation of nature's systems. The imagination is also useful in poetry, because it is a way for the poets to suggest the ineffable, by handling the subtle art of images and metaphors. The imagination is extremely useful in science, where it brings to mind goals and vision, and in engineering, where it bring about inventiveness.

However, the imagination is not welcome in the practice of prayer. We do not have to stumble over images and to give the holy things a face from our daily world. If we do that, we will remain anchored in the material world and we will never reach the heights of heaven. "There are sentries from hell that take up their watch at the gateway of man's imagination" (see Elder Cleopa of Sihastria, 2001)

Prayer is a step forward. It does not need to express the ineffable in images in order to communicate it to others. Prayer is an experience entirely personal; it is a manner of living. The icons are austere. We pray in front of an icon that gives us symbolic elements but we close our eyes and we do not try to imagine the face and body of the Lord or of His saints when we address them. We just feel their presence, a steady and rich presence. We have to learn to dialogue with the abstract, to live with the abstract and to discover gradually the peace and silence of it. They serve as symbols and are not actual faces.

Truly, the idea of God might sound abstract, because He is ineffable, inconceivable, and above everything. However, God is also *very personal*, and our heart, mind, and spirit *feel Him* as a dear presence, a parental presence and at the same time a Master's presence. He sees us everywhere we are and knows the whole of our being, even the most intimate corners of our soul (cf. *Psalm 138/139*). As Our Lord Jesus Christ said, "*the very hairs of your head are all numbered*" (*Matthew 10:30*). These words also bring the message that, being under such attentive care, we should not despair when we are hurt. "*He who endures to the end will be saved*" (*Matthew 10:22*).

PARTICIPATION OF THE BODY. The body is a temple dedicated to the spirit. Many physical gestures or actions of the body are included in the work of the spirit: venerating the icons, kissing the cross, making prostrations, kneeling, being abstinent during lent. When we make the sign of the cross, we make our body part of our soul's prayer. We make the cross by using three fingers because they represent the Holy Trinity, while the meaning of the other two remaining fingers is the double nature of our Savior: the divine and the human nature.

Father Vladimir Lecko encouraged us not to be satisfied with a shallow faith fed by merely going to church Sundays and by a certain respect given to the holy things. This kind of faith is like the horizontal arm of the cross. We should go into the depth of things for gaining the force to rise like the vertical trunk of the cross. Some people compare the shape of the cross with a key that opens the locks of death, reminding us of Our Lord's descent into Hades before the Resurrection, while others see a sword, reminding us of Our Lord's battle with evil. When we make the sign of the cross, we should do it slowly, in order to allow our mind to add to the gesture the exact correspondence of the words. We touch the forehead and pronounce the name of the Father, the lower side of the chest and say the name of the Son, the right shoulder and say the word "Holy," and the left shoulder and say "Spirit," then we say "Amen." These are the unseen four cardinal points of our body and they correspond to the image of the baptism (*Luke 3:21-22*): the Father above, the Son down in Jordan River, the Holy Spirit in the middle floating in the air like a dove with wings outstretched to the right and the left. When we cross ourselves like that, slowly, living its deep meaning, we feel, as the Romanian Hieromonk Daniel (previously the poet Sandu Tudor) used to say, "how this gesture embraces, covers, embodies and comprises us." He also said about the depth of the Divine mystery, "the cross is the Lord's nocturne look at us; '*From the sixth hour until the ninth hour there was darkness over all the land*' (*Matthew 27:45*)". It was Christ, the Son of God, looking unseen to us with sadness, love and mercy, from the world beyond of death (Tudor, 2001).

I remember a little Romanian folk story. A Jewish merchant hired a peasant to move him and his merchandise from the village to the town. The peasant loaded his wagon, the merchant jumped in, the peasant whipped the horses once, and they left in a hurry. They followed the main street, passed through the center of the village, and continued the road over large fields. When they had almost covered half the distance, the merchant asked the peasant to stop and to return to the village. The peasant wondered why. "Because when we passed by the orthodox church in the middle of the village you did not make the sign of the cross. I do not trust people who disrespect their God," the merchant said.

Father Cleopa Ilie advised us to cross ourselves before doing anything: when we depart on a journey, when we begin our chores, when we start to do our school homework, when we remain alone and when we enter society. He said, "Seal your forehead, chest, body, heart, lips, eyes, and ears with the Holy Cross, to avoid any sin with them." Many people do not want to show off and therefore they make the sign of the cross in their mind, or with the tongue. Nevertheless, they are in a state of awe for God at that moment and they ask mentally for His help and blessing.

We say in our morning prayer, "My hope is the Father, my salvation is the Son, and my protection is the Holy Spirit." Saint Theophan the Recluse used to tell his disciples, "We are saved by the compassion of the Father, by the merits of the Son and by the grace of the Holy Spirit." So "we pray *to* God the Father, *through* God the Son and *in* the Holy Spirit" (Ware, 1987).

OVERCOMING THE FATIGUE. At times we grow tired. We keep the same rule of prayer strictly, but on some days, it seems that our heart becomes cold like a stone. Our prayer takes on the appearance of a robotic recitation and it does not echo in our heart. We do not feel the thrill anymore. No repentance, no attachment, no participation, no joy fills our heart. We feel no vibration from the special boundless realm that exists behind each word we say.

This state might worry us very much because, in order to wake our spirit up, God might give us hard trials like those given to Job. In our modern times, these trials came as a world war or as the communist gulag. Before subjecting us to hard trials like those, God keeps us awake with small events that make us cry for help. The remembrance of the difficult moments of our life, the remorse for a serious sin or simply the reading of the Gospel and Holy Fathers succeed very often in melting the cold rigidity of our soul.

Reviving a petrified heart by prayer extenuates the body and mind and robs them of all their power. Therefore, the monks consider praying as a very tedious and exhausting work. Realizing the coldness of their soul, the weaker monks might feel a desire to quit the monasteries, while the stronger ones might need to go and visit other ascetics in order to check the solidity of their faith.

We read many things like that in Patericon about Abba Macarius. Abba Zosima, who met Saint Mary of Egypt, fell into a sort of pride in himself and the Angel of God advised him to go outside the monastery with the same intent - to compare the depth of his faith with that of the other monastics. We, the laymen, might go to the priest to whom we make our regular confession or we might go to the religious services at monasteries, for refreshing and strengthening our soul. However, we have to come back to the labor of prayer.

Retiring into the small intimate room of our soul will eventually fill us with peace, far from the events of the day, from worries, and from any zeal for achievement, with only one goal - to abandon ourselves to a calm and persevering prayer in our nearness to God, Whom we trust as a loving friend.

Many people mention that they come out from the Divine Liturgy invigorated, with a refreshed spirit and a positive attitude toward life. Others come out with a sweet peace from the Vespers, celebrated in a low voice in the mild darkness of the night under the small mysterious light of the candles.

OVERCOMING A BUSY SCHEDULE. Sometimes it is hard to follow the rule of the daily prayers because of a busy schedule during the day, because we are in an improper place, or because we are not alone. However, there are many examples of praying people who always succeed in finding their moment of silence, concentration, and perseverance. A political detainee witnessed how a priest, who was in the same prison cell with a group of several cell mates, was kneeling and praying in the dark of the night when the others were sleeping. The priest stopped every time one of the cell mates woke up to use the pot, and then continued his prayer after that, unknown by anyone. Serge Fudel mentioned an officer in the Russian czar's guard, Khomyakov, who was busy during long days with numerous guests at his dacha, because everyone loved him for his charisma, jokes, dinners and stories (Fudel, 1989). Nevertheless, he always found later, in the silence of the night, a remote corner in his room, where he prayed with tears in front of the icons.

Above the entrance to the church of the Antim Monastery in Bucharest, there is a snail carved in stone. As the snail goes everywhere with his cochlea on its back, the monk carries in his heart the private room that is his world of prayer. *"But you, when you pray, go into your room, and when you have shut your door, pray to your Father who is in the secret place; and your Father who sees in secret will reward you openly,"* Christ said (*Matthew 6:6*). If we cannot keep our discipline of prayer, we can use the Jesus Prayer, as a permanent prayer, and this will temporarily replace the prayers that should be said at a certain time of the day or night.

THE SILENCE OF GOD. Our challenge is not to despair when praying becomes painful. We should not lose our hope. We pray that the will of God be done as He thinks it is good for us. When we act we say, "God willing, I shall do that thing" or "I will do it with God's help". Saint Apostle James advised, *"You ought to say, 'If the Lord wills, we shall live and do this or that'"* (*James 4:15*). Praying persistently (*Matthew 7:7-12*) should be our philosophy of life even if we have to endure harsh events like losses, sickness, invalidity or death of the beloved during our lifetime. We are struck sometimes by the Lord's "silence." Despite our ardent prayer, our virtues and our fasting, we receive no response to our prayers. We feel as if there were a great apathy and indifference in the heavens for our needs. *"O Lord, I have cried to You; hear me; give heed to the voice of my supplication when I cry to You"* (*Psalm 140/141:1*).

The Russian priest Alexander Men, who lived in 1935-1990 and was murdered as a martyr on his way to the church to celebrate the Divine Liturgy, wrote very wise words about the Lord's "silence." So did the theologian Paul Evdokimov (see Evdokimov, 1973).

First, let us not forget Our Lord Jesus Christ's own silence. He preached daily during the three years of His activity, often neglecting to rest or to eat (*Mark 2:23-25* and *11:12-13*). The Gospel records only very little of what He said and did (*John 21:25*). Our Lord was silent throughout almost the whole duration of his confrontation with the priest Caiaphas. He replied very briefly to Pilate but He did not say a word while He was being mocked and beaten. The Lord Jesus was silent all the time that He carried the cross and, with the exception of the few words said to His mother and John, and to the thief on the cross, He was silent during the Crucifixion until the last exclamation when He died.

Father Men (see Hamant, 1995) wondered why Christ, Who preached so long and inspired so many people by His magnificent words, sowing hope and faith in their hearts, remained quite silent these last long hours while the disciples were frightened and discouraged. Yes, we feel sometimes that the Lord is silent and does not answer our prayers about our suffering and needs, ignoring our heart-felt supplications. Our Lord Jesus Christ Who suffered and died in silence for our sins, *does care for us.* He suffers in silence for our weak faith, for our trespasses. He, who was silent on the cross and seems sometimes to be silent in heaven, is truly our Savior, the Person who never abandons us. He is our only Hope.

Saint Isaac the Syrian said we do not have to be sad if the Lord is slow in responding to our request, because He might act so due to His profound wisdom. Everything that is received quickly might be lost quickly. In fact, the life in this world is not only a gift to enjoy, but it is also a chance to work for our eternal life. The Abbott Herman of the Platina Monastery emphasized an important Christian thought: "there will be no *total* earthly bliss during this life, only spiritual trans-cendence." The total bliss is in the Kingdom of Heaven.

DURING PRAYER, WE MIGHT SUFFER INTERRUPTIONS. The Tempter can cause this and in this case, we have to remain calm and to try to resume our prayer with patience and consistence. The interruption can also be a sign from God, a sort of message. In this latter case, we will receive it with love and, immediately that it is over, we will continue with the same patient consistence.

Our Lord, on His way to Jairus' house, where He was going to resuscitate the ruler's daughter (*Matthew 9:18-26* and *Luke 8:41-56*), was interrupted from His intentions by the humble woman who had a ceaseless flow of blood. The Savior welcomed the incident and wanted the healing miracle to be loudly acknowledged. This was in contrast to the resuscitation of the ruler's daughter that followed, which was part of a spiritual process Our Lord wanted to keep secret.

It is obvious that we have to be vigilant to protect the prayer from interruption but in no case, should we fall into becoming angry or impatient. The interruption might be caused by God Who calls us to do something else. Who knows? Maybe it is a reaction to our very prayer. How many miracles have we very likely missed because we refused to answer the Lord's call, pretending that we are busy with something more important?

The man who disturbs us at the time of prayer needs to be treated with kindness if not with genuine love. Because of the very time he comes, we should receive him like an angel, a messenger. Saint Paul wrote in his letter to his disciples, *"Do not forget to entertain strangers, for by so doing some have unwittingly entertained angels"* (*Hebrews 13:2*). This is a reference to Abraham welcoming the three heavenly visitors at the oak of Mamre (*Genesis 18:2*).

Never discouraged by the interruption, regardless of the intruder's intentions, we have to resume our praying as soon as we can. Only death can stop us, but at that time, we are already in God's arms.

SCHOOL FOR PRAYER. Father Anthony Bloom in his booklet "School for Prayer" named five things that we have to keep in mind when we talk about prayer: the absence of God, the knock at the door, the inward work, the discipline at the time of prayer, and the manner of addressing God (Bloom, 1970).

For us regular people, the moments when God reaches us or we reach Him, when we intuit the depth of things or of God's Kingdom inside us, are actually as rare as the opening of the eyes of a man born blind. This happens because usually we leave God aside when we pray. The prayer assumes a <u>full</u> communication. We have to keep in our mind and heart the total certitude of the presence of the person with whom we communicate. Communication is *union*. It is true that we pray with love, passion, and fervor for the help we need or for the help needed by our loved ones. However, we do not realize that we actually care more for the person we are praying for than for God. We may correctly say, as Father Anthony Bloom warned the readers of his book, that in fact we live and pray in the absence of God. This is the cause of the despair felt by the Existentialists - they did not see the forest because of the trees; they did not see God but only the many men around them. The instant Saint Peter realized the glory of the Son of God in the person of Jesus Christ, after the miraculous catch of fish, he knelt and said with awe, *"Depart from me, for I am a sinful man, O Lord"* (*Luke 5:8*). How many times do we realize in depth our sinful nothingness in front of the Lord, Our Savior?

We have to learn to pray with the conviction that, in the very moment of prayer, we are in God's Kingdom. However, in order to reach this condition, we need to be very humble and to realize our frail and sinful nature like the publican who did not dare to walk into the temple and was praying full of repentance at the entrance (*Luke 18:13*). Otherwise, we will see only us and will not let the Lord manifest Himself, not noticing His miraculous intervention in all the circumstances of our life.

As a conclusion to the observation about the absence of God, the Metropolitan Anthony Bloom narrated the spiritual evolution of a faithful woman who fell sick with a terrible and incurable disease. At the beginning, she said that she liked to confront the unbelievers in reference to the presence of God. She was convinced that only stupid people dared to judge the things they do not fully understand. Later, when the disease started to hurt, she wrote that, while her body became weaker and weaker, her spirit gained power, and she perceived with infinite joy a divine presence in her life. When the disease had progressed, she discovered with sadness that the weakness prevented her soul from rising toward the Lord and her thirst for God faded, so she deepened her humility. Then she decided to abandon herself and to receive gratefully anything from neighbors and from God. Extremely ill, left alone by everyone, including her husband, who had tired of taking care of the dying woman, she wrote to Father Anthony that she was completely finished. She could not move any more toward the Lord but *the Lord descended to her*. This is a memorable example of the process of becoming fully conscious of the presence of God and of living in God's Kingdom even here on this earth.

After the first stage consisting in a real understanding of the "absence" of God in our soul, an absence actually never caused by God but by us, we realize that, despite our effort to ascend toward the Lord, we are in fact still outside of God's Kingdom. We should then knock at the door asking for permission to enter. We will be able to go in, provided we take off our shoes and leave them together with all other worldly assets at the door.

We think that our lifetime achievements and riches are the direct results of our own efforts and talents, and we do not realize that they are actually *generous* gifts from the Lord, as a reward for our hard work Do we not remember the outstanding generosity of Our Lord Jesus Christ at the wedding in Cana of Galilee? He gave wine to the participants in an amount that exceeded their needs by far (*John 2:6-7*). After acknowledging the divine generosity and our poor condition, we join in consensus with the first Beatitude: "*Blessed are the poor in spirit, for theirs is the kingdom of heaven*" (*Mathew 5:3*). We do not possess anything. Nothing is under our control. The Lord decides what happens to us and to our belongings.

Everything that we have comes from the Lord's mercy, from His love.

How do we knock at the door of the Kingdom? With the words of prayer, with the words that we think are suitable for a proper offer to God, words that touch our heart and that we fill with the whole power of our mind. They are the words through which we can abandon ourselves in the arms of the Lord and obey His will. This way, despite the fact we do not pray with images, as mentioned above, the certitude of God's presence next to us and in us will gradually grow in our being and it will become material-like.

"Going inward" is, according to Father Anthony Bloom, the third element we have to learn in order to confer efficacy on our prayer. He wrote, "Generally it is the greed, the fear and the curiosity which made us live outwardly." We are too superficial and live too much in the outside world. A mere example in this regard is the fact that, if we remain alone, we cannot find our peace without turning on the radio or the TV. We actually have become strangers to our own person. We get bored to death in our lone presence. There is a great void in us. We forget to feed our thoughts and feelings. We forget to build our own life. We end in being totally dependable on others. We live by reflecting the world around us like a mirror. We do not produce. We just react to the things that surround us. If we create something, it is just an echo of what others have created. We can say, in terms of horse and wagon, that we do not pull the wagon (i.e. an action caused by us) but we run from the wagon of fear not to be run over (i.e. a reaction to others' action).

If we look deep inward, we see naught. Therefore, when we pray and try to concentrate on searching for God inside our being, we fall into despair like the monks who, after trying unsuccessfully hour after hour to progress in their prayers, run out of their cells crying out for help. It is from this interior vacuum that we cry out, with the whole power of our mind and heart, asking God's mercy to fill our void and to give a sense to our being and life. We will persevere in our prayer's labor, fearing that if we are going to abandon it, we will leave the depths and come up again to the surface of our being, and we will live again a reflected life and not a real one. The blind man Bartimaeus shouted unceasingly in the street, disturbing the crowds and Our Lord's disciples (*Mark 10:47-48*), because he was in terrible despair caused by his frightening inner void.

It is out of despondency that the hermits pray to God - they fear they cannot escape from the unstoppable storm of temptations. After the Lord gives them peace by rescuing them from the fire of passions, they pray with even more ardor, fearing to fall again prey to that fire. This way their prayer gains continuity – a continuity sustained by an ardent need. Often the hermits are under the pressure of what the Holy Fathers called a "spiritual greed" – the desire to acquire as much as possible from God's matters, to force His hand and will. We ordinary people living in the common world are unable to struggle toward a real continuity of prayer.

For us, realizing the uninterrupted presence of God in our life might suffice. We might be defeated if we try to pray without ceasing, but as Father Anthony Bloom advised, we have to choose intelligently the appropriate moments for intense prayer. We should live every day as a gift from God – a gift carefully chosen by Him. We should welcome every event and person that the day brings to us, regardless of its nature – sweet or bitter, pleasant or unpleasant, as given from the love and wisdom of the Lord. Such a manner of living can confer on us the much-desired continuity between the few moments of prayer.

Managing the time for prayer represents another aspect discussed by Father Anthony Bloom. We are the slaves of time and very often, in this modern period, our life is a continuous rush, except a few moments of rest when we are too tired and are unable to do something more constructive. However, as Father Anthony wrote, "There is absolutely no need to run after time to catch it. It does not run away from us, it runs towards us." We move so fast from past to future that present becomes tension and hurry, and actually ceases to exist.

HOW OFTEN SHOULD WE PRAY? As often as we can. Saint Paul wrote to the Thessalonians, *"Rejoice always, pray without ceasing"* (*1 Thessalonians 5:16-17*). In order to make His disciples *"pray and not lose heart,"* Our Lord told the parable about a tenacious widow (*Luke 18:1*). Indeed, if the prayer becomes as intimate and necessary as breathing, one can feel abundant blessings by doing it. But how can a man pray ceaselessly? Father Thomas Hopko reminded us of the words of a monk who had a strategy: he was praying when he was awake and the beneficiaries of his good deeds were praying when he was sleeping. However, as the anonymous commentator of Saint Paisius' teachings about the Jesus Prayer wrote in "Sbornik" Sbornik, 1936), "the heart of the advanced bearers of this profound prayer is praying even when the mind is resting, as written in the Holy Scripture, '*I sleep, but my heart keeps watch*'" (*Song of Songs 5:2*).

As Moses, inspired by the Holy Ghost, wrote the book of Genesis, the day started at sunset: "And there was evening and morning, one day" (*Genesis 1:5*). Therefore, according to the rule of prayers of the monastic life, the cycle begins in the evening with the Vespers (at sunset). They are followed by Compline (at bedtime), Midnight, Matins or Orthos (at dawn), First Hour (6 a.m.), Third Hour (9 a.m.), Sixth Hour (at noon, when Our Lord was crucified) and Ninth Hour (3 p.m., when Our Lord died on cross). Saint Ephraim the Syrian advises: prayer should go before all the other activities; if the first gesture when you wake up in the morning is praying, sin will find the soul's door closed. The prayer books for laity have morning and evening prayers, prayers before meals, prayers before work, before travel etc.

DO WE HAVE ENOUGH TIME TO PRAY? Yes, more than we think. Many moments of relaxation or entertainment can become moments of prayer. The worry of the day can open a dialogue with God. The fatigue of the day, that might hinder us in our concentration and in putting passion into our prayer, could become the whisper that elevates our thoughts toward God. Father Cleopa Ilie used to say, "When you think of God, He thinks of you."

Reading an episode of the Scripture and thinking of Christ can very well be a prayer. "There is no human cry that God does not hear," Pope Benedict XVI said. Saint Paul's advice, *"be steadfastly in prayer"* (*Romans 12:12*) and do not stop praying (*1 Thessalonians 5:16-17*) incited the Russian Pilgrim to figure out how that could be achieved. He searched with fervor, wandering on foot enormous distances from skete to skete and from monastery to monastery, until eventually he found the response: living with the Jesus Prayer.

During the day, the fervor of our soul can increase in intensity and in number the words of the prayer that we say in the morning. The monks and hermits teach us also that the consciousness of the permanent presence of God in our proximity, together with love and awe, is like a prayer at the time of the day when we cannot actually pray. In this way we accomplish in our weakness what Saint Paul suggested when he referred to unceasing prayer.

WE NEED TO ESCAPE FROM THE BURDEN OF TIME. I might say, in the terms of Vladimir Lossky's writings, we should try to reach the "continuous present" in which the Lord Himself lives. We have to stand firmly with both legs in the present, in that "now" mentioned by Saint Herman from Alaska while talking to the sailors. He said, "For our good, for our happiness, at least let us make a promise to ourselves, that from this day, from this hour, from this minute we shall strive to love God above all, and fulfill His holy will!" (see *A Treasury of Saint Herman's Spirituality*, 1989).

I was impressed when I immigrated in America to see a sign on an executive's desk saying, "Do it now!" Let us transfer these words into our spiritual life and let us not procrastinate anymore. If our present time is empowered with a spiritual significance, it may become tangent to God's eternity. Father Anthony Bloom wrote, "It is essential to be alert and alive, and at the same time still and relaxed, and this is contemplative preparation for contemplative silence." (Bloom, 1970) We have to receive everything that comes to us with an attentive spirit, without dreaming and somnolence. The French writer Georges Bernanos, quoted by Father Bloom, noted, "All of a sudden I perceived that the silence was a presence. At the heart of the silence there was Him who is all stillness, all peace, all poise." We have to quiet the lips and the body and let the spirit grasp the sweet peace that reigns in the shadow of the Lord.

Spontaneous prayer is powerful only in two cases: (a) when we are full of joy and gratitude and we offer praises and thanks to God; (b) when we are in trouble and cry in despair for an ultimate help from Him. Unfortunately, this sincere and powerful prayer, as a spontaneous shout of the soul, cannot be produced at will, as we turn on a faucet. Many people think that if they do not feel this intensity, the prayer is false and it makes no sense to pray anymore. Father Anthony Bloom advised us to look for the prayers that have roots in a strong faith, prayers such as the Psalms or the liturgical prayers. It is not enough to learn them by heart. We have to try to live them, exactly as we should do with the words and meanings that flow toward us when we read the Bible and other holy writings.

JESUS PRAYER. THE POWER OF NAME. The solution of the unceasing prayer is "Jesus Prayer", which by its short formula can be easily repeated anytime, everywhere. For the hard spiritual workers it becomes as often and as intrinsic to the spirit and the body as breathing. For them it is the blessed Prayer of the Mind or Prayer of the Heart and it can carry the praying soul to the heights of supreme Divine blessings.

The narrator of the Russian spiritual classic "The Way of a Pilgrim" (a booklet that might have been circulated from the Optina Monastery which had been visited in the nineteenth century by Gogol, Kireevsky, Dostoyevsky, Soloviev, and Tolstoy) suggested it. The Jesus Prayer ("Lord Jesus Christ, Son of God, have mercy on me, a sinner") can be easily said many times; it does not need a special concentration of the mind or a strong memory and can function in the background without interfering with the main activity of the person who prays. The Russian Pilgrim was able to say it, without any effort, twelve thousand times a day, i.e. twelve times a minute. The Philokalia contained many writings of the Holy Fathers regarding the practice of the Jesus Prayer.

The outstanding power of the Jesus Prayer consists in the important weight of the name. The name Jesus comes from the Greek *Iēsous* and means "Savior" that is the equivalent to the Hebrew word *Yehoshua*, meaning "Yahweh is salvation." The name Christ comes from the Greek *Christos* that is a translation of the Hebrew word Messiah (*Meshiach*), meaning the "anointed one," "the chosen by God." This latter term was reserved for prophets, priests and kings such as King David and the High Priest Aaron. It refers to the divine origin and mission of Jesus as the Highest Priest and it is connected to the creation of the Church. When Our Lord began His ministry, He went into the synagogue, took the book of Isaiah and opened it at the words regarding Him: *"The Spirit of the Lord is upon Me, because He has anointed Me to preach the gospel to the poor"* (*Luke 4:18*). Our Lord asked His disciples, *"Who do people say that I am?"* He knew that the people wondered. So He asked, *"Is He John the Baptist, Elijah, Jeremiah or another prophet?"* Simon Peter replied to the Lord's question, *"You are the Christ, the Son of the living God"* (*Matthew 16:16*).

Bishop Kallistos Ware drew our attention to several passages of the New Testament showing how the Power of the Name works (Ware, 1986). Jesus said to His disciples, *"Most assuredly, I say to you, whatever you ask the Father in My name He will give you"* (*John 16:23*); *"Go therefore and make disciples of all the nations, baptizing them in the name of the Father and of the Son and of the Holy Spirit"* (*Matthew 28:19*). Christ taught us the Lord's Prayer in which we say to God the Father, *"Hallowed be Your name"* (*Matthew 6:9*). The power of Our Lord's name is revealed by the words of Saint Peter when the rulers and elders asked him by what power or name he preached. He said, *"by the name of Jesus Christ of Nazareth, Whom you crucified."* (*Acts 4:7-10*). It was also revealed by the words of Saint Paul: *"at the name of Jesus every knee should bow"* (*Philippians 2:10*).

Concerning the many meanings included in Our Lord's name, let us also remember the verses of the Akathist hymn: "Jesus, Word uncontainable; Jesus, Intelligence unfathomed; Jesus, Power incomprehensible; Jesus, Wisdom immeasurable;

Jesus, Divinity undepictable; Jesus, Dominion unbounded; Jesus, Kingdom invincible; Jesus, Sovereignty unending; Jesus, Strength sublime; Jesus, Authority everlasting."

As Lev Gillet (Un moine de l'Eglise d'Orient, 1963) remarked in his classic book, by practicing the Jesus Prayer, the name of Our Lord gradually enters and spreads deep in our being, and new meanings of His name are continuously revealed to our mind and spirit. At first, this prayer instills in us the certitude of His presence and the desire to adore Him. Later, the invocation of the name opens an initial understanding of the mystery of salvation. Jesus is the "substance of all good things." He is the help in need. Jesus' name "gives peace to the tempted people." His name calls to repentance and induces the thirst of reconciliation with God after the impurities caused by sin. His name carries the meaning of forgiveness. Jesus' name signifies the incarnation, the meeting between man and God in one body. He is at the same time the complete transfiguration of nature. He reassembles in a single unit, as it was in Paradise, all the three realms: the mineral realm (*"the stones would immediately cry out"* – *Luke 19:40*), the animal realm (He *"was with the wild beasts and the angels ministered to Him"* – *Mark 1:13*) and the human realm. Regarding the human realm His followers first discovered His presence after the Resurrection as a mysterious gardener in the proximity of the tomb (*John 19:14-17*), then as a traveler on the road to Emmaus (*Luke 24:15*) and also as a stranger at the Sea of Tiberias (*John 21:1*). The secret presence of Our Lord Jesus Christ is everywhere around us - in the man or woman we meet on the streets, in the people in the factory or in the office, as the Savior was with the fisherman (*Luke 5:8-10*), with the thief (*Luke 23:40-43*), with the prostitute (*Luke 7:37* and *John 8:10-11*), and with the beggar (*Mark 10:46-52*).

JESUS PRAYER. POWER OF INVOCATION. The invocation of the Holy Name has also an ecclesiastic side. It is our means of connecting with Our Lord (Jesus, the Savior) through His spiritual body that is the Church. Christ is the High Priest, *"according to the order of Melchizedek"* (*Hebrews 5:6*). Through His name and the church, we meet God's Saints and the people fallen asleep in God. Calling Jesus' holy name, "our soul becomes the Upper Room, where Our Lord wants to eat the Passover with His disciples and where the Last Supper can take place" (Un moine de l'Eglise d'Orient, 1963). A spiritual communion is accomplished in that moment and, despite the fact that it does not replace the actual Communion with the Body and Blood of the Savior, it causes a spiritual union. This union responds to our fervent aspiration for the definitive coming of Christ, because the sacrifice of the Eucharist keeps Our Lord with us until He finally comes in glory. It proclaims *"the Lord's death till He comes"* (*1 Corinthians 11:26*).

Invocation of Jesus Christ's holy name also brings the Holy Spirit within us (*John 20:22*) and even God the Father: *"No one comes to the Father except through Me"* (*John 14:6-7*). At the same time, it brings to mind the relationship of Son-Father and Son-Holy Spirit. As Lev Gillet, who signed his book about Jesus Prayer as "a monk of the Eastern Church," wrote, "to pronounce Jesus' name means to pronounce the Word that was at the beginning (*John 1:1*), the Word that the Father speaks eternally." Lev Gillet, concluded that this way, by accumulating all the name's complex meanings in our soul, we can become gradually like Saul, open to the Lord's call, Who made him the Saint Apostle Paul. God said about Saul, *"he is a chosen vessel of Mine to bear My name before Gentiles, kings, and the children of Israel"* (*Acts 9:15*). During the Divine Liturgy we hear twice the words, "Blessed is he that comes in the name of the Lord!"

JESUS PRAYER. SYMBOLS. The Romanian poet and philosopher Nichifor Crainic might be wrong in his belief that this prayer originally came from the Theotokos. But if it is possibly wrong from a historic point of view, he also might be right from a mystical standpoint because, as the well-known author Father Lev Gillet wrote, the Holy Virgin was hearing and repeating continuously inside of her heart the Archangel's words. These words were, *"And behold, you will conceive in your womb and bring forth a Son, and shall call His name Jesus"* (*Luke 1:31*). However, Saint Paisius of Neamţ quoted the words of Saint Gregory Palamas, who wrote that the Holy Virgin Mary used a mental prayer (the Prayer of Mind and Heart) at an earlier age when she was dwelling in the temple, in the Holy of Holies, and was conversing with God, praying for the healing of the suffering human race. Let us also think of the Gospel episode with the blind man of Jericho (*Luke 18:35-43*). He cried out saying, *"Jesus, Son of David, have mercy on me!"* This sounded very close to the words of the Jesus Prayer. Father Kallistos reminded us also of the words of the good thief on the cross, *"Lord, remember me when You come into Your Kingdom"* (*Luke 23:42*).

JESUS PRAYER. BENEFITS. The Jesus Prayer is the prayer that can stay with us permanently, at every event, with every feeling, with every thought. Saint John Climacus noted that one can say it when one eats, drinks, walks, rests, travels, in *any* circumstances. The monks are persistent in practicing it. They have developed certain methods. Father George Calciu admitted that he was not able to pray the Jesus Prayer continuously but the prayer helped him very often. We, the laymen, have to keep the rule of the morning and evening prayers as they are in the "Book of Orthodox Prayers" but, in order to feel the presence of God every day of our life, it is good to say the Jesus Prayer formula anytime we remember. It teaches our soul to pay attention to many things that otherwise might remain unnoticed. Nothing is accidental or random in our life, everything occurs by God's will or allowance. It helps us to say the Jesus Prayer in many circumstances: when we are afraid, when someone bothers us, when we see someone departing this life, when we worry about something, when a good event occurs. We can say it when we leave the children's bedroom seeing them already sleeping, when someone pushes us in a crowded bus or when we wait in line and we would like to swear, when we are tempted, when we are happy, when we travel, when we are in danger, when we are sick. As Metropolitan Anthony Bloom wrote, the advantage of the Jesus Prayer consists in the fact that it is not a discursive prayer and it does not move from one thought to another, but remains in the same unmodified formula, focusing on the same Being: the Being of God.

The Jesus Prayer can increase the receptivity of our soul while reading the Gospel, because the Gospel is not only a message of wisdom but also a message of love – a love for Christ. The Jesus Prayer reveals to the person who uses it the fragility of his/her being, and how worthless many desires, moods and conceits are from an existential standpoint.

By this prayer, we remain connected to the Lord during all the time of our existence. We can address Him as it is said in the verses of the Akathist Hymn: "Jesus, Protector of mine infancy; Jesus, Guide of my youth; Jesus, Boast of mine old age; Jesus, my Hope at death; Jesus, my Life after death; Jesus, my Comfort at Your Judgment." The complete formula "Lord Jesus Christ, Son of God, have mercy on me, a sinner" can take various shorter forms. One of them brings a nuance that includes our neighbors as well: "Lord Jesus Christ have mercy on us." Father Arseny Boca, who suffered much persecution and long detention from the Romanian communist authorities for his faith, and received many gifts from the Holy Spirit, prayed with the following words: "Lord Jesus Christ, I lie every minute; please make the prayer of Your Holy Name to work in my mind faster than the lightning in the sky, in order to avoid any darkening shadow of my evil thoughts." Father Ambrose of Optina was asked if one should place the emphasis on the word "Jesus." He replied that it is better to emphasize the word "sinner."

THE SPIRITUAL LADDER OF PRAYING. The Bishop Theophanes described the stages of the prayer. His words have been included in the "Sbornik" (Sbornik, 1936). The first stage is the *prayer of the body*. It is done in a standing position, loudly and with many prostrations. It brings patience, sweat, fatigue. Man needs this hard labor in order to get closer to God. The second stage is the *prayer of the thoughts*, when the mind utters the words of the prayer in a profound peace, without any distraction. We feel the words written in the prayer book as if they were our own and we are thrilled by the shadow of great silence behind each uttered word.

The third stage, according to Bishop Theophanes, is the *prayer of the feelings*. The heart warms up. The person who reaches this stage prays without words. The words become useless "because the Lord is the God of the heart." The desired effect of the prayer, the enriching of the soul, actually starts only now. The person who is praying goes from one feeling to the other and advances toward the divine presence. The *spiritual prayer* that is the fourth stage starts when the depth and fire of feelings achieve unceasing prayer. This prayer is a gift of the Holy Spirit that prays in the human soul. Father

Theophanes mentions a possible fifth stage that the holiest humans might reach. It is the last stage that the human spirit is able to experience. It is the *prayer beyond the limits of what the mind can comprehend*, as Saint Isaac the Syrian calls it. Therefore, this kind of prayer cannot be described in words.

Writing about the stages of prayer, Vladimir Lossky quoted Saint Isaac the Syrian (Lossky, 1997). The prayer starts with requests, like a search for God and actually marks a gradual rise toward Him. Then the Christian ceases to ask for something, deciding to yield to the Divine Will that he learns to identify and understand. This is the moment when the prayer becomes a *pure prayer*. Later, a synergy takes place between man's will and God's will. The mind's movement slows down, the discursive prayer stops but the mental prayer (the contemplation) starts. This prayer is "said" in the complete silence of the mind, in communion with the energies of the Holy Spirit. It is a state that some people call ecstasy, when the mind is ravished and a profound silence becomes dominant. Man does not belong to himself anymore. He loses his own initiative and pride and even the consciousness of his own freedom. He lets himself be led by the Holy Spirit. Some people have told me that they reached this intense moment in the loneliness of the communist prison. However, according to Saint Simeon the New Theologian, quoted by Lossky, the ecstasy and ravishment are for the beginners, for the uninitiated. The spiritually advanced people acquire a life in the uncreated, i.e., the dimension that is "not of this world." I think that this is the condition when an uncreated light appears on the face of the chosen ones. This is a light seen only by the witnesses chosen by God (see the story told by Father Calciu in the following chapter).

3. Discovering the Sacred Time.
The Divine Being and the Human Nature.

A Christian life helps us to understand things that we never could explain before and brings wonderful revelations to our mind. *"Behold, You love truth; You showed me the unknown and secret things of Your wisdom"* (*Psalm 50/51:8*). It leads us to comprehend the beauty of the Creator and the Creation, which will flood our heart with its supreme, ineffable harmony, joy, and happiness. *"And I know such a man – whether in the body or out of the body I do not know, God knows – how he was caught up into Paradise and heard inexpressible words, which it is not lawful for a man to utter"* (*2 Corinthians 12:3*). Father Cleopa and other fathers who reached higher spiritual levels and were "caught up" closer to the Kingdom of God for a few minutes or hours through the depth of the Prayer of Heart, said that the state they were in was so full of sweet light and happiness that they wanted never to come back to the earthly reality.

A Christian life allows us to learn to know God, to meditate in depth about Him, <u>to discover the sacred time of our own life</u> and to elevate our soul much closer to the blessed touch of Divinity.

3.1. The Holy Trinity.

CREATION OF THE WORLD. There are numerous aspects regarding Genesis that a scientific debate could touch upon, including the possible correlations between the succession of the days of creation on one hand and the cosmic events and geological eras on the other hand. However, despite all the astronomical discoveries and the evolution of the scientific concepts of the universe, "the theology does not need to change anything in the story of Genesis or to care about the salvation of the potentiality that beings live on Mars," as Vladimir Lossky wrote very correctly in his book about the Mystical Theology of the Eastern Church (Lossky, 1997).

If we insist in explaining Genesis in the terminology of the science of today we always risk finding links that are missing or do not match, and this might hinder us from paying attention to the essential things. Another "Scopes Monkey Trial" is actually a waste of time and a futile effort. It is *by faith* that we accept Genesis as we read it in the Holy Scripture. *"By faith we understand that the worlds were framed by the word of God, so that the things which are seen were not made of things which are visible"* (*Hebrews 11:3*). The Bible says this in a very beautiful and richly nuanced manner: *"God by wisdom founded the earth and prepared the heavens with discernment. With perception the depths were broken up and the clouds flowed with dew"* (*Proverbs 3:21-22*).

We have to read the Book of Genesis, written by Moses at the inspiration of the Archangel Gabriel, as a theological text. Vladimir Lossky was right when he affirmed that we have to see in the book of Genesis the creation of our earthly world and not the creation of the universe, because "the church reveals the mystery of our salvation and not the mysteries of the universe that do not need a salvation effort."

The Russian theologian noted that the human spirit, like Faustus' restless spirit, is looking with avidity toward new scientific discoveries and meanings of the cosmos. However, man can understand only the disintegration aspect of the cosmos that corresponds to our nature after the fall from

Paradise. These words of Lossky show an extraordinarily deep insight. Let us consider that the second law of thermodynamics refers actually to an "aging" (entropy non-conservation) of the universe. It is no wonder then that Paul Florensky suggested a return to a geocentrical cosmology, leaving aside our scientific knowledge about the solar system. Such a cosmology reflects better the profound significance of the spiritual relationship between man and Divinity. Paul Florensky, who lived in the first half of the twentieth century, was not an ordinary man: he was a brilliant Russian scholar with a Renaissance type of education (great theologian, mathematician, and physicist), who died as a martyr in a labor camp, and was canonized as an Orthodox saint.

Vladimir Lossky pointed out an interesting idea from the writings of Saint Basil the Great and Saint Gregory of Nyssa: the process of Creation that was described in the Book of Genesis, as a story unfolded in six days, actually occurred in a simultaneous manner on the very first day. This thought makes sense, if we remember the words of Saint Apostle Peter: *"with the Lord one day is as a thousand years, and a thousand years as one day"* (*2 Peter 3:8*). And of the psalmist: *"For a thousand years in Your sight are like yesterday, which passed and like a watch in the night"* (*Psalm 89/90:4*). God has His own measures that are different from ours. The six-day description might be like watching something in slow motion for a better understanding of the process. Is this not the way the creation of woman was described in the Holy Scripture? The details written in *Genesis 2:18, 21-24* do not contradict what is written in *Genesis 1:27* ("*So God made man; in the image of God He made him; male and female He made them*") but are details of the latter. The Lord did not create gradually but at once, for good and forever. Lossky noted that in God nothing stops and nothing ends while in the created world His word comes and does not pass. The Lord *"established the world, which shall not be moved"* (*Psalm 92/93:1*).

By reading Lossky's writing, we might think of the idea of a dichotomic structure of nature. There is an uncreated nature and a created one. The created nature is divided into an intelligible nature (the material world) and a sensitive one (the spiritual world). The sensitive nature consists of heavens and earth. The earth consists of our earthly life and the eternal life in Paradise or Inferno which are not *locations* but *states of being*. However, affirming that might be a little overwhelming for our mind and spirit. Where do the souls go after the death of the body? Do they go up or go down? It is hard to understand because we cannot think in other terms than those of time and space.

The human being is situated between the intelligible, material world and the unintelligible, sensitive world, and has a structure more complex than the angelic spirits because the human reunites both worlds in one single specific unit. Vladimir Lossky quoted Saint Maximus the Confessor: "All that was created by God in various natures (essences) is gathered together within the human being as in a melting pot in order to reach an outstanding perfection." Despite the fact that we are talking here about the spiritual part of man I think it is not wrong if we add the aspect of the biological nature of man that should be regarded as a synthesis and a peak of perfection of the whole living world. The geneticists found great similarities in the human DNA structure to that of other creatures. However these similarities do not support the naïve Darwin-like idea of an imaginary evolution from simple to complex, from worms, through fish and birds, to mammals and man.

Vladimir Lossky concluded in the following terms: the world was created from nothing by God's will – this is the *origin*. The world was created to participate in the plenitude of the divine life – this is its *vocation*. The world was also created as a call to freely accomplish the union with God – this is the *mystery*.

HOLY TRINITY AND GENESIS OF THE WORLD. As soon as we open the Holy Scripture we find a mention of the Holy Trinity. *"God* [the Father] *made heaven and earth"* (*Genesis 1:1*). The Son of God is the creating Word of God (*John 1:1-3*); this is how we read the verse *"Then God said, 'Let there be light'"* (*Genesis 1:3*). The Holy Spirit was also present; *"The Spirit of God was hovering over the face of the water"* (*Genesis 1:2*). Saint Basil said that according to the account of the Creation, the Father is the *first* cause, the Son is the *building* cause, and the Holy Spirit is the *accomplishing* cause.

By reading what Saint John the Apostle has written, we learn that the Son of God is the Word: *"In the beginning was the Word, and the Word was with God, and the Word was God"* (*John 1:1*). Through Him, God the Father has created the world. He was with God from the very beginning. *"All things were made through Him, and without Him nothing was made that was made"* (*John 1:2-3*). We also read in Saint Paul's epistle to Colossians: *"For by Him all things were created that are in heaven and that are on earth, visible and invisible"* (*Colossians 1:16*).

The frescos at the Romanian Monastery of Sucevița show Our Lord Jesus creating the world and blessing the realm of plants and animals.As Father Seraphim Rose from the Monastery of Platina in California commented, the traditional Orthodox iconography does not represent the creation as Michelangelo depicted on the ceiling of the Sistine chapel: God the Father, millennia old, followed or not by angels, dividing light from darkness, creating the sun and planets, dividing the waters from earth. The Orthodox tradition depicts the creation as something accomplished through Christ, the Word, within the perfect harmony proper to the Holy Trinity. "The Father has spoken, the Son has created and the Holy Ghost has participated," Saint Ephraim the Syrian wrote.

THE NATURE OF HOLY TRINITY. As we read in Lossky's book, while the very essence of the created beings was caused by a *change* (the transition from non-being to being) and consists of a persistent change and spiritual evolution, the Holy Trinity reveals an absolute *stability*. The creature, changeable by nature, is able to reach an eternal stability by grace in order to enjoy an infinite life in the light of the Holy Trinity by an apophatic contemplation of the mystery of the Trinity and not by a rational approach. As Lossky further wrote, the ultimate term of the Christian spirituality is, according to the tradition of the Eastern Church, the Heavenly Kingdom (Lossky, 1997). However, the happiness of being in that Kingdom "is not seeing the essence that is the Being, but first of all the participation in the divine life of the Holy Trinity," so much as this is given to us by grace, by His uncreated energies.

According to Saint Gregory of Nazianz, quoted by Lossky, the Father is *the source* of the Divinity, the Son is *begotten* from the Father, and the Holy Spirit *proceeds* from the Father. When we talk about the three Persons of the Holy Trinity we have to keep in mind Saint Thomas Aquinas' words: "Persona est relatio" (the term "person" implies relationship). Saint John the Damascene underlined three hypostases (existences) that co-exist within the Holy Trinity. These three hypostases belong to a single nature and they have only one will, only one power, only one work to accomplish. The principle of unity within the Holy Trinity is the Father's Person, according to Saint Gregory of Nazianz (quoted by Lossky), because the three Sacred Beings are gathered into a single Lordship and Divinity. If there is no Father, there is no Son and no Holy Spirit. The Holy Spirit is not the result of the reciprocal love between Father and Son because the Father is the only hypostatic source of the Holy Spirit. Therefore, we Orthodox believers, do not agree with the principle "Filioque" (which says that the Holy Spirit proceeds not only from the Father but also from the Son). This latter principle, adopted by the Roman Catholic Church, impairs the monarchy of the Father. Neither the Son nor the Holy Spirit could exist without God the Father.

Saint Maximus commented that the Father identifies the hypostases of the Holy Trinity "by an eternal movement of love." The Word and the Spirit, i.e. the Son and the Holy Ghost, are, according to Saint Gregory of Nazianz, "like two rays of the same sun or, better to say, like 'two new suns' who are not separated during their work, being two Persons proceeding from the same Father" (see Lossky, 1997).

WHY A TRINITY? Why three – a triad? By reading Vladimir Lossky's important book of mystical theology, we learn that a *monad* is incompatible with the multitude of God's faces. The *dyad* is used by philosophers in all the antinomian pairs applied to the nature of this world, but it cannot characterize the Divinity that is above everything, above matter and form. The *triad* is the correct formula for, as a Trinity, the Godhead does not remain limited within Its boundaries and neither does It spread infinitely. The triad as a unit would be a Judaic monotheistic concept while as three separated persons would be a Greek polytheistic concept. Lossky wrote the following about the mystery of the number three, which is applicable to the Deity: the Divinity is neither one nor a multiple. The real perfection is superior to the multiplicity of the Gnostic dyads generated by a duality, because *two* is the number that splits, while *three* is the number that goes beyond the separation. We venerate the Holy Trinity as a Divine Family and as a divine unit, not as three gods. In fact, it is very difficult for man to fully understand the mystery of the Holy Trinity. Lossky wrote that the "dogma of the Trinity is a cross for human thought. An apophatic ascent is like walking up Golgotha (Lossky, 1997). This is why no philosophical speculation is able to reach the height of the mystery of the Holy Trinity."

Saint Gregory of Nazianz, who is often named "the minstrel of the Holy Trinity," wrote that, historically for humankind, the knowledge of the Divine Trinity was achieved gradually. The Old Testament talked clearly about God the Father but in an obscure manner about God the Son. The New Testament revealed the Son but barely mentioned the Holy Ghost. Today the Holy Ghost abides among us and is clearly manifest, speaking to us through the Saints. Man has therefore learned about each Person of the Holy Trinity one by one, throughout history. There is an objective order in the theology that we have to be aware of, and this order prevents us from learning everything at the same time and always leaves something obscure.

In Romania, along the old dirt roads between villages, there are "troitsas" where the travelers stop, think of God, and say a short prayer. These are either bare crosses of wood or stone exposed to the outside conditions, or crosses with a hanging vigil lamp protected by a little shelter. The Slavic word "troitsa" means Trinity.

The beginning prayer for all our prayers contains the concept of the Holy Trinity. This is expressed by the Trisagion: "Holy God, Holy Mighty, Holy Immortal, have mercy on us." Some people use the Trisagion as a permanent prayer instead of the Jesus Prayer. This is followed by words addressing again the Divine Triad: "O Most Holy Trinity, have mercy on us. O Lord, cleanse our sins. O Master, pardon our iniquities. O Holy One, visit and heal our infirmities for Thy name's sake." We also say in our morning prayer, "My hope is the Father, my salvation is the Son, and my protection is the Holy Spirit." The elders emphasized, "We pray *to* the Father, *through* the Son, *in* the [Holy] Spirit" (Ware, 1996).

THE ATTRIBUTES OF GOD THE FATHER. "O Lord our God, Thy power is incomparable, Thy glory is incomprehensible, Thy mercy is immeasurable, Thy love for man is inexpressible," the priest chants before the First Antiphon during the Divine Liturgy. And later, at The Anaphora Prayer, he says the following: "For Thou art God ineffable, inconceivable, invisible, incomprehensible, ever-existing and eternally the same." God the Father, *"the King eternal, immortal, invisible,"* (1 Timothy 1:17) is *"the King of Kings and Lord of Lords, who alone has immortality, dwelling in unapproachable light, whom no man has seen or can see, to whom be honor and everlasting power" (1 Timothy 6:16).*

God, the Lord, *"who gives life to the dead and calls those things which do not exist as though they did" (Romans 4:17),* is God the Father, the Creator we know so little about. He creates by calling things from non-existence to existence. To him no boundaries exist between the uncreated and the created world. Nor are there boundaries between the invisible created world and the visible created world. "Thou it wast who brought us from nonexistence into being, and when we had fallen away didst raise us up again, and didst not cease to do all things until Thou hadst brought us up to heaven, and hadst endowed us with Thy Kingdom which is to come," the priest says during the Eucharistic Anaphora. The Orthodox Church talks about a direct connection between creation and salvation.

Saint Athanasius of Alexandria taught us that Son of God, the Word, is the means of this connection.

Am I wrong if, by using ordinary words, I am saying that the world was created in the biblical account in Genesis and that this world is now simply undergoing a process of maintenance, as for instance the management of the birth and death of people? This "maintenance" should not diminish the importance of the essence of creation which continues to unfold, for a new baby is conceived every second in this world, and in this way each of us was brought, one by one, from nonbeing into being.

The Lord is infinite, omnipresent, without any limits of time. He is also in *an absolute silence* and *His stability is perfect*, as the Russian theologian Vladimir Lossky wrote (Lossky, 1997). He is not cognoscible and He might be in a continuous repose. We can know Him from His active energies manifested in the world and we aspire to unify with them, by grace, as a result of our laborious process of deification.

The created beings are (1) limited and (2) in movement, because "where there is diversity and multiplicity there is movement" and because God "induces in the beings created by Him the love that moves them towards Him," according to Lossky's quotes from Saint Maximus the Confessor's writings. This is a spiritual definition for the *space* (we are limited) and the *time* (we are in movement), in which man and the other living creatures live.

We should try to avoid understanding *ad litteram*, the characterization of the Lord that we read in the Old Testament: jealous (*Exodus 34:14*), angry (*Exodus 32:9* and *Deuteronomy 32:21*), swearing (*Isaiah 45:23*), mocking (*Psalm 2:4*), sleepy and like a drunken man (*Psalm 77/78:65*), quick to take offense and vengeful. How can we describe God in such a human way, Him who is "ineffable, inconceivable, invisible, incomprehensible, ever-existing and eternally the same"? He is *"The Lord, the Most High who dwells on high forever, the Holy One among His saints, whose name is the Lord Most High"* (*Isaiah 57:15*). But man does not have adequate terms to express God's will and therefore he uses human attributes in order to render God's action easier to comprehend, because we all need to speak of our Lord and our Master.

Vladimir Lossky referred to Saint Basil who wrote that all the characteristics we attribute to God the Father "unveil His energies that descend to us but do not bring near His inaccessible Being." (Lossky, 1997) Dionysius Pseudo-Areopagite, quoted by Lossky, defined God in an apophatic manner, "of an unknowable nature, the Lord of Psalms, who made the darkness His shelter" (see *Psalm 17/18:12*). As Lossky wrote, Moses experienced on Mount Sinai his "helplessness of knowing God ... when he entered the darkness of His inaccessibility," while Saint Paul realized his powerlessness "when he heard the words that expressed the divine inexpressiveness" (see *2 Corinthians 12:4*).

WE CAN NEVER KNOW GOD IN HIS VERY ESSENCE that consists in inaccessible "unions" proper to the unity of the Holy Trinity. As Saint Gregory Palamas wrote, our only chance to know God is through His uncreated energies. These energies, according to Pseudo-Dionysus the Areopagite, reveal the many names given to God as "Wisdom, Life, Power, Justice, Love, and Being." These divine names or "characteristics" are as numerous as the energies. We use all these names to describe God by perceiving the exterior manifestation of the energies, while the real nature of God's Being, which is the source of the energies, remains incomprehensible to us like "a deep darkness covered by an abundant light," as Lossky wrote. We call these energies "uncreated energies" because they do not belong to the created world, to the created nature. They belong to the intimate nature of God, Who is the Creator.

The divine "energies" are the actual manifestation of the Lord in relation to the created universe and they represent His glory. The glory of the Divinity shows up through "revelation, appearance, reflection, and cover of the inner perfection" and its supreme expression is Light. As Lossky quoted Saint Maximus, the Lord, God the Father, did appear in glory to the faithful of the Old Testament. The human nature of Christ was penetrated by this glory with its eternal Light, which revealed Christ's divinity in front of the disciples, at the Transfiguration on Mount Tabor. The same glory is the grace of the Holy Spirit Who is uncreated but makes possible the deification work of the Saints of the Church. The Saints will shine like sun in the Heavenly Kingdom, as it is written in *Matthew 13:43*.

The Church teaches us to say the following words in our Sunday morning prayer: "Truly my heart is full of joy and content when I think that only You, Lord, are holy, wise, merciful, kind, righteous, strong, infinite, and, in a few words, you do not lack any gentleness, power and glory." However, according to Lossky, it is important that the Lord is actually not definable by any of His attributes described by man. When we say that God is Wisdom, Life, Truth, Justice, and Love, we name aspects of the energies that come from His Divine Being; they are indeed natural manifestations but they are actually only an exterior expression of the real essence of the Holy Trinity, which remains mysterious to humankind. Therefore, Serge Bulgakoff was wrong when he identified Wisdom (Sophia) with the very principle of Divinity, because wisdom is only an aspect of the energies, and not a feature or a component of the Creator Himself. The energies come from God the Father through the Son and are communicated by the Holy Spirit.

We might be tempted to think that the "uncreated energies" coming from God have built the world. We also might think that Genesis did not happen as a necessity but as a generous spread of God's nature. Lossky wrote that the creation, the Genesis, was not a spread or a spill of His fullness but *a free and conscientious action* of God's will. Indeed, we frequently find in the Book of Genesis the words *"Then God said"*; this expression means "action." The words *"Let Us make man in Our image, according to Our likeness"* (*Genesis 1:26*) indicate that the creation of man was preceded by a conversation among the three persons of the Holy Trinity, like an "eternal and unchanging Counsel of God." Therefore, we can conclude that an initial idea led to a decision materialized into the "free and considered act" of creating man, a creation that used the image of the Holy Trinity as a possible model.

HOW CAN WE KNOW GOD THE FATHER? The Lord, the Father, made Himself known to the people only by facts, because no one knows what He looks like. "*No one has seen God at any time. The only begotten Son, who is in the bosom of the Father, He has declared Him*" (*John 1:18*). However, God the Father *touched* the people's *eyes*, as in the case of Moses (*Exodus 1, 3, 4:1-17, 33:18-23, 34:29-35*) and of Elijah on Mount Horeb (*1 Kings 19:11-13, Isaiah 6:1-5*). He also *touched* the people's *ears*: as at the Epiphany (*Matthew 3:17*), at the Transfiguration (*Mark 9:7*), or when He answered Our Lord's request for glorification (*John 12:28*).

Nevertheless, no one *saw* the person of God. Moses and Elijah had to hide in the same crack in the cliff in the mountain, because, as a consequence of the original sin, man cannot look at God without substantial damage *("You cannot see My face and live" – Exodus 33:20).* Neither can a regular man hear Him. Only Saint John the Forerunner and Jesus' three preferred disciples heard God's voice - at the Baptism and on Mount Tabor respectively. God's voice sounded like meaningless thunder to the crowds in Jerusalem *(John 12:28-29).* God the Father sent His Son to the world *(John 3:16-17)* and, this way, He made it possible for the people to know Him through Our Lord Jesus Christ. *"He who has seen Me has seen the Father,"* Lord Jesus said to Philip *(John 14:9).* Unfortunately, only a few could realize that truth because not many believed in Jesus Christ. That is why Jesus said, making reference to the senses of the people gathered around: *"He who has _ears_ to hear, let him hear!"* *(Matthew 11:15* and *13:9).*

Because of all the things mentioned above, God the Father cannot be depicted in icons. However, sometimes man does not resist the desire of representing Him. It is the case when God's eye is painted within the frame of a triangle, corresponding probably to the Holy Trinity, on the inside-facing wall of the entrance tower of the monasteries (usually a bell tower), in order to be seen only by the monks – a non-sleeping eye that watches them unceasingly.

Some Orthodox painters represent Him as an old man with white hair and a long white beard, *The Ancient of Days,* probably in accordance with some verses in the *book of Daniel 7:9 and 13* and in *Revelations 1: 13-15.* However, according to schemamonk Constantine Cavarnos, "The Ancient of Days" is actually the icon of Christ, Son of God, through Whom we can see the Father. As the Orthodox commentators say about Holy Scripture's symbolic references, God the Father's eyes might signify knowledge, His voice - authority, His hand - power and His feet - stability. God the Father is the very *Existence,* the essence of existence. "This essence is like a boundless sea, containing all things yet not contained by anything" (see notes in the Orthodox Study Bible, 2008, p.69). Nor can His name be contained in human words. "*I AM the Existing One,*" He said to Moses (*Exodus 3:14*). This is the translation of YHWH, i.e. Jahve or Jehovah, a name that no pious Israeli has ever pronounced. But Our Lord Jesus Christ has a name accessible to men because the Son of God has shown Himself to man by taking a human body. The core prayer in the Orthodox Church, was built upon this very name.

With difficulty, we attain proper knowledge of God the Father by knowing God the Son through Jesus Christ and by being taught and ignited by the Holy Spirit that works in the world. Therefore it is so important that the Son of God was incarnated taking a human body and ascended back to heaven in that transfigured body. The faithful man's way to go to God the Father will be through His Son. Our Lord said to Thomas, "*I am the way, the truth, and the life. No one comes to the Father except through Me*" (*John 14: 6*).

Paul Evdokimov commented that God the Father is the *Silence* while God the Son is the Word (Evdokimov, 1973). We need silence in order to reach the state of God's revelation; this is why Noah was enclosed in his ark, Jonah was held in the belly of the monster fish, and the High Priest Zachariah was reduced to muteness when he heard about Saint John Baptist's birth. When injustice strikes the world and triggers great tragedies, when one feels that Heaven's Hand does not intervene in punishing the unjust, when any Christian logic is denied, the faithful people think that it is God's silence that is revealed and not the Word, as usual. At that very moment we communicate with the part of the Holy Trinity that is God the Father and not with the Son Who might be more understanding because, by the incarnation, He showed Himself to the mortal people in a perceptible manner.

HOW DO WE APPROACH GOD THE FATHER? God the Father is above everything in this world. We can raise our voice of supplication to the Lord only by using the prayers that Christ's church teaches us. It is good to avoid any improper communication in order to avoid all disastrous consequences possible. Let us think of the harsh punishment the wedding guest, who did not put his festal shirt on, was subjected to (*Matthew 22:12-13*).

In reference to what is allowed and what not, it is instructive to reflect a moment on something that happened on Alaska's Spruce Island. A faithful woman asked her husband to bring some water from Saint Herman's spring. The man believed in God, belonged to a protestant church, and was a nice person. He traveled to the island where the Saint had lived. When he arrived at the spring that had a miraculous power of healing, he realized that he forgot to take a clean bottle for the water. So he drank all the wine from the bottle he carried in his backpack and tried to fill it with the blessed water of the spring. To his and all the others' great surprise, when he dipped the bottle in the spring, the water became dirty, strangely colored and totally undrinkable. This thing frightened all the people present and since then everyone has approached the spring with great respect. This is quite a clear warning about the danger of the liberties that we are sometimes tempted to take in handling sacred things. The Orthodox Church is kind and gentle with everyone's weaknesses, but we are not allowed to make our own rules, disregarding the Church's recommendations.

Let us also remember how a man of King David was punished: *"And when they came to the threshing floor of Chidon, Uzza put out his hand to hold the ark, because the oxen stumbled. Then the anger of the Lord was aroused against Uzza, and He struck him because he put his hand upon the ark"* (*1 Chronicles 13: 9-10*). He was punished because he mishandled a sacred thing, ignoring the way God commanded people to carry the holy ark. The explanation comes later in the text: *"As Moses commanded, in accordance with the written word of the Lord, the sons of the Levites took the ark of God upon their shoulders with bearing-poles"* (*1 Chronicles 15:15*).

We also address the Lord with the following words: "Light without beginning and end in which there is no change or shadow." We say that based on the Holy Scripture's words: *"every good gift and every perfect gift is from above, and comes down from the Father of lights, with whom there is no variation or shadow of turning"* (*James 1:17*). We talk in a quite similar way when we pray for the souls of those departed into eternity. Toward the end of our regular morning prayers we say, "Our Lord Jesus Christ, the true Light, who sanctifies and enlightens every man that comes into this world, let the Light of Your Face cover us, enabling our soul to grasp the unapproachable light." We venerate Christ, Who is the Light that brightens man's darkness.

At vespers we sing, "O Gladsome Light of the holy glory of the Immortal Father, heavenly, holy, blessed Jesus Christ. Now we have come to the setting of the sun and behold the light of evening. We praise God: Father, Son and Holy Spirit God…" I heard Father Cleopa Ilie emphasizing the beauty of the description of this moment at dusk, when a group of us visited him at Sihăstria Monastery in the summer of 1969. The mystery of God's light blends into the picturesque nature and the soul feels the beneficent effect of the manifestation of His divine energies.

I remember the profound peace that flooded my heart, under the gentle light of the sunset in the blessed environment

3. DISCOVERING THE SACRED TIME | 253

of Meteora, in Greece. The valley was filled with isolated column-like cliffs with monasteries at the top. They seemed to be sacred crumbs from the mountain, ordered in a long line like an articulated hymn unfolding toward the remote horizon of the plain, a broad transcendental space. I had the chance to revisit Meteora after a decade on a crisp morning after a cold rain that covered the surrounding high peaks with powdery snow making them shine under the gradually increasing light. The same sweet peace was submerging our souls but this time it was coming from the morning sun that was climbing in the sky and splitting the long shadows of the cliff columns. The sacred peace of Meteora under the miraculous power of the evening or morning light induced an unforgettable emotion that persisted a long time in our hearts, and we felt it later while saying our morning and evening prayers. *"In the sun He set His tabernacle"* and the sun is *"like a bridegroom coming forth from his bridal chamber"*; *"its rising is from one end of heaven and its circuit runs to the other end"* (*Psalm 18/19:6-7*).

THE SON OF GOD AND THE HOLY SPIRIT. Our Lord Jesus Christ, The Son of God, is "the only begotten of the Father before all ages" and is "of one essence with the Father, by whom all things were made," as The Creed Prayer says. According to Saint John the Damascene (quoted by Lossky, 1997), the Son was *begotten* of the Father "as a work of the eternal Being." This is a very different phenomenon from the human birth.

We live now in the era of the Holy Spirit that followed the era of the Old Testament, describing the manifestation of God the Father, and the era of the New Testament, describing the manifestation of God the Son. *"I came to send fire on the earth and how I wish it were already kindled,"* Our Lord Jesus Christ, the Son of God, said (*Luke 12:49*). Saint Symeon the

254 | HORIA ION GROZA

New Theologian, quoted by Lossky, saw the Holy Spirit in this fire (Lossky, 1997). I wonder if the Burning Bush from Mount Sinai was not the manifestation of the Holy Spirit. In this case, we have the whole Holy Trinity represented in the icon of the Theotokos at The Burning Bush: God the Father by his unseen but felt presence, God the Son by the presence of the Theotokos and the child, and the Holy Spirit by the presence of the kindled fire. Our Lord Jesus Christ healed the possessed in cooperation with the Holy Spirit (*Matthew 12:28*). The goal of a Christian life is to acquire the gift of the Holy Spirit, as Saint Seraphim of Sarov said

"*He put all things under His feet and gave Him to be head over all things to the church, which is His body, the fullness of Him who fills all in all*" (*Ephesians 1:22*). Here, in this text, we have the whole Divine Trinity: The Father (the first He), the Son (under Whose feet the things were put and Whose body is the Church) and the Holy Spirit (Who fills all in all). We also learn from Lossky's book that the Church is the body and Christ is her head, while the Holy Spirit brings the fullness by filling her with divinity. The Holy Spirit's work in the world before or outside the Church is different from the work done in the Church which started after the Pentecost. "*For the Holy Spirit was not given, because Jesus was not yet glorified*" (*John 14:39*). The Holy Spirit comes in the name of the Son in order to witness for the Son, as the Son came into the world in the name of the Father in order to make the Father known (Lossky, 1997).

As Saint John the Damascene, quoted by Lossky, wrote, "the Son is the image of the Father, and the Holy Spirit is the image of the Son." Indeed, it is so if we think of the Savior's words: "*You know neither Me nor My Father. If you had known Me, you would have known My Father also*" (*John 8:19*). "*However when He, the Spirit of truth has come, He will guide you into all truth; for He will not speak on His authority, but whatever He hears He will speak, and He will tell you things to come. He will glorify Me, for He will take of what is Mine and declare it to you"* (*John 16: 13-14*).

The Holy Spirit is at the same time "*the Spirit of wisdom and understanding, the Spirit of counsel and might, the Spirit of knowledge and godliness, the Spirit of the fear of God*" (*Isaiah 11:2-3*). He is the deifying grace feeding the Christians' souls from the natural abundance of God, but He remains unknown and does not manifest Himself directly (Lossky, 1997). Our Lord Jesus Christ, Son of God, taught us how to pray to God the Father (*Matthew 6:9-13*), but only if we are devoted followers of Christ, the Lord deems us worthy to call Him "Our Father" like His real Son. And in order to be Christ's good followers we have to be Christians, members of Christ's body that is the Church, because only through the Church we receive the Holy Spirit Who leads us to Christ. "*You received the Spirit of adoption by whom we cry out, 'Abba, Father'*" (*Romans 8:15*).

Christ's work addresses the *general* human nature that is recapitulated in His hypostasis. By contrast, the Holy Spirit's work addresses the *individual* human nature, being applied to each person (Lossky, 1997). When Our Lord Jesus breathed on His disciples and said, "*Receive the Holy Spirit*" (*John 20: 22*), He created their first communication with the Holy Spirit. This was a *functional communication*, a general one, because by it, He enabled the Apostles to be priests with the power of forgiving and not retaining sins (*John 20:23*). It was a gift to the whole Church, as a body. When the Holy Spirit descended at Pentecost like tongues of fire, the communication was a *personal communication*, with each of the Apostles. The Holy Spirit Himself comes to persons, marking every member of the Church with the seal of a personal and singular relationship with the

Divine Trinity. For us, the Christians of today, the Holy Spirit descends at baptism through the sacrament of chrismation.

I think the story of healing the man born blind (*John 9:1-38*) illustrates the journey from the revelation that occurred at the opening of eyes that had never seen to understanding and faith, when the healed man said, *"'Lord, I believe!' And he worshiped Him"* (*John 9:38*). Faith is the response given in eternity's terms by our soul to Christ's appeal and to the healing of our blindness. Lossky wrote, "We confess the Son's divinity shown to our mind by the Holy Spirit who dwells within us." Let us not forget that Saint Apostle Paul first lost his sight in order to be converted to the faith (*Acts 9:3* and *7-8*). Only later, after Ananias was involved, he was *"filled with the Holy Spirit,"* and *"immediately there fell from his eyes something like scales, and he received his sight at once, and he arose and was baptized"* (*Acts 9:18*).

3.2. God is Light. He Brings the Sacred Time.

GOD IS LIGHT. After the Lord created the heavens and earth, the first matter was the *light*. It was the concrete expression, like a beneficent spring, of an essential attribute of the Divine Nature that is the Spiritual Light (*Genesis 1:3*). The Light did not cease to accompany the Creator but helped the created world even after man, its pivotal element, fell away from the Eternal Truth that is God.

Hell, the dwelling place of death, is the opposite of God's Kingdom and therefore is a denial of the Light. It is the Dark - a frightening, compact darkness, a state of eternal suffering. It is the very dark that results from the refusal to respond to the loving call of God. As Father Kallistos said, the gates of hell are locked from inside, by those who live in it. Hell is a tenebrous, murky, gloomy place, full of pestilential odor, a place of torture and infinite pain. Light has certainly a direct physical meaning as the light of sun or candle, and it provides a necessary condition for our eyes to see. It has also a profound metaphysical meaning. Saint Matthew the Evangelist started his story about Our Lord's spiritual work in the world by mentioning the Prophet Isaiah's words: "*The people who sat in darkness have seen a great light, and upon those who sat in the region and shadow of death, Light has dawned*" (*Matthew 4:16*). The manifestation of God in the world is affirmation, is Light. By His incarnation, the Son of God made this light perceivable by the human race.

Vladimir Lossky mentioned a manuscript, a Hagioritic Tome, from Mount Athos that distinguished three categories of light (Lossky, 1997). The first two belong to the created world: *the visible light* (the physical, material one) and *the light of comprehension* (the intuition of mind that notices God's work, presence, and influence). The third category belongs to the universe beyond this world. It is *the uncreated light* of divine nature, which is superior to the first two. The uncreated light illuminates the truth that the faithful people seek with the light of comprehension.

Saint Gregory of Nazianz, the hymn-praiser of the Holy Trinity, quoted by Lossky, wrote toward the end of his life of intense prayer and spiritual struggle (podvig), that even the unclear shadows of the Trinity, not comprehended, have filled his heart with light and great emotion. This is a magnificent image - *white* shadows in the Light's blinding *white* space. It is the meeting place between man and God, in His uncreated light. Let us think for a moment of the miraculous light wrapping the whole body of Saint Seraphim of Sarov during his conversation with Motovilov. The Romanian philosopher Constantin Noica brought to our attention a quote from Louis de Broglie: "The material universe could have been born by the condensation of the light and could die by expanding back into the light." (Noica, 1991) This thought might illustrate very well the Christian idea of the incarnation of Son of God. "Light of Light, True God from True God." The Uncontainable was contained in a human womb as "the Son of God becomes the Son of the Virgin" (the Troparion of Annunciation), and the people "saw the inaccessible God as a man accessible to all" (the Akathist of Annunciation). The thought might also illustrate His return to God the Father, His ascension, when the contained went back into the Uncontainable, with important consequences for us Christians. "When You had fulfilled the dispensation for our sake, and united earth to heaven, You ascended in glory, O Christ our God, not being parted from those who love You, but remaining with them and crying: 'I am with you and no one will be against you'" (Kontakion of Ascension).

GOD'S LIGHT IS ACTION. God is affirmative action, a positive act, creation. Therefore His attribute is *Light*. The darkness is antithetic: denial, destruction, annihilation. The Gospel's expression *"The light shines in the darkness, and the darkness did not comprehend it"* (*John 1:5*) is not a tautology. It makes sense because Light like Peace is also a symbolic term; both of them characterize secret features of God's presence. The Son of God is, as we learn from the Creed, "Light of light, true God from true God." We, the humans, are made in the image and resemblance of God. Therefore we hear from Our Lord Jesus Christ: "*Take heed that the light which is in you is not darkness*" (*Luke 11:35*). "*Now you are Light in the Lord. Walk as children of light*," Saint Paul told his disciples (*Ephesians 5:8*).

The Romanian theologian André Scrima noted that the Lord's word *"let there be light"* opened the room that the creation needed in the originary space (Scrima, 2000). The creation is actually neither the earth as a planet nor the cosmic universe, but the possibility of manifestation of an unpredictable and overwhelming freedom. We might then say that the light is our bridge of communication with the Creator through the freedom given to man. There is light in all the icons of the Saints; it is present in the background that symbolizes the heavenly kingdom and in the halo around the Saints' heads that represents God's individual blessing.

After Our Lord answered the disciples' question why a certain man was born blind, He said, "*As long as I am in the world, I am the light of the world*" (*John 9:5*). He anointed the blind man's eyes with mud – the same material God the Father used to mold man. Then Jesus told the blind man to go to wash his mud-covered eyes at the Pool of Siloam.

Therefore what the man saw first, after the complete dark that had covered him since he was conceived in his mother's womb disappeared, was not Our Lord Jesus Christ, although he heard His word, but the world, God's creation. Only after he passed, with the persistent sound of God's Word in the back of his mind, through the examination imposed by the Pharisees, he reached the maturity necessary for intuition of the Divinity. When, eventually, he met Christ, the true Light, his intuition became fact - he believed and worshiped Him. This way, not only his body but also his soul was healed. We can say, as Saint Matthew did, that because his eyes were now healthy, his whole body began to be filled with light (*Matthew 6:12*). By contrast, the Pharisees remained buried in their sin; their foggy eyes could not open the gates of their soul to let the outside human-loving Light enter (*John 9:40-41*).

Saint Gregory Palamas taught us about the incogno-scibility of God's nature and that our only access to Him becomes possible through the uncreated energies, i.e. through

His work in the world. "God is Light, not according to His being but according to His work" (as quoted by Lossky). This is the part of the Lord that the faithful and the people most pleasing to God are enabled to know. The most worthy ones, the Saints, were blessed to see the Heavenly Kingdom even while living on earth (*Mark 9:1*). Such an event happened with Saint John the Apostle. Christ's Light at Transfiguration was perceptible by His three disciples, Peter, James, and John on Mount Tabor. Vladimir Lossky noted that the Divine Light will become visible to all, in proportion to everyone's diligence and merit, on the Eighth Day, at the Second Coming of the Son of God.

One day a Bahai teacher explained to his students that the truth comes on different paths. These paths, he said, are like the windows that let the light of truth enter a dark room. The names of the windows are Confucius, Mohamed, Buddha, and Jesus. One of the students was a Christian. He said, "Jesus is not just a simple window for the light of truth. He is the Light Himself. He is the sun who shines through all the windows of the world," for Jesus Christ is the Truth. He is True God from True God as the Creed says (see Coniaris, 2001).

GOD'S LIGHT TRANSFORMS THE HUMAN BEING. Our human being needs the physical light for the body and the spiritual light for the soul. In the Kingdom of God, we will not have the burden of the body so our being will continue to live only with the spiritual light. An evening prayer says, "O Our Lord, the bodiless powers of heavens praise you unceasingly. They do not need the physical light because they were given the eternal brilliance of Your impenetrable glory." The Angels perceive the light that feeds everything in God's Kingdom and they praise His glory in their songs. God is Light, as He is Peace and Love.

The divine uncreated light that became manifest to humans was of two kinds: (1) a burning light, as unbearable to the human eyes as the sunlight when we look directly at the sun; and (2) a warm and gentle light, coming from a fire without flames - an unearthly light, smooth and mild. The Light irradiating from the Savior in the icon of Transfiguration painted by Andrei Rublev is a solar light, explosive like the act of joy. It floods and conquers everything, and it burns so intensively that two disciples turn their face away from it. It is a light a bit reminiscent of the damaging light of God's presence when He was talking to Moses or Elijah. By contrast, the Light painted by Theophanes the Greek in the icon on the same topic, is uniform, smooth and sweet, mysterious, whitish-blue, like the legendary Easter Light that comes every year to the Church of Holy Sepulcher in Jerusalem. However, because the source of this miraculous light is the Savior's body, it is still hardly bearable for the disciples' eyes. Despite its gentleness, this light carries a divine power that overwhelms the humans.

Only two persons were enabled to endure the direct brightness of the Divine Light, without being harmed. Moses saw it in the Burning Bush. Elijah disappeared in the clouds in a carriage of flames. This fact might be another reason why Moses and Elijah were present with the Savior when His face and body were transfigured on Mount Tabor – they had already experienced the fire, they could take it and they could witness it.

Mary Magdalene at the Savior's tomb might have seen a combination of the two kinds of light mentioned above. First, a powerful, striking, blinding light struck her eyes. *"An angel of the Lord descended from heaven and came and rolled back the stone from the door, and sat on it. His countenance was like lightning and his clothing as white as snow"* (*Matthew 28: 2-3*). Then, a gentle and smooth light comforted Mary's eyes. *"As she wept, she stooped down and looked into the tomb. And she saw two angels in white sitting, one at the head and the other at the feet, where the body of Jesus had lain. Then they said to her, 'Woman, why are you weeping?'" (John 20: 11-12). "They went in and did not find the body of the Lord Jesus. And it happened, as they were greatly perplexed about this, that behold, two men stood by them in shining garments" (Luke 24: 3-4).*

The Light of Resurrection that mysteriously filled the tomb was, according to Saint Gregory Palamas (quoted by Lossky), a light that made everything visible inside despite the darkness of the night. This mysterious light that predicted the coming of the bright light of the day, allowed Mary Magdalene to see the angels and to talk to them. The light coming from God reveals to men profound meanings and, like a fire, kindles in them the power of understanding. The immaterial fire of Divinity landed on the Apostles' heads like tongues of fire and illuminated their minds and spirits with a sudden deep comprehension of Christ's words and deeds. The same light spoke to Saul, illuminated his mind, and blinded his eyes. This secret fire was partially perceived by Saul's companions, unworthy spiritual vessels seeing the light and hearing the voice without understanding a word (*Acts 9:7* and *22:9*). Saint Simeon the New Theologian wrote that the few who are blessed could see God as a powerful Light and, because the Light of His Glory precedes the image of His Face, it is impossible for them to discern Him in another way than within the Light.

Saint Gregory Palamas said that the person who meets the divine energy ends in being a glowing light himself, when he becomes united with the Lord's Light and is completely conscious that he sees things which remain hidden to those who lack this grace. There is an old icon that was venerated at Antim Monastery in Bucharest. It represents the Prayer. The *Prayer of the mind* is in the upper right side: the Theotokos holds the Holy Child on her right, the foreheads united. The next step of prayer is the *Prayer of the heart* that is depicted in the upper left side of the icon: the Theotokos holds Our Lord on her left next to her heart. This prayer is the Royal Prayer. The Holy Child is blessing the praying people. He and His Holy Mother bear crowns on their heads. A wall surrounds them, because this prayer is in the very inside of the human being. Our Lord taught the disciples: *"When you pray, go into your room, and when you have shut your door, pray to your Father Who is in the secret place; and your Father Who sees in secret will reward you openly"* (*Matthew 6:6*). The Angel of Silence stands in the middle of the icon. He corresponds to the mystery of the inner prayer said in the profound silence of the soul, and represents the Savior, Jesus Christ Himself. The Mother of God with her face all red, burning with the inner fire of the Prayer of the Heart, is depicted in the lower left side of the icon. Several saints can be seen in the lower right side; they are bearers of an intense prayer of heart, the Jesus Prayer.

Moses' face was shining when he came down from the mountain with the Tablets of the Law. He *"did not know the skin of his face was glorified while God talked with Him"* (*Exodus 34:29*). This is another example of uncreated light seen on the body of the Saints. As we read in the Philokalia, the prayer of the mind is unstable but accessible; it is like a fire with pinewood – it starts easily and ends quickly. The prayer of the heart is stable and powerful but is hardly accessible and takes a long while for its fire to start. However, the fire in it lasts indefinitely and burns with high flames. The prayer of the mind ignites the prayer of the heart.

As Lossky described, since the schism of 1054, the Western Christians are accustomed to showing their devotion and profound belief in Christ by meditating at the Savior's agony and His suffering in the nocturne solitude in

Gethsemane. Often the Catholic Saints acquire the stigmata of the cross in their palms like Saint Francis. The Orthodox Christians direct their attention to the light of Our Lord's Transfiguration and their Saints become united with God in light. Saint Seraphim of Sarov answered the question N. A. Motovilov asked about the presence of the Holy Spirit as follows: "My friend, we both are now in God's Spirit. Why do you not look at me?" That moment Motovilov turned toward Saint Seraphim and saw his face brighter than the sun with flame-like eyes. Motovilov could still see in that light only the movement of the Saint's lips, could barely hear his voice, and could only guess the shape of his hands. All this time the powerful light was spreading very far out around the saint. Saint Seraphim asked, "What do you feel?" Motovilov answered, "An infinite kindness."

Father George Calciu Dumitreasa narrated how he saw a discrete warm light covering the body of the gentle Father Benedict Ghiuş when they were at the Cernica Monastery. The Elder was resting his fragile body, weakened by age, by the treatment in the communist prisons, and by severe fasting, on a little chair in a corner of the altar room. The light lasted the whole length of the Divine Liturgy. When he came to take the communion, his hands were hands of Light.

A young Romanian hieromonk, Father Anthony, who was close to Father Cleopa for a while, said that when the prayer done in mind becomes a prayer of the heart, the labor and severe discipline of prayer are not anymore a burden for the praying person but a very great joy. It is a joy above any worldly happiness and pleasure, a joy that, with an unceasing thirst, man wants to last forever. Unfortunately, this state lasts a relatively short time – from a few seconds to a few hours and then man falls back into the hard work and sweat of the praying mind. According to Bishop Theophanes's terms, the prayer of heart corresponds to the prayer of feelings (Sbornik, 1936, chapter 2). The very place where those moments of very intense fire and joy intersect is the meeting space of the fine matter of physical light with the spiritual energies, resulting in a substance like the mysterious silken blue light at Easter in Jerusalem that flows over the bodies of the faithful without burning them but kindling the candles.

This happy status, that one wants to never end, derives from the feeling of the peace that Our Lord was referring to, while telling His disciples, *"My peace I give to you"* (*John 14:27*). It is the peace that the priest invokes several times during the Divine Liturgy while blessing the attending faithful people, with the cross, because at that time they are like the Lord's disciples. *"You are My friends if you do whatever I command you. No longer do I call you servants, for a servant does not know what his master is doing; but I have called you friends, for all things that I heard from My Father I have made known to you"* (*John 15: 14-15*). Saint Simeon the New Theologian, quoted by Lossky said that the Person who is God by nature speaks to the faithful persons who are made gods by grace, as a friend speaks with his friends - face to face (Lossky, 1997).

Those who struggled to walk on the earthly narrow trail to God will fully share a sacred light in the eternal life. *"Then the righteous will shine forth as the sun in the kingdom of their Father. He who has ears to hear, let him hear,"* Our Lord said (*Matthew 13:43*). The Evangelist's words are symbolic: "*The lamp of the body is the eye. If therefore your eye is good, your whole body will be full of light*" (*Matthew 6:22*). In order to be able to receive this powerful light we need to live in virtue and purity; otherwise, the sunbeam of God's love cannot enter the temple of the human body and soul, without the risk of shaking and disturbing it. Light works in a unit with love. Only then, the body and soul are blessed with plenitude and splendor. "*He who says he is in the light, and hates the brother, is in darkness until now*" (*1 John 2:9*).

This is why we sing at the Divine Liturgy, after taking Communion of the Body and Blood of Our Lord and being united with the Divinity, "We have seen *the true light*! We have received the heavenly Spirit! We have found the true faith! Worshipping the undivided Trinity, who has saved us." Lossky wrote that those who were not in this true light had not passed properly the gate of penitence. I think that probably he referred, in the case of communion, to the sincere and penitent confession that takes place before it. The burning candle that we hold in our hand when we go to receive the communion might be announcing the unseen light, the true light that we are going to be offered.

ETERNITY, THE SACRED TIME. During the Divine Liturgy, we hear frequently the words "now and ever and unto ages of ages." The psalmist said, "*from everlasting to everlasting You are*" and "*a thousand years in Your sight are like yesterday which passed and like a watch in the night*" (*Psalm 89/90: 2 and 4*). We also find the following words in *Ecclesiastes 3:15*: "*What is has already been and what is to be has already been*". Certainly, these words from the Holy Scripture sound stunning, unreal, or confusing to us for whom time flows and life passes as a sand glass empties. Swimming in temporality, we are tempted to build all kinds of theories about past, present, and future. These biblical sayings warn us about the very different kind of time that is in God's existence and work. It is the *sacred time,* which is secretly present in our life, hidden behind the perishable one.

The Church brings the breeze of eternity into our daily life. I remember how my heart reacted when our priest started his Easter sermon in a simple and direct way: "We are immortal." God has planted in us a soul that has eternal life. *"He made everything beautiful in its time, and He indeed put eternity in their hearts in such a way that man may not find out the work God made from the beginning to the end"* (*Ecclesiastes 3:11*).

"Thou it was who brought us from nonexistence into being," the priest says in his prayer in front of the altar, before the hymn of Hosanna that precedes the Holy Sacrifice. God has brought each of us from nothingness to life, and this life is eternal because the earthly life that we are experiencing is a prelude to the life beyond earthly life.

SPIRITUAL SPACE AND TIME. According to Saint Maximus (quoted by Lossky), all created beings "are first of all defined as limited beings. Their end is outside themselves. They tend toward somewhere else and are in a continuous state of becoming. This limitation and this movement of becoming are the forms of space and time. Only God remains in absolute repose and His state of perfect stability places Him above time and space. God produces love in the created beings and this love makes them tend towards Him. His will for us is a mystery." Consequently, from a spiritual standpoint, we might say that in our universe of created beings, the cause of movement expressed in parameters of reference like space and time, is our conscious or unconscious yearning for God. God is not in movement toward a point because He is everywhere. Not God but *we* are moving and this spiritual movement is manifest in the diversity and the multiplicity of our human nature.

The concept of space comes from our limitation; God is unlimited. The concept of time comes from our conflict with changes – the diseases and death that our body suffers. God alone is stable, above time, while our soul is eternal only after we are brought to life by God. "Created in order to be deified, the world is dynamic," Lossky wrote in the spirit of the Eastern Church's tradition. Therefore, these might be some things to think about: the world has *time* because it is dynamic and undergoes an evolutionary process; the world has *space* because it needs a unit to measure its evolution.

When I was young I almost contaminated my spiritual tutor, Ștefan Todirașcu, member of the Burning Bush group, who was a wise old man and a bright intellectual of profound Christian knowledge and faith, with my enthusiasm for Teilhard de Chardin's philosophy. However, I felt in him a stubborn hesitation: something was incorrect in the system suggested by the Jesuit scholar. Unfortunately, I lost the chance to find out what his opinion was - he died after the terrible earthquake that shook Bucharest in 1977. I think a major error came from the thinker's confusion of three terms: (1) the evolution of species (the transformism) that Teilhard de Chardin studied as a paleontologist, (2) the evolution as a process of growth and development, and (3) the spiritual evolution of mankind toward a universal Christ.

Teilhard de Chardin supported in a way the idea of an evolution of the human species. He discovered some intermediary forms like the Peking man and the Piltdown man. The authenticity of both these forms was later contested, as Father Seraphim Rose noted. I think Darwin's theory of the evolution of species is false, despite its apparent "logic" and "scientific arguments." This idea comes actually from a good systematic classification of the living organisms from simple to complex, initiated by the Swedish taxonomist Carl Linnaeus. On the contrary, there is a genuine evolution of every individual within a species. This is an ontogenetic process of growth and development and it is real. However, the intraspecific evolution of an individual does not simulate the "evolution of species" from one to another as many scholars siding Darwin's ideas think when considering the cellular transformations of embryos.

Teilhard de Chardin's theory about the evolution of the whole of humankind toward the central point Omega, as a "sanctification of the world" might seem valid. A spiritual evolution is very possible. It can be part of the mysterious work of God who first created man according to His image and likeness, then sent His Son to be incarnated in this created structure. Let us not forget that Christ ascended to the Divine Kingdom in a human body. God the Father will send His Son again at the Second Coming and He will be the judge. Even the angels go through a continuous process of spiritual growth but with very different parameters than humans. Nevertheless, I think Teilhard de Chardin creates here a confusion between the deification process that the Orthodox Christian chooses to follow by enduring the harsh conditions of the podvig, and the general state of the human world that continues to live in pleasure and sin and refuses to involve itself in the work of purification and ascent toward God.

Father Kallistos, who signed several of his books as Timothy Ware, wrote that nothing in nature, including the stars, moon, rivers, woods, and animals should remain a stranger to man, because we are saved _with_ the world and not _from_ the world. When Our Lord was baptized He entered the water as part of the created universe. The water is a primordial element present in all living organisms. Saint Apostle Paul said, "_For the creation was subjected to futility, not willingly, but because of Him who subjected it in hope; because the creation itself also will be delivered from the bondage of corruption into the glorious liberty of the children of God. For we know that the whole creation groans and labors with birth_ *pangs together until now"* (*Romans 8:20-22*). The animals wait for man to accomplish his work of regaining his resemblance to God. "When man will become spiritually uncorrupted the whole creation will become new," Saint Symeon the New Theologian wrote.

Teilhard de Chardin died on a very blessed day - Easter, April 10, 1995, in the midst of a very busy metropolis of the modern world - New York. He lived in our corrupted contemporary social environment but he was always a man pleasing to God.

3.3. God is Love. He Did Not Create Evil.

GOD IS LOVE. "Love is the very life of the divine nature" of the Holy Trinity, as Saint Gregory of Nyssa wrote. *By love* we have been created, *by love* we are watched and protected. A beautiful poem of Paul Evdokimov refers to the Lord's love as follows: "His love is more than simple love; the love's kingdom breaks the limits of the universe and enters the Lord's immensity. At His supper that will last eternally, there will be always an empty chair for the rich people and for the beggars. The wine cup is unceasingly full like something that never ends and the bread multiplies like the wheat grains in the golden ears. Crumbs fall from the table and cover the sky like the stars. Even the smallest glitters of this immense Joy cross the firmaments and look like the sun's purple light that chases the darkness." (Evdokimov, 1971)

"As the Father loved Me, I also have loved you; abide in My love," our Lord Jesus Christ told the disciples (*John 15:9*). The love that comes from the Father goes through the Son (and the Holy Spirit) to the people most pleasing to God who are the Saints, and then it flows through them to reach all of us, the ordinary people. Therefore, we are on a straight axis of love.

The beacon of the warm light that fills our soul comes a long way from God the Father and its shape and density starts to be defined better and better as it comes closer to us. This is how the divine light, after it passes through Our Lord, the Apostles and the Saints, becomes accessible to our common human senses of mind and heart. The whole sphere of the creation whirls in perfect balance around this huge axis of love.

"For as rain comes down, or snow from heaven, and does not return until it saturates the earth, and it brings forth and produces, and gives seed to the sower and bread for food, so shall My word be, whatever proceeds from My mouth," said the Lord (*Isaiah 55:10-11*). What a beautiful image for the beneficent will of God and for His Word that makes the faithful soul become fertile! His Word does not rise to heaven before being assimilated by man. In a similar manner, the earth is penetrated by rain water and snow; then it returns to the clouds of the sky through the vapors from the surfaces of streams and lakes and from the steam from the perspiration of the vegetation.

The Lord is Justice but He is also Love. In fire, God descended upon Mount Sinai when He prepared the people of Israel for receiving *the Tablets of Law* (*Exodus 19*). A dark cloud, thunder and lightning, clouds of smoke as from a giant furnace, and loud sounds of a trumpet blast announced His coming to speak with Moses in front of the people. However, also in fire, as a burning bush, never consumed, God appeared to Moses on Mount Horeb to make *His call of love* and to show His intention to deliver His people out of the hand of the Egyptians and to bring them to *"a land flowing with milk and honey "*(*Exodus 3:17*). Lev Gillet noted that both Sinai and Horeb are two different peaks of the same geographic mountain unit and the difference between them has a profound spiritual significance (Gillet, 1976).

God is Love, but if man's spirit is not burning with the fire of faith, man cannot receive God's love in his soul. Therefore, man has to go through a learning process in order to reach the spiritual maturity that makes his soul ignitable, receptive to the fire of God's word as Moses was. First, God called the unsteady people to the School of the Ten Commandments, in order to reach *the level of fearing God*. This would lead to the profound understanding, the strength of virtues, and the cleanness of the soul, needed by man to reach the superior spiritual *level of loving God*. This is why, at the time of the incarnate Son of God's coming among us, people heard the ten Commandments of the Law summarized in only two simple rules of love: love for God and love for neighbor (*Matthew 22: 37-40*).

OUR RECIPROCITY OF LOVE. Here I can find another answer to the question I asked Father Thomas Hopko a long time ago: "Has God created us to glorify Him as the angels do? Did the Lord need this? Is this indeed our role?" I think Father Hopko was right when he said that God does not need praises but we glorify Him out of our gratitude. I think he was right because "gratitude" does not merely mean "to be thankful" for the fact that we have been created. Gratitude is actually *a reciprocity of love*. As Lossky quoted Saint Pseudo-Dionysus, *we are animated by the divine love*. Love is sharing, so we respond with love to God's love. It was often said that the most terrible torture in hell is the remorse that we have rejected God's love.

As Father Hopko told us in a conference, the Holy Scripture is full of nuptial terms, which might sound erotic to some unbelievers. The reason for using the nuptial terms is to properly express a union fed by love. This love is manifested mainly by the first two aspects – *agape* and *philia*, and not by *eros*. In other words, it is a sacrificial and brotherly love, not a sensual one.

As Pseudo-Dionysus the Areopagite wrote, every creature responds to love in the specific manner of its nature. "All the creatures are called to a full union with God and this union is accomplished in synergy" (Lossky, 1997). Therefore, because we are in the midst of the universe of Divine Love, I think we might say that our labor of deification (defined by our striving to be nearer God, to be in touch with His energies and to prepare our soul to receive the grace of the Holy Spirit) is measured in units of love for our neighbors. "He produces in the created beings the love that makes them attracted to Him" (Saint Maximus the Confessor, quoted by Lossky). However, we should not forget that man's freedom of decision might lead to a conflict between his will and the very essence of his own real nature and, consequently, he might ignore the seed of love that had been planted deep in his soul.

Let us remember that *"the great commandment in the law"* is love, as Our Lord Jesus Christ pointed out, because on the two commandments of love *"hang all the Law and the Prophets"* (*Matthew 22:36,40*). These were already formulated in *Deuteronomy 6:5* and *Leviticus 19:18* and were well known by the Pharisees, when they decided to test Jesus: *"You shall love the Lord your God with all your heart, with all your soul, and with all your mind, and your neighbor as yourself" (Luke 10:27; see also Matthew 22:37-39).* But what kind of love should that be?

On the shore of the Sea of Tiberias, Our Lord asked Peter three times if he loved Him. Obviously, in order to absolve Peter, Christ repeated His question as many times the disciple had denied Him in the courtyard of the high priest (*John 21:15-17*). However, there was another reason for the Teacher's insistence. Love can be manifested under three aspects: the passion of the body (eros), the fire of the heart (philo), and the flight of the spirit (agape). Our Lord used the term "agape" when He asked Peter because only with this unique kind of love man should approach God. We have to love God like nobody else. *"The Lord is one"* (*Mark 12:29*). Solely *agape* can elevate the soul toward God, can support the work of deification. Peter answered with the term "philo" which is proper for the love of the neighbor, a love directed to all humans including himself. Our Lord realized that His disciple is not able to understand the depth of His call. Therefore, the third time He asked, He condescended to Peter's level of love by using the term *philo*. Nevertheless,Christ added some words about the way Peter would die, because He knew that eventually Peter would glorify God with the highest level of love, the divine *agape*.

DID GOD CREATE EVIL? A friend brought to my attention a text from *Isaiah 45:7*: *"I form the light, and create darkness: I make peace, and <u>create evil</u>: I the LORD do all these things."* This is the King James Version that uses harsh words. What it is written here is really frightening. Should the Scripture mean that it is not the fallen angel that brings evil in the world but it is God Himself, known by definition to be only love and justice, who then corrupts humankind and strikes the Christians with misery, tragedy, and disaster, even if they did not sin? The case of Job, who was a virtuous man and most pleasing to the Lord, could bring forth an argument supporting the idea of such an unjust treatment.

I think we should be cautious when we start to launch ourselves into this kind of reasoning. The good and evil were expressed by the tree of knowledge Good and Evil in Paradise, and Paradise was created by the Lord. God is love, by definition. He did not create us to be like an interesting toy that

He can put under favorable and unfavorable circumstances to see how it reacts, as some have interpreted Job's story. How could we deny the Lord's love when we know that He sent his Son, one of the Holy Trinity, to the human world to help, to teach, to heal, to suffer with it and for it, and to save it from the fall that resulted from a wrong option taken by the human's free will?

Does the Lord enjoy harming us and striking us with evil? No, because He is love. Might He do that as a punishment because He is also justice? No. I wrote about that in a previous chapter. The so-called "punishment" is not a consequence of a correct and cold judgment of the Lord. As the Holy Fathers said, if the people were to be punished for the wrong things they have done no one could stand. Fortunately, God is a forgiving Master. This is why we are Christians and have hope and faith in Christ, our Savior. The "punishment" is actually an effect of our disrespect of the laws and order of the universe. If a child does not believe his parent's preventive advice and puts his finger into the fire, his finger will burn according to the laws of Physics.

Sometimes our mind's logic cannot bear another hard question. Can God, Who created everything, including good and evil, decide to let the evil be manifest in our life? Does He, Who knows perfectly our future, our "destiny," plan a definitive fall for us? Did the Lord establish Judas' destiny to sell the Savior, at Judas' very birth? Did Judas not have any chance to defend himself against his "destiny" and change the end of his life?

The Orthodox Church teaches us that God does not predestine people to do evil and consequently to go to hell. Man has his freedom of decision and how he acts in his life is the result of his own decision. However, the Lord can foresee what decision man will make.

Let us not forget that Judas had several warnings and chances to avoid his sin of betrayal. Judas had a chance to be saved even after he had fallen into such a terrible sin. Let us think of the repenting thief dying on the cross who was forgiven, as we read in in the Gospel (*Luke 23:40-43*). Peter truly repented for his denial and he was absolved, while Judas went and hanged himself. Maybe it would be interesting here to share a story about Judas. The villagers of Oberammergau, in Bavaria, vowed in 1634 to enact the Passion of Christ in a gesture of gratitude to God who eradicated a terrible bubonic plague epidemic that killed thousands of people. Later they decided to enact the Passion of Christ drama every ten years. The play lasts six hours; it has been staged many times since that year, and the people of the village interpret all the characters of the story. After ten years the play will be resumed in a new distribution; the interpreters remain marked by their roles. Everyone loves the man who played Jesus and everyone hates the man who played Judas; sometimes this antipathy is so strong that the latter prefers to leave the village and move to a different location as far away as possible.

Is the Lord truly good to some and malicious to others? Does he pre-establish who will be saved and who will be condemned? Does He consider evil as an intrinsic part of our imperfect being? The Orthodox philosopher Nicholas Berdiaeff debated this subject which seems to be tragic and without a clear conclusion (Berdiaeff, 1935). Therefore, some critics classified the author as an existentialist and his work as the tragic absurd. He considered that "tragedy is always linked to freedom" and "if the antique tragedy was a tragedy of destiny, the Christians' tragedy is one of liberty." Freedom, Berdiaeff thought, preceded the whole creation and preceded being. It is being that resulted from freedom, and not vice-versa. God created man and enabled him with a free will. God does not experiment with man in order to verify His anticipative calculation, as the atheists affirm. It is the manner in which man uses freedom for bringing significance to the notions of good and evil that counts and that could generate life's tragedy, the tragedy of "destiny." The notions of good and evil are actually simple antinomian categories and do not mean fortification or destruction.

Surprisingly, Berdiaeff considered that "the greatest human tragedy is connected with the suffering caused by good" and not by evil. He meant that the conscience of the good that we do not accomplish causes deep remorse which tears our heart. I remember that Father Kallistos said at a conference that the suffering in hell is in essence the soul's refusal to accept the love and peace offered by God, and the preference for its own ego which ends by devouring itself. I think a significant example of rebellion against a correct knowledge of good and evil, as the Lord's commandments defined these two categories, is the relativism promoted nowadays by the post-modern man who uses his individual freedom in a selfish manner. He says that what is good for him is what suits his goals and aspirations. If this kind of good hurts others it is not his fault but theirs because they do not understand and do not love him. According to the post-modern man, every individual has the right to have his own definition of good, different from the others.

Therefore, I think some Bible translations prefer to formulate the highly troubling text from *Isaiah 45:7* with other words than the classic King James Version. So is The Orthodox Study Bible (2008), based on SAAS (Septuagint), as mentioned in the Introduction of this book: "*I am He who prepared light and made darkness, who makes <u>peace</u> and creates <u>troublesome things</u>. I am the Lord God who does all* *these things."* The unselfish *peace* is actually the good while the *troublesome things* are the range of trials that teach us how to distinguish the good from evil and to fortify our soul's virtues. One thing is clear: by nature, God cannot create evil. Evil is the result of the will of man cooperating with the evil spirit's deception.

CAUSE OF HUMAN TRAGEDIES. Abominable things happen in our world and they fill our soul with terror. People are killed in terrible accidents, in earthquakes, tornadoes, and hurricanes, in explosions and fire. Some, without any guilt, are arrested, tortured, persecuted, and executed. Others are murdered by mad people. Our mind finds some reasons: all these atrocities are caused by the fact that we all sinned and we are punished. However, he who harms others brings unhappiness to himself. *"It is impossible that no offenses should come, but woe to him through whom they do come,"* Our Lord Jesus said (*Luke 17:1*).

There are numerous mass tragedies in this world, when many people suffer and are killed. Several tragedies are due to a natural cause: they are part of the order of the universe's life and their effect can be partially diminished by man but cannot be avoided. So are the earthquakes, the volcanic eruptions, the flooding, the hurricanes, the tsunamis. As the British physicist and priest John Polkinghorne commented, science knows that Mother Nature comes to us with good and evil in the same package (see Polkinghorne and Beale, 2009).

Let us talk for instance about earthquakes. If God had covered our planet with a solid, continuous, and deep crust, it would not have been good for us. The tectonic plates, which move to adjust to each other over the spaces between them and produce damaging earthquakes, allow the mineral resources to move up to the surface of earth through those free spaces.

Without a refreshment of the mineral resources, life on the surface of our planet would not be able to continue. On the other hand, many mass tragedies are the result of man's striving for better comfort; so are the crash of planes, the derailment of trains, the sinking of ships, the collapse of dams, the crumbling of mine galleries. Tragedies are the result of man's interference with nature's flow; so are the epidemics, radioactivity and pollution of the air, water, and soil. They might be caused as well by man's selfish passions and lack of love for others; as are the wars, political persecutions and prisons and the undermining of the economy of other states.

Other mass tragedies are due to the Divine Will. They can be the effect of the rules of a well-adjusted functioning of the universe, as we could see in the examples above. In this case, the Lord decides to finish the people's lives in an abrupt manner in order to protect them from a long intense suffering. Tragedies also can be the effect of the evil produced in the world by human free will. In this latter case, the Lord decides to stop the spread and aggravation of the moral corruption caused by man in order to save the world. Consequently, He ends the life of those people who are so deep in sin that there is no more hope of their correction, while He warns and reproves those whom He keeps alive, giving them a chance to correct. The Church thinks that the reason why Our Lord Jesus decided to bring the widow's son back to life was not only the compassion for her grief and despair but also the will to give the young man another chance to properly live his life (*Luke 7:11-15*).

"It is a fearful thing to fall into the hands of the living God," Saint Apostle Paul wrote (*Hebrews 10:31*). *"The fear of the Lord hates unrighteousness, and both rudeness and arrogance, and the ways of wicked men; and I hate the perverted ways of evil men"* (*Proverbs 8:13*). At the same

time, fear is a good teacher and eases comprehension. *"The beginning of wisdom is the fear of the Lord; a good understanding is in all who practice it,"* the Psalmist said (*Psalm 110/111:10*). We read in the book of Proverbs, *"The fear of the Lord is the beginning of wisdom, and the counsel of saints is understanding"* (*Proverbs 9:10*).

Respect of the laws saves us from harm. *"What you are doing is no good. Should you not walk in the fear of our God because of the reproach of the nations, our enemies?"* (*Nehemiah 5:9*). Therefore, keeping order and avoiding corruption is the attribute of people with a wise mind. *"All wisdom is the fear of the Lord, and in all wisdom there is the doing of the Law"* (*Wisdom of Sirach 19:18*).

Man learns by aging in the school of life. *"The crown of old men is great experience, for their boast is the fear of the Lord"* (*Wisdom of Sirach, 25:6*). This advice hides a promise that should guide us for everything we do. *"Now let the fear of the Lord be upon you. Take care and so do it, for there is no wrongdoing with the Lord our God, neither partiality nor taking of bribes"* (*2 Chronicles/2 Paraleipomenon 19:7*). We should proceed as Jehoshaphat commanded the people of Israel, *"Thus you shall act in the fear of the Lord faithfully and with a mature heart"* (*2 Chronicles 19:9*). Saint Apostle Paul was absolutely right when he wrote to the Corinthians, *"Having these promises, beloved, let us cleanse ourselves from all filthiness of the flesh and spirit, perfecting holiness in the fear of God"* (*2 Corinthians 7:1*).

What is entirely amazing in all these mass tragedies is the fact that several people escape untouched by the disaster. So are the few houses that are protected by air drafts and humidity and remain unburnt in the midst of a broad zone destroyed by fire, or the little child, a few months old, found alive under a two-yard thick pile of debris carried by the wrath of the tsunami in Japan. This proves that God's love *works*. Unfortunately, we notice the Lord's love only under extreme circumstances. We ignore His love when we are busy with our daily life as we ignore the benefits of health as long as we are healthy. "Plant, O Lord, the roots of the good things and the fear of Thee in my soul. Make me, O Lord, to love Thee with all my heart and with all my mind and to do everything upon your will," we say in the morning with the words of Saint John Chrysostom's Prayer. Truly, man's love for God should be combined with fear, because the latter makes man pay attention and it prevents him from being carried into moral corruption by irresistible temptations. As long as man's love for God and man's care to avoid sin increase, the raw fear becomes respect and trust in God's will.

WHY DO THE INNOCENTS SUFFER? We might ask, "Why do the innocent people, as the children are, suffer and die?" Our Lord told the disciples, *"Let the little children come to Me, and do not forbid them; for of such is the kingdom of God"* (*Luke 18:16-17*). Little girls are kidnapped, raped and murdered; some children die of cancer after long periods of unimaginable pain, others die of heart anomalies; some children suffer from asthma, diabetes, or epilepsy from a very early age; others are handicapped and carry this yoke their whole life, etc. It is a fact hardly acceptable by our heart and mind. *"Rabbi, who sinned, this man or his parents, that he was born blind?"* the disciples asked Our Lord Jesus (*John 9:2*).

This is exactly the burning question asked by the priest Paneloux, a character in the book "The Plague" written by Albert Camus. Surrounded by dying people, he decided that there is evil doing in the world, which functions reasonably as a necessary punishment for sinning grown-ups, but he wondered why the punishment happens also to the innocent children. Facing this overwhelming tragedy, what should we do? Should we deny God's love? Probably we will say like Paneloux, "We must believe everything or deny everything, and who would dare to deny everything?" We would risk losing our faith, and without faith we cannot go further and struggle for our life. This is our challenge. In my translation from French his words sound as following: "A child's suffering is humiliating for the heart and the mind. But just because of that we have to go through it... The children's suffering is our bitter bread, but without this bread our soul would perish by spiritual hunger... The love for the Lord is a hard love... However, only this love can reconcile the children's suffering and death, only this love can make them necessary; otherwise it is impossible to understand them and the unique thing that we are able to do is not to want them" (see Camus, 1947).

The Serbian Father Dane Popovic suggested considering the response he found in the Holy Fathers' writings. The innocent children die because the Lord wants to protect them from an overwhelming evil in their future life. He foresees the trials and temptations that will challenge the grown-up child and He also foresees the child's weak resistance and terrible fall. I remember how the little miracles seem very "natural" *after* they happen but never *before* – that is why they are *miracles*. I trust that this hardly explainable suffering of innocent people will look normal to us when we are in eternity, beyond the limits of this world, because in eternity the perspective becomes much more all-inclusive.

The Lord sees the defeat of the growing child ahead of time with the same great wisdom He sees the future resistance of those who will overcome their martyrdom with faith and confidence, with joy to be in God's care. It seems so sad and unbearable when one of our very dear friends or relatives suffers from a terminal disease for an extremely long period, but this situation gives us a chance to prepare the soul of a person nearing the end of his life and, at the same time, it strengthens the caregiver's heart in the love and power of sacrifice. The faith that characterizes the Christian's spiritual maturity confers endurance in tribulations, peace, and courage in losses, moderation in happiness, excitement in monotony, and patience in delays.

OUR THINKING IS NOT GOD'S THINKING. In his little book about the school of prayer, Metropolitan Anthony Bloom wrote that sometimes we feel that Christ does not care that we are in trouble, despite the fact that a single word would be enough to help us, as happened to the centurion, whose servant was healed just with a word from Christ. With just one word we could be healed and saved. How was it when the disciples were disappointed that Our Lord Jesus was sleeping and did not care that they might perish in a terrible storm? He stood up and ordered the wind to calm down and then He scolded them for being unfaithful (*Luke 8: 23-25*).

The reality is that we understand too little of God's will and how it works. Paul Lungin, the director of the Russian movie "The Island (Ostrov)," made in 2006, emphasized the fact that none of the needy people coming with a request to the holy man, the main hero of the story, received the expected response despite the fact that something miraculous happened. God has His own ways to solve our problems; we do not know what actually is best for us.

When Elijah was running for his life far from Queen Jezebel's wrath, he was frightened and he forgot that God had given him so much power that he was able to bring fire, drought, or rain. The Lord could punish Jezebel striking her directly, but He chose to tell Elijah to go anoint Hazael, Jehu, and Elisha,

because their sword was going to punish her and the people of Israel (*3 Kingdoms or 1 Kings 19:15-17*). Our problem is that our faith and devotion to God is too weak. We have to live by God's ways and not ours, and it will be for our good.

3.4. God is Truth. He is the Savior.

THE TRUE GOD. We should avoid building our own God by imagining Him as we like and as it suits our manner of life. As Father Thomas Hopko used to say, the Lord is *only one* and we have to learn to know Him as *He really is*. This is actually the Truth, the essence of life and the universe, the essence of everything that the Scriptures talk about and that the man searches for with continuous scientific and spiritual efforts. We need perseverance, humility, love, and patience for advancing in our knowledge. By striving for this Truth, the meaning of our earthly life, as a part of our soul's eternal life, starts to make more and more sense. *"And this is eternal life, that they may know You, the only true God, and Jesus Christ whom You have sent,"* the Savior said in His prayer done in Gethsemane garden (*John 17:3*).

Did we not notice a peculiar nuance in Christ's words that summarize the Ten Commandments, protected by Law, at a higher spiritual level in only two, wrapped in love, He said, *"You shall love the Lord your God with all your heart, with all your soul, with all your strength, and with all your mind, and your neighbor as yourself"* (*Luke 10:27*)? He emphasized four times how to love God. Why? Because we have to love Him as no one else - *as He is*, without any modification. He is perfect and our love should be perfect – a devotion of our whole being, of our mind, heart and soul. By contrast, we love our neighbor as ourselves, with a love that aims for a continuous improvement of our beings.

GOD IS THE TRUTH. Pilate asked Jesus, *"What is Truth?"* (see *John 18:38*). The Holy Fathers said that he had to ask correctly, *"Who* is the Truth?," because the Savior had explained to him before, *"You said rightly that I am a king. For this cause, I was born and for this cause, I have come into the world, that I should bear witness to the truth. Everyone who is of the truth hears My voice"* (*John 18:37*). Jesus said to Thomas, when he asked Him about the way to go, *"I am the way, the truth, and the life"* (*John 14:6*).

We learn from the Holy Fathers that the Truth is God the Father; God's Word is the Son Who tells the people about Truth, and the Holy Spirit is the Truth through Whom the faithful listen to God's voice. Consequently, let us try to learn the Truth, personified by the Holy Trinity, as it really is and not as we like to imagine it. Saint Gregory of Nazianz, quoted by Lossky (see Lossky, 1997), wrote, "The Father is He who is True, the Son is Truth, and the Holy Spirit is the Spirit of Truth." Christ tells the Samaritan woman at the well, *"God is Spirit, and those who worship Him must worship in spirit and truth"* (*John 4:24*). His words tie the two notions together, as the Christian prayers have to respond to the attributes of the Divine Trinity. It is specific to the Christian religion that the Truth is represented by a Person in three hypostases; the Truth is not an abstract notion. God knows us *entirely* by His nature of a Creator, while we know *only a part* of Him by grace.

The Orthodox Christian is called to go through a deification process. Striving to accomplish this process the Christian follows Christ and as he knows God more intimately and accurately, his podvig's burden, cumulated before time, becomes lighter. *"If you abide in My word, you are My disciples indeed. And you shall know the truth, and the truth shall make you free,"* the Savior told the Jews who believed Him (*John 8:31*). The teaching work of the incarnate Son of

God on earth was continued by the Holy Spirit, as Our Lord Jesus indicated: *"When He, the Spirit of truth, has come, He will guide you into all truth; for He will not speak on His own authority"* (*John 16:13*). The whole Holy Trinity is revealed in the truth, as Our Lord emphasized: *"He will glorify Me, for He will take of what is Mine and declare it to you. All things that the Father has are mine. Therefore I said that He will take of Mine and declare it to you"* (*John 16:14-15*).

LIVING IN TRUTH. If God is Truth, we, the created sons of God, have to live in truth all the days of our life. This is a frightening task and a hard responsibility given to us by God, as a very pious friend of mine used to repeat often. But what does "living in truth" mean? What is the untruth? It is *a deformation of the truth*, a lie, as the serpent misleading the first human couple said in Paradise: *"you will be like gods, knowing good and evil"* (*Genesis 3:5*). Did man really know good and evil after eating the forbidden fruit? No, he probably was only *aware* of them. He did not understand them, because he lacked the appropriate spiritual maturity. The untruth can also be *a denial of the truth*, which causes a void, a nothingness, and destroys the being. The untruth is promoted by the fallen angel who is man's enemy. In conclusion, to live in truth means *to live in God* – to listen to His commandments, to watch His will, to resist the lying or nihilistic temptations, and, at the same time, to communicate with God by constant prayer, by the joy of feeling His protective presence, by the tonic feel of awe.

The truth *"enters the sheepfold by the door"* like the shepherd. The lie *"climbs up some other way"* like the thief and the robber. Our soul hears the Shepherd and recognizes Him, as the Truth. He calls our soul by name and leads us out with Him (see *John 10:1-5*).

THE SALVATION OF MAN BECAME VERY NECESSARY after his fall. Sin drowned him in confusion, in untruth about soul, life, and world. Sin leads him to spiritual death. *"For the Lord knows the way of the righteous, but the way of ungodly shall perish"* (*Psalm 1:6*). *"For God so loved the world that He gave His only begotten Son, that whoever believes in Him should not perish but have everlasting life"* (*John 3:16*). This love is of such large dimensions that *"neither death nor life, nor angels nor principalities nor powers, nor things present nor things to come, nor height nor depth, nor any other created thing, shall be able to separate us from the love of God which is in Christ Jesus our Lord"* (*Romans 8:38-39*). Here, in the text, "principalities" and "powers" are superior categories of angels, and "height" and "depth" are the beings invisible to man – the good and evil spirits.

After the fall from Paradise, man was separated from God by a triple barrier – nature, sin, and death. Lossky quoted Saint Nicholas Cabasilas who said that the Son of God as Our Lord Jesus Christ had defeated these barriers one by one – "the nature by His incarnation, the sin by His death and the death by His Resurrection." (Lossky, 1997) This was achieved by Christ's divine will, which was the result of a will common to the three hypostases of the Holy Trinity: the will of the Father (the source of the will), the will of the Son (the free obedience), and the will of the Holy Spirit (the accomplishment).

As we learn from Lossky's book, a tremendous distance grew between the created and uncreated, between man and God, due to man's fall into sin and death and due to the resulting alteration of his nature. It became an impassible abyss. Man could not pass it to accomplish his journey toward his Master and Creator, despite his intimate call to the vitally needed deification. The Son of God, through the person of

Christ, gave man the chance of Salvation, as a bridge over the separating gulf, helping the *reunion* with God. Thus He reestablished the *authentic human nature* by defeating the alteration through the incarnation of His divine essence. He reestablished the *human being's purity* by defeating sin through His death on cross. He reestablished *the eternal being* as Adam should remain by defeating death through His Resurrection. All these can be expressed, according to Saint Maximus, quoted by Lossky, by the three successive stages of salvation work that reestablished the *being*, the *well-being*, and the *eternal being*.

At crucifixion, Our Lord Jesus Christ united Paradise, the dwelling place of the first people, to the Earth, the place of the people of today. At burial, He illuminated the prisoners of Hades' darkness. At Resurrection He gained victory over sin, decay, and death. At Ascension, He united the earth with the heavens, restoring the whole universe. Saint Paul wrote in his epistle to Romans, *"Do you not know that as many of us as were baptized into Christ Jesus were baptized into His death? Therefore, we were buried with Him through baptism into death, that just as Christ was raised from the dead by the glory of the Father, even so we also should walk in newness of life. For if we have been united together in the likeness of His death, certainly we also shall be in the likeness of His resurrection"* (*Romans 6:3-5*).

WAS CHRIST'S SACRIFICE NEEDED? We still might ask a question from our human standpoint: why was Our Lord's sacrifice needed? Was His glorious blood shed for us as an offering to someone and why? The priest says in the altar at the Prothesis Service, which precedes the Liturgy of the Catechumens and the Liturgy of the Faithful, "He is brought as a lamb to the slaughter". These words correspond to what is written in the Scripture: *"He was led as a sheep to the slaughter, and as a lamb is silent before his shearers, so He opens not His mouth."* (*Isaiah 53:7*) Later, the priest says, "The Lamb of God is sacrificed, He who takes away the sins of the world," traces a cross on the bread, and makes an incision by piercing the right side of the Lamb (see Cabasilas, 1977).

Saint Gregory of Nazianz, quoted by Lossky, commented that we are corrupt and bound by our sins to evil and Jesus saves us. But to whom does the ransom paid for our freedom go? It cannot not be to the evil one! It is a ransom consisting of God Himself! Then, does it go to the Father? Why? Did He keep us prisoners? No. The answer is that the Father does not receive the sacrifice because He asked for it or because He needed it, but because this is part of the process of regaining the original human nature that did not know sin.

THE INCARNATION OF SON OF GOD. As part of the Holy Trinity, the Son of God was begotten of the Father, not made. For the incarnation He chose to be born but this was a very different phenomenon from the regular human birth. It occurred through a pure Virgin who remained Virgin and the seed was from the Holy Spirit. The salvation of man is a synergistic process depending not only on God's will but also on man's will. Nicholas Cabasilas, quoted by Lossky, wrote that the incarnation was not only the result of the work done by God the Father, His Son and the Holy Spirit, but also the result of the will and faith of Saint Virgin Mary. It is very frightening to think that if Saint Mary had not said, "Yes," to the appeal of God's Messenger, Our Lord Jesus Christ might not have been among us for thirty-three years. As Saint Dimitry of Rostov noticed, six thousand years were needed for the chance of the existence of a maid, so pure as to be a bodily cradle for the Holy Child.

We might say that this long period was a preparatory time, marked by a long chain of people pleasing to God. Noah, Abraham, Moses and David were among them. The Old Testament presents a sacred history that predicted Christ's body in a "providential and messianic" manner. The Church's tradition through the Holy Fathers considers the Mother of God descending from David, as Saint Paul wrote: *"Jesus Christ our Lord, who was born of the seed of David according to the flesh"* (*Romans 1:3*). Regarding Saint Joseph, betrothed to Saint Mary, Holy Evangelist Matthew emphasized from the very beginning of his Gospel the three ranges of fourteen generations from King David to the incarnate King of the universe (*Matthew 1:1-17*), while Holy Evangelist Luke tracked Our Lord's genealogy all the way back to the first man (*Luke 3:23-38*).

We note that numerous successive purifications and numerous selections of virtuous sons of man were needed along all the generations descending from Adam, the first sinner, in order to reach such a perfectly clean soul and body as that of the Holy Virgin and to offer a sacred ground to the seed of the Holy Spirit. All this careful preparation was necessary for the birth of the Person who is completely without sin, totally untouched by Adam's original sin and able to restore the primordial immaculate status of man in Paradise. The Holy Fathers brought another important observation to our attention: by His birth from a Virgin, Our Lord Jesus destroyed the separation of the human nature into male and female occurred after the original sin. The two reunited into a unique being, called to participate in the work of God.

It is with deep emotion that we read about the presentation of the infant Jesus to God in the Temple (*Luke 2: 21-38*). Two female persons with names of profound resonance partake in the event: Mary (Mother of God) and Anna (the prophetess, whose name reminds us of Saint Mary's mother). The Son of God meets God the Father. Two parental lines merge - the prestigious genealogical line of the mother and the sublime unearthly line of the Father.

The Mother of God and Our Lord Jesus Christ were prefigured in the Old Testament. Father Anthony Michaels said in his sermon at Saint Andrew's Orthodox Church in Minocqua that, from the very beginning, God the Father saw in Eve, the future Virgin who would come and would give birth to Jesus (as Elder Cleopa Ilie also wrote). When God cursed the serpent He said, *"I will put enmity between you and the woman, and between your seed and her seed. He shall bruise your head, and you shall be on guard for His heel"* (*Genesis 3:15*). What is the seed of the woman? The woman does not have seed, she has ovules - the eggs. The seed comes from man. However, the seed God was referring to, did not come from any man but from the Holy Spirit who overshadowed the Holy Virgin. The serpent's seed is the human progeny who rejects Christ and follows the evil angel. Christ will smash the serpent's head under His heel.

The Protestant Churches, in opposition to the Catholic Church, do not venerate the Holy Virgin Mary as the Mother of God, the Theotokos. For protestants, the father and mother signify the beginnings, and therefore, because at the beginning of the universe there was only God, the Creator, there is only a Father without any mother. We, the Orthodox, venerate the Holy Virgin Mary as the Mother of God because she carried in her womb the Son of God, a hypostasis of the holy Trinity. In contrast to the Catholic Church, a traditional church like our Orthodox Church does not accept the idea of the Immaculate Conception and we believe that the Holy Virgin Mary was conceived in a human way. This fact has an extraordinary importance because, if a human being was pure enough to carry the body that the Son of God assumed, it means that all of us have the theoretic chance to carry God within us, in other words to walk the road of deification, a process so vital for our spiritual life.

THE IDEA OF REINCARNATION IS NOT A CHRISTIAN IDEA. The heretics say that man lives several lives and the goal of this successive reincarnation is a continuous spiritual improvement in a move toward God Who is perfection. One of their arguments is the question Saint John the Baptist was asked by the priests and Levites who wondered if he is Christ, Elijah or the Prophet (*John 1:19-21*). Their presumption seemed to be supported by Our Lord's words addressed to the multitude about the future coming of Elijah, *"For all the prophets and the law prophesied until John. And if you are willing to receive it, he is Elijah who is to come"* (*Matthew 11:13-14*). This confusion also persisted in regard to Jesus' identity as mentioned in Luke's Gospel (see *Luke 9:7-8* and *18-20*). They do not see a spiritual continuity but a reincarnation – John from Elijah or another Prophet, and Jesus from Elijah, from another Prophet or even from John risen to life after beheading. The heretics do not see the spiritual work of God along the generations through His chosen saints. They disregard the fact that, according to God's wisdom, the Savior was born from a Virgin at the end of a long genealogical line coming from King David. Some heretics suggested that Christ is a reincarnation of Adam, based on Saint Paul's words, *"The first man Adam became a living being. The last Adam became a life-giving spirit"* (*1 Corinthians 15:45*). They did not understand what the Church actually teaches about Christ, Who is spiritually the new Adam. Our Lord Jesus cannot be a reincarnation of a human person, because these are distinct natures. Man *received* life by God's breath blown on the clay of man's body, while Christ is the Son of God and *has the life-giving spirit*, as we can see at His meeting with the disciples after Resurrection (*John 20:22*). In fact, the whole idea of reincarnation is a great heresy. As Father Mark Malone observed, Christianity emphasizes the uniqueness of the person. The person is transfigured and not obliterated. The goal of the oriental religions is the dissolution of the individual person.

TWO NATURES BUT A SINGLE HYPOSTASIS. The incarnation of God the Son gave man the chance to dialogue *directly* with the Holy Trinity through Our Lord Jesus Christ. This might already sound like a common thing for a Christian but, if we go into the depth of what it means, our mind fails in awe and our heart becomes incandescent. Vladimir Lossky quoted Saint Maximus the Confessor when he wrote, "the union of the divine and human nature has been decided by the everlasting counsel of the Holy Trinity, because the union is the final goal for which the world was made out of nothing." As the Divine Trinity is one nature but three hypostases, Our Lord Jesus Christ has two different natures but a single hypostasis. When we make the sign of the cross, the first three fingers held together remind the Holy Trinity, and the last two fingers the double nature of Our Lord – divine and human. The union of the two natures, as we learn from Lossky's book, is apophatically expressed by four negative adjectives: "not mixed, not changed, not divided, and not separated."

While Our Lord was among people as a material person, one could notice two distinct aspects in every work of His, as Saint Maximus (quoted by Lossky) commented. For instance, in the case of the Jairus' daughter (*Matthew 9:25*), Christ's human hand lifted up the young girl and the Divinity resurrected her. In the case of Jesus walking on the See of

Galilee (*Matthew 14:25*), His human feet walked upon the water and the Divinity made that possible. Saint Maximus compared this work of the two natures of Christ with the efficiency of a sword reddened by the fire: the iron cuts and the fire burns.

J.A.T. Robinson, quoted by George Every, Richard Harries and Kallistos Ware, wrote about Our Lord Jesus, "He is a perfect man and perfect God – not as a mixture of oil and water, of natural and supernatural – but as the embodiment through obedience of 'the beyond in our midst', of the transcendence of love." (Every *et al*, 1984) Christ's nature is 100% divine and 100% human. This is one of the mysteries of our faith.

Surely, Nikos Kazantsakis' passionate idea to make Jesus half-human and half-divine person sounds interesting but the Greek writer is extremely wrong and his idea is a great blasphemy and heresy. Kazantsakis intended to suggest the Lord's closeness to our human way of suffering and, consequently, to increase our love for Him. He imagined even an earthly love of Our Lord for Mary Magdalene. This idea was quickly embraced by the Hollywood moviemakers, who are ever open to shocking the public in order to make more money. Some scholars pleaded that Our Lord Jesus' knowledge came from the Essenes, and others thought that He learned from the Indian religions in His youth. All these forget the fact that Jesus showed a deep knowledge of the Scripture even when He was only twelve years old and was teaching the wise men in the temple (*Luke 2:46-47*). Truly our Lord was 100% man and 100% Son of God from the moment He was conceived. He said to his earthly parents, *"Why did you seek Me? Did you not know that I must be about My Father's business?"* (*Luke 2:49*). All these stories that are dangerous to the spirit made possible the very damaging aberrations of the books and films of today claiming to unveil secrets of "Leonardo's code" about the person of Our Lord Jesus Christ. They are the result of the very subtle and treacherous work of the evil tempter on the imagination of man's mind.

Exasperation (*Mark 9:19*), anger (*Matthew 21:12-13*), tears of sorrow (*Luke 19:41*), sad groans (*John 11:33* and *38*), and a voice crying aloud (*Matthew 27:46*) revealed a human manifestation of Our Lord Jesus. However, this should not encourage us to try to define the human contour of His soul.

THE WAY TO GOD'S KINGDOM GOES THROUGH THE SAVIOR. Jesus told Thomas, "*I am the way, the truth, and the life. No one comes to the Father except through Me*" (*John 14:6*). The meaning of Salvation is not only the forgiveness for our sins but also the reunion with God at the end of our road of deification. Therefore, the Jesus' Prayer practiced in the Orthodox Church is so powerful. Through it, we feel unceasingly the Lord's presence and our soul builds slowly, with a lot of sweat and with Christ's help, our own ladder to the heights. Our spirit goes up "through Him, with Him, in Him" in a continuous and humble process of returning all we were given, with a joyous tone of praise, as the Orthodox priest says, during the Anaphora, after the words of the Last Supper: "Thine own of Thine own, we offer unto Thee, on behalf of all and for all." Jacob saw, full of awe, in his dream, a ladder set up from earth to heaven, on which the angels were ascending and descending (*Genesis 28:12*). He said then, filled with fear, "*How awesome is this place! This is none other than the house of God, and this is the gate of heaven*" (*Genesis 18:17*).

Christ, as Son of God, showed Himself to the saints, in His full glory, on a ladder linking earth with heavens. He told Nathaniel, "*Most assuredly, I say to you, hereafter you shall see heaven open, and the angels of God ascending and descending upon the Son of Man"* (*John 1:51*). Christ, our Savior, comes down to meet the man and, with His Saints, gives man a hand pulling him up. The Kondakion of the Ascension Day, when the Son of God, as Christ, returned to heaven in a human body, sounds as follows: "After fulfilling for us Your plan of redemption and joining the things of earth with those of heaven, O Christ our God, You gloriously ascended without abandoning us, but remained with us forever and reassured all who love You by telling them: 'Behold, I am with you, no one has power against you'."

The tradition of the Orthodox Church has many other nuances in the complex meaning of a spiritual ladder. One meaning nuance is that represented by the sacred person of Mother of God who is a bridge between man and Son of God, between earth and heaven. Therefore, she is depicted above the altar. A ladder is drawn on her breast in the well-known icon of the Burning Bush which illustrates, within a symbolic star, Moses' vision on Mount Horeb mentioned in *Exodus 3:3*. In the same sense, the Theotokos is praised with the following words in Eikos 2 of the Annunciation Akathist: "Rejoice, heavenly ladder by which God came down! Rejoice, bridge that conveys us from earth to heaven!" Another nuance of this complex spiritual meaning refers to the ladder of virtues, purification, and transcendence, described by Saint John Climacus. This ladder, where the last step, the 30th, is faith, hope and love, is in iconography a live ladder with an unceasing traffic of angels who symbolize our own tireless prayers, as Father Anthony Coniaris wrote (Coniaris, 1998).

THE WORK OF CHRIST DEPICTED IN THE DIVINE LITURGY. One classic interpretation of the Divine Liturgy considers that all the above-mentioned things are illustrated by its structure. Thus, the Divine Liturgy starts with the Old

Testament. It passes to the New Testament in the middle of the second antiphon, with the words "Only begotten Son and immortal Word of God, Who for our salvation didst will to be incarnate of the Holy Theotokos and ever-virgin Mary." It travels then with Our Lord Jesus, starting with the Sermon on the mountain at the time of the third antiphon, The Beatitudes, which is sung while the priest comes out from the altar holding high the Scripture; this signifies the entrance of the Word in the world to preach and teach the people. Then the Epistles and Gospel are read, and the word of Christ's teachings is spread. The Great Entrance, preceded by the Cherubic Hymn, brings the offering, the Holy Gifts as bread and wine, to the altar. It signifies the journey of Our Lord through the world to the place of sacrifice on Golgotha. In Romania the priest, walking through the church, touches the head of the kneeling people with the chalice as Jesus was healing the sick and forgiving the sinners, and the people kiss his vestments as the woman with the flow of blood did (*Luke 8:43-48*). Then the people affirm their faith by saying the Creed, and the choir sings with the hymn of Palm Sunday, "Hosanna in the highest!" (*Matthew 21:9*).

The Sacrifice follows, with the words Our Lord said at the Last Supper. By the power of this Sacrifice, which is the central part of the Eucharist, we become sons of God through Jesus Christ. *"Because you are sons, God has sent forth the Spirit of His Son into your hearts, crying out 'Abba, Father'. Therefore you are no longer a slave but a son, and if a son, then an heir of God through Christ"* (*Galatians 4:6-7*). We ask God to make us worthy to call Him Father and, without condemnation, to say The Lord's Prayer. At the beginnings of Christianity, only those who were baptized were allowed to learn this Divine Prayer. As we used the word "I" when we chanted the Creed, now we use the word "we" when we chant the Lord's Prayer. We are not alone anymore, separated individuals; we are now all together in a single Christian hypostasis - one mind, one heart, and one soul, united through Christ. We are part of the Church. We are sons of God.

Then the process of deification starts by our Communion with the Mysteries of the Savior's Body and Blood. The process will continue the rest of the week until the next Sunday Liturgy, under the blessing given by the Prayer before the Ambo when the priest says, "O Lord, who blessest those who bless Thee, and sanctifiest those who trust in Thee, save Thy people and bless Thine inheritance." This way, although we leave the Church as separated individuals again, we keep Our Lord's teachings and blessings deep in our heart all our days, and sanctify the new week we have just entered.

INCARNATION AS A TIME FLOW. *"I came forth from the Father and have come into the world. Again, I leave the world and go to the Father,"* the Savior told the disciples before going to pray in Gethsemane garden (*John 16:28*). There is a time flow here: the descent from eternity into temporality, living in temporality and the departure back into eternity. Vladimir Lossky noted that the body of the Lord's rest in the tomb on Holy Saturday corresponds to the day of rest during the Creation. For Our Lord Jesus Christ, the Holy Saturday was the day of rest from all His work in our material world, although He descended into Hades that day to rescue the souls of the reposed. We see that the Son of God's work by His incarnation followed the pattern of the Creation, in order to open the road for the final stream of all the living creatures toward the Heavenly Kingdom.

For us Christ is Alpha and Omega, the beginning and the end (*Revelation 1:8*). *"In the beginning was the Word, and the*

Word was with God, and the Word was God" (*John 1:1*). He was the Word when the world was created and, behold, the end is also with Him, the Word, when He will be the Judge. The whole life of humankind is under the sign of the Son of God Who passed for a short but ever remembered period, as Jesus Christ, among the people on earth. Some Holy Fathers considered that, even in the absence of Original Sin, the incarnation of the Son of God would have taken place, as a part of the wise work of the Holy Trinity. They said that, when God the Father created man in His image and likeness, He might have in mind the body that the Son would assume.

THE TWO FUNDAMENTAL TREES. The enigmatic book of Revelation is rich in significances. We read at the beginning of the last chapter of the Revelation, the following, in the King James Version: *"And he showed me a pure river of water of life, clear as crystal, proceeding out of the throne of God and of the Lamb. In the midst of the street of it, and on either side of the river, was there the tree of life, which bare twelve manner of fruits, and yielded her fruit every month, and the leaves of the tree were for healing of the nations"* (*Revelation 22:1-2*). If the Holy Scripture starts in Paradise with the *tree of knowledge* of good and evil (*Genesis 3*), it ends back in Paradise with the *tree of life* (*Revelation 22*).

The first man and woman had not the appropriate spiritual maturity to eat the fruits made by the tree of knowledge. After the tests of good and evil in a life of challenges, suffering and hard work, under the care of God the Father, the Son and the Holy Spirit, with Whom man had a continuous dialogue, humankind will be able to access the tree of eternal life from which the first man was prevented to eat. In all this long hard process of man's spiritual evolution, a central place is taken by the Cross, the *life-giving tree*, on which Christ, the Son of God and man, was crucified. Due to his originally sinful choice man cannot go from the tree of knowledge to the tree of life without the sacrificial tree of reestablishing life brought by the incarnated Son of God. The road of returning to Paradise is impossible without it.

On the day when the Elevation of the Holy Cross is commemorated, a Hymn is sung in the Romanian Orthodox Church. In English translation, it would sound as follows: "My soul glorifies the most venerated Cross of God. Mother of God, you are a Paradise full of mystery, who without sin has given birth to Christ, through Whom *the life-bearing tree of cross* was planted on earth. For this, now when the cross is elevated, we bow in front of it and we glorify Him." At the Vespers of the Third Sunday of Lent, The Adoration of the Holy Cross, a special hymn is sung in the American orthodox churches. "Rejoice, O *life-bearing Cross*, O bright paradise of the Church, O *Tree of incorruption*, thou who didst bring forth for us the enjoyment of glory everlasting, through whom the hosts of evil are driven out, the ranks of angels rejoice together, and the congregations of believers celebrate, O unconquerable weapon and impregnable foundation, the triumph of kings and the pride of Priests, grant us to apprehend the Passion of Christ and His Resurrection."

As Our Lord Jesus is the second Adam who expiated the original sin and blessed man on his way of deification, the Mother of God is a second Eve, because by the gift announced by the Archangel she was overshadowed by the Holy Spirit and remained pregnant with the Holy Child sent for the salvation of humankind. The second Eve contrasts to the first Eve who conceived after listening to the serpent's word, which brought about the lack of obedience, sickness, tragedy, and death to humankind.

"**WHERE DO WE COME FROM? WHAT ARE WE? WHERE ARE WE GOING?**" is the title of a famous and enigmatic painting of Paul Gauguin. What is the sense of man's life? What is the message of all the events of man's existence? What should be the most important goal of man's journey on this earth? Humankind came from a nature made with love in the image and likeness of the Creator of the universe; it is now in a nature deformed by some of man's acts that are not right, and it should change into a transfigured nature close to the one that man came from.

Each of us, as individuals, has to pull out of the false order of the present world in which we were born. We have to leave the empire of passions that our mother brought us into, when we began our personal existence. We have to discover our real nature and the harmony of the creation that was covered by humankind's misery. We have to work spiritually to reach a maturity of thinking and feeling that confers the right understanding of our earthly presence. We have to aspire to the final grace of eating from the tree of eternal life. We will accomplish all these by living in Jesus Christ. A new life marked by repentance, asceticism (i.e. purification), prayer, humility and love, will enable us to discover new resources in the midst of the corrupted world we were born in. This transformation will reward us with a quiet peace and joy, with the love for others, and with the actual sense of happiness.

The tree of eternal life grows next to a river with crystal clear water that comes from the deep and undisturbed peace of God the Father and of His Son. According to Saint Andrew of Caesarea, quoted by Archbishop Averky Taushev, this tree is Christ Himself and the twelve fruits of the tree are the Holy Apostles (Taushev, 1995). The tree brings fruits twelve times a year, which are "the most perfect knowledge revealed in the age to come." Its leaves "will be for healing, that is, for

302 | HORIA ION GROZA

cleansing away the ignorance of those people who are lower than others in the accomplishment of virtues."

The verses of the Apocalypse remind us of *Psalm 1* that compares the man pleasing to God with "*a tree planted by streams of waters, that produces its fruit in its season; and his leaf shall not wither and whatever he does shall prosper*" (*Psalm 1:3*). Patrick Henry Reardon, actually sees in that blessed man paralleled with a fruitful tree, not the "human being," the "man" (*Adam* in Hebrew or *Anthropos* in Greek) but "the male" (*is* in Hebrew and *aner* in Greek) who is the Mediator between God and man, i.e. the Son of God and the Son of man - Our Lord Jesus Christ (Reardon, 2000). This is another proof that all the Bible episodes are tied together in carrying a unique, mysterious, and profound meaning. "*The fruit of the righteous is a tree of life; and he that winneth souls is wise,*" King Solomon wrote (*Proverbs 11:30*, King James Version).

Father Dumitru Staniloae, quoted Saint Maximus the Confessor's comments about the Paradise tree of knowledge and suggested that its fruits offered the notion of good in spiritual terms and the notion of evil in bodily terms (Staniloae, 2002). Saint Maximus said that the **tree of life** was the mind of the soul where the throne of wisdom is placed, while the **tree of good and evil** was the feeling of the body, a feeling from which God wanted to protect the man. The *mind* has the ability to distinguish between perishable and everlasting while the *feeling* has the ability to distinguish between bodily pleasure and pain. By eating the fruit of good and evil, man acquires the irrationality of the senses as the only modality of discerning between what is favorable and unfavorable for the conservation of the body. I think we could add here also the discernment between good (pleasure, joy) and not good (pain, sickness, death). Maybe this is why Adam and Eve discovered that they were naked after eating the forbidden fruit - they acquired the consciousness of the body, of its feelings.

THE TWO ADAMS. Like Father Staniloae, Vladimir Lossky also made comments based on Saint Maximus' writings (Lossky, 1997). According to St. Maximus "the first man was called to unite in his being the whole of created beings." We know that man named all the living creatures (*Genesis 2:19-20*). "Man had to achieve a perfect union with God and then to confer his deified state to all the creation. He had to destroy in his own nature the distinction between the two sexes by living a life without passion according to the divine archetype. He had then to be able to reunite paradise with the rest of the earth, to transform the whole earth into paradise. He had to overcome the spatial order, not only for his mind but also for his body, by reuniting the earth and heaven. He would then surpass the margins of the sensible world and penetrate an intelligible universe by a good knowledge similar to that of the angels' spirit, with the goal to reunite within himself the intelligible world and the sensible one. In the end, as nothing would remain outside himself but only God, man had to dedicate himself completely to God in a flux of love and thus return to Him the whole universe united within his human being. God, in His turn, would then give Himself to man who would detain by virtue of this gift, i.e. by grace, all that God detains by His nature."

Adam, the first man, did not accomplish this condition but the second Adam, Christ, accomplished it. "*And so it is written, 'The first man Adam became a living being. The last Adam became a life-giving spirit*" (*1 Corinthians 15:45*). "Life," which is God's breath in man, has communicated in Christ's body with the Spirit of Life. Under the sign of Christic communication, man, the follower of Jesus the Savior, does his work of deification and he progresses due to the grace of God.

THE HUMAN BODY AND SOUL. The body has to be fed by the soul, the soul by the mind, and the mind by God – this is the order that should fit the immortal nature of man. The sin caused the mind to distance itself from God and therefore a reverse order was triggered. The mind started to be fed by the soul, and the soul to be fed by the body that is the source of passions; the body, remaining without any internal resources, started to be fed by the inanimate matter where sickness and death grow. This is why the harmonious human complex enters a decomposing process (see Lossky, 1997).

Man exercised his free will by sinning. The original sin was lack of obedience, the refusal to follow the road of deification. Then the sin began to enlarge like a snowball. Instead of repenting, Adam blamed Eve, and the two sexes that were one single unit split. Eve, in her turn, blamed the serpent. As Lossky noted, "by man's will, evil becomes a power that contaminates the creation" and the ground is cursed because of man who has now to produce his food from it by hard work (*Genesis 3:17*). From the moment of the fall until the Day of Pentecost when the grace of Holy Spirit descended upon man, the divine energy remained a stranger to human nature and worked only from outside. Fortunately, what the first man, Adam, was supposed to do by participating in God's work, was accomplished by the incarnation of the Son of God - by Christ, the second Adam.

Lossky quoted the Holy Fathers when he spoke of the human body. "Nothing of the body – neither the shape, nor the volume, nor the bulk, nor the weight, nor the color, nor other features taken in part, is the body. They are only realities perceived by thought. However, when they are structured and tied together they form a bodily unit." Lossky also mentioned the teachings of Saint Gregory of Nyssa: "Every element of the body is guarded by a sentinel, which is the thinking power of the soul that marks it with its seal, because the soul knows her own body even when the elements are spread throughout the world... The spiritual nature of the soul will know to find these elements at the time of resurrection in order that a 'spiritual body' may be assembled. This body is indeed our true body distinct from the grossness of our previous earthly body dressed in the 'garments of skin', which God made for Adam and Eve after they sinned."

Saint Paul wrote, *"For our citizenship is in heaven, from which we also eagerly wait for the Savior, the Lord Jesus Christ, who will transform our lowly body that it may be conformed to His glorious body, according to the working by which He is able even to subdue all things to Himself"* (*Philippians 3:20-21*). Saint Makarios from Egypt, quoted by Lossky, wrote, "The resurrection itself will be an expression of the inner state of the beings, because the mysteries of the soul will be visible through the bodies."

"But someone will say, 'How are the dead raised up? And with what body do they come?' ... *There are also celestial bodies and terrestrial bodies; but the glory of the celestial is one and the glory of the terrestrial is another... It is sown a natural body, it is raised a spiritual body"* (*1 Corinthians 15: 35, 40, 44*). Therefore, the Orthodox tradition discourages the cremation of dead bodies, instead of their natural decay, because like the seed that is sown and dies by decaying in order to emerge into a plant which will yield, as stated by Saint Paul: *"the body is sown in corruption, it is raised in incorruption. It is sown in dishonor, it is raised in glory. It is sown in weakness, it is raised in power"* (*1 Corinthians 15, 42-43*).

The soul will find the bones and will put them together in a spiritual body. The Old Testament shows us the power of God Who can re-create a material body out of bones: *"Thus says the Lord to these bones: 'Behold, I will bring the Spirit of life upon you. I will put muscles on you and bring flesh upon you. I will cover you with skin and put my Spirit into you. Then you shall live and know that I am the Lord"* (*Ezekiel 37:5-6*). Although the process at resurrection is different and so is the resulting spiritual body, these verses of the Old Testament tell us a little about the transformation a body can undergo. The practice of cremation, as Father Mark Malone said, seems to be motivated by pride, a desire for control, a false sense of ecological awareness, or the cost and convenience.

It is very important that Son of God, Who took a human body by living on earth, ascended to heaven in a human-like body. Our Savior's body after Resurrection was not one hundred percent similar to our human body and was different from the body of those He raised from the dead as the widow's son, Jairus' daughter, and Lazarus. Our Lord Jesus' body after resurrection was *transformed*. He entered the room where the disciples were gathered *through* closed doors (*John 20:19*) and He disappeared after He blessed and broke the bread at Emmaus (*Luke 24:31*).

3.5. The message of Orthodoxy.

SPECIFICS OF ORTHODOXY. As already emphasized in the first chapter of this book, Orthodoxy is the only Christian faith that pleads for deification. There are three fundamental elements of our Orthodox faith: (1) The incarnation of the Son of God; the Hebrews deny that Our Lord Jesus Christ is Messiah, the Muslims consider Jesus a prophet, the free thinkers in Western Europe think He was a mystic, the heretics affirm that He was 50% man and 50% God, while we apophatically believe that He was 100% God and 100% man. (2) The Resurrection of Our Lord Jesus Christ; the Hebrews contest it, while we not only believe it, but our entire spiritual life is built around the Resurrection that defeats sin, sickness, and death. (3) The deification of man; it is denied, ignored or "negotiated" by other churches, while for us it is the essence of our Christian thinking and feeling, the sense and the goal of our life. Many vital nuances can be unveiled from each of these three fundamental elements.

One of the Saints who protects the Moldavian province of Romania is Saint John the New, of Trapezunt. His relics are in Saint John the Baptist's Church in Suceava. He suffered a martyr's death in 1332 from the Tartarian pagans who captured him. A Venetian catholic sailor, navigating on the Danube, entered into an argument with Saint John who defended the *concept of deification*. Defeated in the conversation, the angered sailor decided to deliver Saint John to the Tartarian pagans, misleading them by slyness. The pagans tortured and killed Saint John. A column of light rose from Saint Martyr John's dead body thrown outside the city, and the people could see angels, like white-dressed priests, censing his body. Frightened, the pagans allowed the Christians to bury the deceased. After a long while, recognizing John's holiness, the catholic sailor came back and tried to steal the relics, piously kept in an orthodox church, to take them to Genova or Venetia.

There are so-called traditionalists (conservatives) and modernists (progressives) within the large family of the Orthodox churches. The traditionalists do not want to change anything, even the calendar which they want delayed thirteen days behind the modern calendar. They are focused only on the old writings of Holy Fathers like Saints Basil the Great and John Chrysostom, and do not accept more recent writings.

Many faithful people are discontent with this philosophy because they do not receive an answer to their modern-era specific problems. The modernists try to express everything in terms of their time and bring more vigor to the terminology, meanings, and symbols. This is to the satisfaction of numerous faithful people who find a manner of expression closer to the vocabulary of their time.

In fact, the actual sense of the term "tradition" signifies a continuous renewal within the inherited patterns. The Russian theologians living in France like Nicholas Berdiaeff and Paul Evdokimov, the American theologians of European origin like Alexander Schmemann and John Meyendorff, the British theologian Timothy Ware (Father Kallistos) and the Romanian theologian Dumitru Staniloae (unanimously considered one of the greatest theologians of the twentieth century), are adepts in the modern way of thinking and feeling.

Some theologians innovate and deviate from the permanent teachings of the Church; they are only partially accepted, like Serge Bulgakoff and Paul Florensky from the Orthodox Church or Teilhard de Chardin from the Catholic Church. In the United States, there was a debate between the conservatives like Fathers Seraphim Rose and Herman Podmoshensky from Platina Monastery and the modernists like Fathers Schmemann, Meyendorf and, more recently, Thomas Hopko from Saint Vladimir's Seminary in Crestwood, NY.

THE ORTHODOX AND CATHOLIC CHURCH. The whole history of the Church recorded heretical movements but the words of the Saints, the few chosen of God, were heard and followed, and this fact kept the Church out of the doubts and disputes. Stability is the advantage of the two traditional Churches, Catholic and Orthodox, which have behind them centuries of spiritual existence. However, the Orthodox Church did not make reforms like the Catholic Church and her Synods identified the heresies with promptitude. Therefore, the Orthodox Church succeeded in keeping the apostolic line intact, which is a guarantee that we are on the right track. The balance within a Church between the conservative and the progressive trends is maintained, as Father Vladimir Lecko used to say, by the monastic life which is the source of the true spirituality and authentic living in faith in every country.

The idea of a union between the two traditional churches – Catholic and Orthodox, always sounds attractive because unity makes Christianity stronger. However, the union became impossible due to the numerous differences that developed along the centuries. The five major differences are: the Papacy, the Filioque, the Purgatory, the Indulgences, and the Immaculate Conception.

The Orthodox Church is democratic and despite her organic unity, it kept an autocephaly for each country. The Orthodox Liturgy was maintained as it was inherited from Saint Apostle Jacob, through the rules established by Saints Basil the Great and John Chrysostom, without the major simplifications made in the Catholic Church. Very important are the differences regarding the concept of the Holy Trinity (according to the Orthodox Church the Holy Spirit proceeds only from the Father, as it is said in the Creed) and of the Mother of God (according to the Orthodox Church she was conceived in a natural human way). Due to her purity, the Holy Virgin became a human vessel for the Holy Child. Therefore, she remains a model for all the Christians who have to strive for dispassion and virtues in order to become a proper vessel for the Holy Spirit. There are no women priests in the Orthodox Church because the High Priest was Jesus Christ (*Hebrew 4:14-15*) and all those who represent Him on earth in this position should belong to the masculine gender.

ORTHODOXY VS. NEW WAYS OF CHRISTIAN THINKING. We can say with the psalmist, "Lord, You made man '*a little lower than the angels; You crowned him with glory and honor. You set him over the works of Your hands; You subjected all things under his feet, all sheep and oxen, and besides these, also the animals of the field, the birds of heaven and the fish of the sea, and the things passing through the paths of the seas*'" (*Psalm 8:6-9*). This is man's place, *our* place. It shows the trust the Lord had in man, together with the gift of the liberty of choice and action. Therefore, we love Him as a son loves his father who encourages him in doing good things and makes him feel stronger. But should this trust provide us the authority, as a recent new wave in the inspirational literature does, to imagine dialogues between man and God, in a very attractive, modern and natural manner? These books have great success and their philosophy is contagious. Among the authors, we can find writers such as Paul Ferrini and Neale Donald Walsch (see Ferrini, 1994 and Walsch, 1996).

Back in Romania, one used to say about good Christians that they are people "with fear of God." Who is first? God or man? Saint Apostle Paul confessed, "*I take pleasure in infirmities, in reproaches, in needs, in persecutions, in distresses, for Christ's sake, for when I am weak, then I am strong*" (*2 Corinthians 12:10*). We do not have to push the asceticism as far as Saint Paul did and the monks do. They battle the weaknesses of the fallen human nature in order to regain the purity of the original human nature which had the seed of God's likeness. We are not that strong, we are fragile, and therefore we try to do as much as we can, while following our road of deification with the firm hope in God's forgiveness. What did Saint Paul mean by writing, "*when I am weak, I am strong*" (*2 Corinthians 12:10*)? He meant that when he renounced imposing his strong will, looking like a weak man in the eyes of the people around him, when he preferred to rely on Christ and follow His path, he actually was strong. Without God, there is nothing, and nothing is possible (see *John 15:5*). Let us not forget that Saint Paul encouraged his young disciple Timothy, telling him, "*God has not given us a spirit of fear, but of power and of love and of a sound mind*" (*2 Timothy 1:7*). That makes us understand better the expression about Christians: "*men with fear of God.*" We do not rely on ourselves because all our struggles are leading nowhere if God does not bless them. We fear God's decision but we know that His decision is for our good and we act accordingly. We trust Him and we follow Him. We do not impose our will on God. We do not offer any reproach for His decisions.

N.D. Walsch dares to imagine a dialogue with God Who talks with man as a parent or an older brother, on a mild and wise voice, and man (the author) has the calm boldness to talk with Him on an equal footing (Walsch, 1996). This way of thinking is inspirational, tells us about the Lord's love, and makes us "understand" and love Him. Let us be careful, nevertheless. Do we say, "understand?" The whole teaching of the Church is full of mysteries because who can know "the ineffable, the incomprehensible, the inconceivable?" We are in touch only with His energies. We will never be able to know His very being. How then can we "understand" God, how can we know what words we might imagine putting in God's mouth?

Both authors, Walsch and Ferrini, are fascinating. They seem to satisfy well the Christian's need of a response from the Divinity to his prayers and questions. They try to dissipate the discontent and confusion produced by God's "silence." Metropolitan Anthony Bloom noted in his book about prayer that the Lord's silence might seem often harder to bear than

His apparent refusal to act. However, he wrote that after a long time standing in God's presence, the silence during the prayer becomes more expressive than the talking and, consequently, the intimacy with God's presence speaks more than any word can speak. In the first chapter, I mentioned the thoughts of Fathers Coniaris and Kallistos about the divine message that we receive during our prayers. Certainly something is wrong, misleading and subtly heretical in the kind of books this new wave is promoting.

One can read in the Patericon about a monk, John Cyprian, who lived in the eleventh century and was a good scholar. Because he opposed and spoke against the Law and the Scripture, he had to endure harsh punishments. It is not allowed to take from the Holy Scripture or add to it, because the Scripture was written under the guidance of the Holy Spirit. I remember that Father Vladimir Lecko talked about a priest who had translated a part of the Bible and while he was worshiping in the Church, he was reading from his own translation with joy and sincere persuasion. However, that translation had not been submitted to the Church for approval. When the Bishop heard what the priest was doing, he forbade the priest to serve the Liturgy ever again. We may not imagine with our limited human mind what Jesus would have said in addition to what was written in the New Testament. It would be like the trap people fall into when they represent Christ in paintings by taking a certain man as a model, or in movies by selecting a certain actor. We cannot replace the image of Savior's divine person with a human face. Therefore, the Orthodox Church respects an abstract typology in painting the icons of Christ and the Saints by using a symbolic spiritual language

Both authors, Ferrini and Walsch, make a mistake by having the certitude that what they think and feel is truthful and justifies them to put their words on God's tongue. Talking to people, as one thinks that He would talk, ends by mixing human ideas with the sacred things and can lead to heresies. This is actually how a new denomination starts: a smarter and more charismatic preacher presents and treats God according to his own ideas and a multitude of naïve people gather around him, listen to him and follow him. I remember the humor of the popular movie "Forrest Gump," where the main character needed an emotional relief and decided to run long distances. Many people ran behind him across America venerating him as new guru, being curious to hear his words of revelation.

By listening to the teachings of the Holy Fathers, which are a spiritual treasure that started with the Apostles and continued along many centuries, the traditional churchgoers avoid the risk of a fundamental spiritual error. The great reliability of the traditional Church teachings is based on the confirmation brought by the miracles performed by God through the saints whose wisdom we absorb. As Saint Mark the Evangelist wrote about the disciples after the Savior ascended to the heavens, *"And they went out and preached everywhere, the Lord working with them and confirming the word through the accompanying signs"* (*Mark 16:20*). Saint Paul wrote, *"I make known to you, brethren, that the gospel which was preached by me is not according to man ... but it came through revelation of Jesus Christ"* (*Galatians 1:11-12*).

It does not matter how smart or charismatic a preacher is, the gospel comes from God and its deeply meaningful content can be revealed and explained only by the Church that is the Body of Christ. What did the Ethiopian Eunuch say when the Apostle Philip asked him if he understood what he was reading from Isaiah. He said, *"How can I, unless someone guides me?"* (*Acts 8:30-31*). The guide is the Apostolic Church.

There is another important thing in the heretical books.

The author considers himself, consciously or unconsciously, to be equal with God, and consequently conducts the conversation in his own terms. *"Professing to be wise, they became fools, and changed the glory of the incorruptible God into an image made like corruptible man – and birds and four-footed animals and creeping things"* (*Romans 1:22-23*). To whom do they give human attributes, as jealousy, anger, doubt, etc.? To the Lord! They forgot that Moses, a wise and faithful man so close to Him, was not able to learn even what His name is: *"I AM the Existing One"* (*Exodus 3:14*). Therefore, we need to be careful when we open the two books mentioned above. They lack a fundamental Christian virtue – the humility.

We must never consider ourselves equal to God, to argue with Him, to blame Him for being unjust, to show Him where he made "mistakes." Otherwise, we would repeat Adam and Eve's error, when they listened to the voice of the tempting serpent to eat the fruit that would make them like God.

OTHER RELIGIONS. What position should a Christian have when he is confronted with the non-biblical and pagan religions? The atheistic Marxists have attacked the religion. They considered it "opium for controlling the people." They found several similarities between the Mosaic and Christian religions on one side and the non-biblical religions on the other side. They accused Christianity of borrowing elements from other religions in order to build a false conception about the world.

"The first expression of the meeting between man and God is found in the pagan religions," Jean Danielou wrote (Danielou, 1956). The pagans feel a mysterious force behind the natural phenomena like the sun's heat and brightness or the storm's destructive power, and they express it in hierophanies, as the historian of religion Mircea Eliade, quoted by Danielou, wrote. A religious attitude is proper to the human being and God takes care of all the people on earth (*Matthew 5:45*). God is "*who in bygone generations allowed all nations to walk in their own ways. Nevertheless, He did not leave Himself without witness, in that He did good, gave us rain from heaven and fruitful seasons, filling our hearts with food and gladness*" (*Acts 14:16-17*). This was the way Barnabas and Paul spoke to the pagans in Lystra who saw the miraculous healing of the crippled man and tried to venerate them saying, "*The gods have come down to us in the likeness of men*" (*Acts 14:11*). Saint Paul preached about God and His works to the wise Athenians of the Areopagus Hill. "*He has made from one blood every nation of men to dwell on all the face of the earth, and has determined their preappointed times and boundaries of their dwellings, so they should seek the Lord, in the hope that they might grope for Him and find Him, though He is not far from each one of us. For in Him we live and move and have our being*" (*Acts 17:26-28*).

The historians often link the Christian religion to the pagan religions in an *evolutionist* idea, considering that one is developed from the other, or in a *syncretistic* idea, considering a simultaneous appearance of different forms of religious aspiration, which are interacting with each other. This is a profound error, because Christianity and Judaism are not the result of a mere manifestation of the human religious genius, but the spiritual human receptivity to the direct interventions of God in man's life, which opens access to domains otherwise completely inaccessible to the human spirit. If the Christians who know the true God should become unstable in their faith and should compromise with other beliefs, they will not be forgiven. "*Because what may be known of God is manifest in them, for God has shown it to them. For since the creation of the world His invisible attributes are clearly seen, being understood by the things that are made, even His eternal power and Godhead, so that they are without excuse, because although they knew God, they did not glorify Him as God, nor were thankful, but became futile in their thoughts, and their foolish hearts were darkened. Professing to be wise, they became fools and changed the glory of the incorruptible God into an image made like corruptible man – and birds and four-footed animals and creeping things"* (Romans 1:19-23).

The Christian is responsible, attentive to God's laws and teachings. The Ten Commandments given to Moses on Mount Sinai and engraved on stone tablets are not only the manifestation of the well-intended Divine Will but they are a living principle because, as Jean Danielou wrote, God's finger which is the Spirit, has engraved them on the tablets of human hearts. The Christian believes in God and he does not dissect Him with the blunt and rusty lance of his mind but tries to understand Him with the fine love of his heart.

The thirst for salvation is the core of the Christian's life experience. As Jean Danielou wrote, the Christian and the Saints of Christianity might be inferior in mystical geniality to great religious personalities like Buddha or Mahomet, but they believe and live God's Word. The Lord spoke for the first time to people through the power of the cosmos and through the conscience, before speaking through Moses and Jesus Christ. After the fall from Paradise, humankind was blessed with intelligence and conscience but needed the objective support of a *positive revelation,* which for Christians was Our Lord Jesus, and the interior support of a *powerful grace,* which for Christians was the faith in Christ and His Church. The whole experience of the non-Christians was marked by the endeavor to find the Divinity who directed the universe. As soon as the real God Who is Truth revealed Himself, all other beliefs should have been abandoned. Christianity is the only possible religion because it brings Salvation. As Jean Danielou commented, Buddha, Zoroaster, and Confucius can be considered precursors of Christ but it is proper to the precursors to step aside when the One they announced appeared. Otherwise, they become adversaries.

PAGAN BELIEFS AND ORTHODOXY. Man was continuously impressed by the surrounding universe. "The stars and the regularity of their movement, the sun and its brightness, the storm and its damages, the rock and its stability – all these are hierophanies," Jean Danielou wrote. These are manifestations of the Divinity and give symbolic dimensions to the cosmos. "*The mountains saw Thee and they trembled; the overflowing of the water passed by; the deep uttered his voice and lifted up his hands on high. The sun and moon stood still in their habitation*" (*Habakkuk 3:9-11* in King James Version). "*Let the glory of the Lord be forever; the Lord shall be glad in His works. He looks upon the earth and makes it tremble; He touches the mountains and they smoke*" (*Psalm 103/104:31-32*).

For a Christian the succession of revelations undergoes an important spiritual transfiguration. The last revelation does not deny the previous ones but links them together into a coronation. "Christ did not annihilate the law but brought it to completion," Jean Danielou wrote. The seasonal pagan feasts were substituted by the Hebrew Feasts of Pascha, Pentecost, and Tabernacle; the prophets of Asherah by Elijah. The day of the Lord's Nativity is celebrated after the winter solstice. It replaced the Romans' Feast of Sun (*Natale Solis invincti*), which marked the beginning of the lengthening of the day, because God Himself is Light and brings light to the creation.

PRIMARY RELIGIONS. Two sacred elements of the pagan religions play an important role in the Christian religion: *the stone* and *the rain*. The rock is a symbol very much preferred in the Holy Scripture in the effort to express God the Father: *"He is the Rock, his work is perfect: for all His ways are judgment; a God of truth and without iniquity, just and right is He"* (*Deuteronomy 32:4*, King James Version). The rock is also a symbol for God the Son: *"... and that rock was Christ"* (*1 Corinthians 10:4*). Christ is *"the stone which the builders rejected"* and *"has become the chief cornerstone"* (*1 Peter 2:7*; see also *Matthew 21:42-44*). The whole Christian faith is built on that cornerstone, as the Church has the Apostles' witness as her foundation: *"And I also say to you that you are Peter and on this rock I will build My church and the gates of Hades shall not prevail against it"* (*Matthew 16:18*).

The rain in the pagan religions expresses God's blessing that covers the drought-suffering ground. This symbol will be repeated in the Bible for describing a spiritual blessing: *"Let heaven above be glad and let the clouds sprinkle righteousness"* (*Isaiah 45:8*). *"For as rain comes down or snow from heaven, and does not return until it saturates the earth and it brings forth and produces and gives seed to the sower and bread for food, so shall My word be, whatever proceeds from My mouth"* (*Isaiah 55:10-11*).

MYTOLOGIES. The myths explain the relationship between God and cosmos and they cover many aspects regarding the origin of all things in this world, including numerous basic elements of human life. For some philosophers, religious scholars and writers, the cosmic pagan myths do not differ in essence from the Christian mysteries.

As Jean Danielou mentioned, Simone Weil in her "Lettre à un religieux" connected the grapevine of Dionysus with that of Saint John, and the cosmic tree with Christ's cross. In a similar manner, we might connect the myth of the Thracian knight in the old Romanian province Dobrogea with the veneration of Saint George by the local population. However, as Jean Danielou emphasized, "the Biblical and Christian revelation does not owe anything to the myth." The only possible connection is the common background of the spiritual expression of the human mind and heart. The vocabulary of the latter ones is limited, and this is why we confer to God human attributes like anger, jealousy, impatience etc. We lack terms to describe the One who is above everything, is ineffable, inconceivable, everywhere and everlasting.

The veneration of Saint Virgin Mary does not address the feminine element of the divinity like the virgin mothers in Hellenism and Hinduism, nor as the psychiatrist and philosopher Karl Jung insinuated, but addresses her as a unique part of the Salvation process (see Danielou, 1956). Christ's cross does not represent the cosmic symbol of the four dimensions of the universe but the wood on which the Savior was crucified. The grapevine does not express the Dionysian immortality but the unique event of sacrifice offered by God for the people of Israel and Christians. The Resurrection does not signify the vernal cyclic victory of life over death but the introduction of humankind into the sphere of the Holy Trinity's life.

While the myths explain the general relationship between God and cosmos, the rites refer directly to the functionality within this relationship. In contrast to the pagan cosmic rites that deal with the life of nature, the Christian sacraments are ministered in relation to the historical actions of God. Besides the categories of myths and rites applied to the human communities, there is the category of the mystical experiences specific to each individual who establishes a very personal relationship between the human soul and the Divinity. In this category are included, besides Christians, other more advanced religions that practice asceticism like the Japanese Buddhism, Greek Orphism, and Semitic Shamanism. Prayers under different forms – praise, gracious action or requests express the piety specific to these religions. Piety is an element common to the pagan and biblical religions but <u>the unique particularity of the piety of the biblical religions is the revelation of the Salvation event</u>.

MORE SOPHISTICATED RELIGIONS. Animism personifies the natural objects and phenomena and gives them a soul. Religions more sophisticated than animism are polytheism, pantheism, and dualism. They also produce a deformed idea of Divinity. The *Polytheism* of the Greek-Roman mythology and of the Indian mythology fills the world with gods and goddesses, often in a hierarchic order. Humankind needed two thousand years to root monotheism into the polytheist peoples. The popular paganism was the largest obstacle to the spread of the Gospel. The Romanian people maintained many pagan habits and beliefs despite the fact that they were among the first Gentile Christians and had martyrs after Saint Apostle Andrew's passage through the Thracian territories. Even now, the Romanians have a pagan alternative name for several great Christian Feasts as Holy Nativity, Pentecost, Saint John the Baptist's birth etc. The Christian believes, like the pagans, that mysterious beings are guardians for springs and forests, families, villages and cities, but these are not gods and goddesses; they are angels who are created beings like man, but invisible (see Danielou, 1956).

Pantheism is man's metaphysical temptation to erase the limits that separate God from what is not God, and actually to see not only God's fingerprint in every created thing but the very Person of God. The motherland of such a concept is India. According to it, God is everywhere in an undifferentiated form in nature, and in a more personal way in the people's souls. By contrast, for the mystical Christian, God remains eternally transcendental and inaccessible. Man cannot reach God. He can know the Lord only through the uncreated energies in accordance with the access given to him by grace. The bridge built by love ("Agape," not "Eros") between God the Creator and man with his free will, provides the way for this grace to come. It is a union of love between a Divine Person and a human person who remain distinct. The Pantheism does not consider the act of Creation a conscious act of God that generates distinct categories of things and beings, as the Christians do. In a pantheistic system, the Being is undetermined; it is a defect or impurity in the midst of the pure Non-being.

The *Dualism* is, as Jean Danielou commented, "the third perversion of the cosmic religions." This religious system opposes the principles of Good and Evil, of Light and Darkness, and both terms of these antinomian pairs are equal in power (see Mazdaism or Zoroastrianism, and Manichaeism). The dualists are monotheists because God is not the principle of evil. Neo-Platonism and Hinduism consider the presence of Evil to be an illusion, destroyable by knowledge. By comparison, the Christians think the existence of Evil is a consequence of the liberty of the created beings: an angel chose evil by denying God and became Lucifer. What might have happened if Adam, after eating the forbidden fruit from the tree of knowledge of good and evil, had used his right of free choice and had opted for evil, and then afterwards had eaten from the tree of eternal life? Would the sinful Adam have become everlasting? Then he would have risked following the same road as Lucifer, and this could have been the catastrophe of catastrophes: the destruction of the human being, the loss of any possibility of uniting with the Creator.

The dualistic vision of the structure of the universe imagines evil with its own existence, independent from God and man, as a force equal with God, and as part of the notion of the Universal Being. Christianity does recognize the mystery of evil and Lucifer's fall, but refuses to see in him a positive and essential principle. The Christians disagree with the dualists' idea of making the good perfectly equal with the evil. For Christians, evil is a secondary appearance. In the present time, man is a prisoner of the evil who is the Prince of this sinful world, because despite his good nature and his aspiration to do good, man is continuously tempted by the evil spirit and is often trapped, risking the health of his harmonious nature. Fortunately, he is released and healed by Christ, the Savior.

MYSTICISM is a transcendental fusion and it is superior to the primary cosmic religions which search for God in full darkness groping with hierophanies that degenerate into idolatries as the personification of the elements of nature. Unfortunately, ordinary mysticism is limited to a divinization of the human spirit, as Plotin and Buddha do, by dragging the Lord down to earth. It is true that "Saint Gregory of Nyssa and Saint Augustine used Plotin's terms about knowing God by a pure soul's mirror, but they gave a sense totally different to these terms", as Jean Danielou wrote by quoting his other book "Platonism et téologie mystique." "The goal of Christian mysticism is to learn about the Divine presence as it is and not degrading it into an earthly presence."

Jean Danielou commented that in the mystical or religious conception, "the soul aspires to merge with God beyond this world and beyond the human limits." A young friend told me that actually the main preoccupation of a Christian should be confession and repentance, because this is the way to obtain forgiveness and to prepare for the Last Judgment.

According to my young friend, the Communion is only an authentication of the forgiveness. It is false. The work of salvation does not reside only in forgiveness, in absolution. Many blind, invalid, or sick people were healed by Our Lord Jesus and the Saints, but this does not mean that they did not sin again. The work of salvation consists in the whole process of deification, a process very important for the Orthodox believers. It is the process of coming closer to God, the process of merging with His uncreated energies.

Therefore, our goal when we fast is not only the asceticism for the education and cleaning of our spirit and body, but also the preparation for being united with the Body and Blood of Our Lord. The Communion with the bread and wine that have been consecrated at the Eucharist is the peak moment of the Divine Liturgy. How can we be with Christ if we refuse His offer of unification every time the Liturgy is celebrated?

HOW SHOULD WE TALK WITH THE NON-BIBLICAL RELIGION ADEPTS? With much condescension and without any hatred, aggressiveness or inconsideration, but trying to explain who, and more important, Who is the Truth, in the unceasing research that the human being has been doing for millennia. How will the Lord judge the people belonging to religions different from the Christian one? According to the sins committed against their own conscience, because all people were created in the image and likeness of God, regardless of what religion they were born into, were raised in or lived in. Are those who switched from Christianity to Buddhism, Islamism, Hinduism right? No, because these people were not ignorant like the others; they knew the truth but deliberately went away from it. *"Whoever denies Me before men, him I will also deny before My Father who is in heaven"* (*Matthew 10:33*).

HOW CAN WE CONCLUDE THIS BRIEF EXCURSUS done with the help of the remarkable theologian Jean Danielou's book? When we are accused by the atheists and free-thinkers that the Christian religion has borrowed elements from other religions in order to build a powerful system that the leaders and the rich classes could use in oppressing the poor multitudes, we can reply that the Christian religion did not take anything from any other religion.

The possible similarities are fortuitous and are caused by the general human nature that has the intuition of the transcendent and tries to understand and express it in the very limited language that man has available for expressing the ineffable of the spiritual domains. This is actually why the Orthodox Church prefers an apophatic approach.

In the end, a little story about religions, found in the book of Father Anthony Coniaris (Coniaris, 2001). A man fell into a deep pit where, on the muddy bottom, there was a giant snake. An Animist, i.e. a man worshiping the elements of nature as some Native Americans do, passed by. He looked in the pit, saw the snake, felt a shock, and ran away as fast as he could in order to avoid any risk of being pulled down by the evil spirit. A disciple of Confucius passed by. He said, "The wise men never fall into a pit. Walk carefully and watch where you put your foot."

A Hindu passed by. He saw the man and said, "My brother, you think that you are in a big dark pit but this is only an error of your perishable mind. All is Brahman and Brahman is all, the exterior world is an illusion. Think a little bit: there is no pit, there is no pit, there is no snake, there is no snake, and all will be good. A beneficent peace will cover you."

A Muslim passed by. Full of care he said immediately, "Man, do not worry. I will help you." He lay down on the ground on the border of the pit, stretched, grabbed the man's arm, and started to pull him up. When the man was half out, the Muslim asked him holding a knife in the other arm, "You will become a Muslim, will you not?" The man refused, so the Muslim let him fall back into the bottom of the pit.

This story reminds me of an article that I read in a newspaper of March 2006 about the Afghan Abdul Rahman who was convicted to death because he converted to Christianity while working with a humanitarian foreign group who was taking care of the sick Afghans from Pakistan.

To continue the story: A Buddhist passed by. Full of empathy he said, "My dear, you suffer bitterly there in the dark of the pit and the reason why you suffer is that you want to get out. Your very desire makes you to feel miserable. Quench all desire; you will feel much better and you will not care anymore that you are in a pit." Eventually Jesus passed by. He looked down with infinite love and descended into the pit, between the man and the snake. The powerful snake immediately struck Him. Feeling the venom spreading in his body, Jesus, with weakening arms, pushed the man out of the pit. Father Coniaris concluded his story, "Confucius died and was buried, Buddha rotted with food poisoning, Mohammed went the way of all flesh, leaving behind a harem, but Jesus Christ rose from the dead and by His resurrection He demonstrated that He was indeed the 'Son of God Who comes with power'... Other religions may have bits of truth, but only Christ has, or rather, is the Fullness of Truth."

Conclusion

If we use Mircea Eliade's terms, we can say that, for a person who believes in God, there are two kinds of time: a sacred time and a profane one. The sacred time is the time of God, of the Creator; it is *chairos* and it is eternal. The profane time is the historical time, the time of the creation, of man and of all living creatures; it is *chronos* and it is the quotidian time that flows unceasingly. Our soul is immortal and its time ever since we were conceived is eternal. Our body is perishable and its time is transitory. Eliade named the manifestation of the sacred in the ordinary world of creation with the term "hierophany." (Eliade, 1987)

The incarnation of the Son of God is a hierophany. By incarnation, the Son of God, a Divine Person living in the eternal time, entered into the world of creation, sanctifying the historical time. Therefore, a Christian is called to discover the eternal time of his soul, and especially the sacred aspect of it, due to the awareness of the permanent presence of God abiding with humanity, of the sacrificial work of the Savior and of the vital necessity to follow God's commandments and Jesus Christ's teachings. *"O Lord, You became a refuge to us in generation and generation... From everlasting to everlasting You are"* (*Psalm 89/90:1-2*). As the Church says, God is "our only refuge" because He "exists outside time," above our daily trials and tribulations.

Today the sin is between man and God. That began when Adam disobeyed in Paradise and it continues every day with our own sins. Because of the sin, man cannot look at God without being hurt. Origen noticed that we, the Christians, confirm the truth in Plato's statement that it is difficult to see the Creator and the Father of the universe. However, Origen wrote further, He can be seen because we can read in the Gospel, *"Blessed are the pure in heart, for they shall see God"* (*Matthew 5:8*), and, in addition to these, Our Lord Jesus Christ, Who is the image of the invisible God, said, *"He who has seen Me has seen the Fa*ther" (*John 14:9*). God the Father remains inaccessible to us in regards to His being, but our heart can feel Him by His uncreated energies that descend to us. We can intuit His wonderful greatness by contemplating the order and the harmony of His creation.

Therefore if, for a fraction of time, we have eyes and ears, we can discover God's presence within each of us. This is the discovery of the sacred time of our life. The emotion of this discovery will be almost as strong as that felt by the two travelers to Emmaus, after they saw the Savior blessing and breaking the bread. *"Then their eyes were opened and they knew Him; and He vanished from their sight"* (*Luke 24:31*). Just as they lost Christ's presence after that revelation, we quickly lose that deep insight into our neighbor's and our soul, and are burdened again by the weaknesses of our sinning human nature and by the nothingness of the daily chores.

Let us make the effort to discover the sacred time of our life behind the quotidian events of our earthly existence and let us try to adjust and live it fully, with the richness of every minute, not forgetting that the supreme goal of our spiritual existence is deification. Let release a little bit the gates of the dam we have built in our minds and hearts and allow a drop of eternity to enter the flow of our historicity. Our reward will be a better understanding of things and an unshakeable peace accompanied by hope. If this book helps you to think about this continuous discovery, it will have fulfilled its purpose – a call to step forward nearer to the Kingdom of God that waits for you and whose secret seed hides deep in yourself.

Bibliography

*** 1936: Sbornik, Sortavalassa Oy Raamattutalon kirjapainossa [Teachings of the Holy Fathers about Jesus Prayer]. Valaam Monastery, transl. in Romanian in 1946 at Antim Monastery, Bucharest, Romania.

*** 1975: *The Sayings of the Desert Fathers* [part of Patericon, Egyptian Patericon or Apophthegmata Patrum], transl. Sister Benedicta Ward, The Sisters of the Love of God, Cistercian Publications, Kalamazoo, Michigan.

*** 1989: *The Living God. A Catechism for the Christian Faith*, transl. Olga Dunlop, St. Vladimir's Seminary Press, *SVP*, Crestwood, New York.

*** 1993: *Athonite Fathers and Athonica,* Holy Hesychasterion of St. John the Theologian, Souroti, Greece.

*** 1995: *Proloagele* [Book of Prologues], Ed. Bunavestire, Bacău, Romania.

*** 1999a: *Patericul* [Patericon, Egyptian Patericon or Apophthegmata Patrum], Editura Reîntregirea, Alba Iulia, Romania.

*** 1999b: *Schema-Abbot John of Valaam. Valaam Patericon,* in *The Orthodox Word*, Platina, California, No.206-207, p.185

*** 2000: *Elder Cleopa of Romania, The Truth of Our Faith,* transl. Peter Alban Heers, Uncut Mountain Press, Thessalonica, Greece.

*** 2001: *Elder Cleopa of Sihastria, In the Tradition of St. Paisius Velichkovsky*, transl. Mother Cassiana, New Varatec Publishing of Protection of the Holy Virgin.Orthodox Monastery, Lake George, Colorado.

*** 2011: *Eternity Hidden in the Moment. The Life and Recollections of Elder Arsenie (Papacioc)*, in *The Orthodox Word*, Platina, California, No.281, p.302.

Alfeyev, Met. Hilarion, 2000: *The Spiritual World of Isaac the Syrian*, Cistercian Studies 175, Kalamazoo: Cistercian Publications, 2000. (Posted under the title "Audacity of mercy," on 2/6/2012 on http://glory2godforallthings.com).

Augustine, Saint, 1984: *Confessions*, Penguin Books Ltd., London, England

Bălan, Ioanichie, 1996: *Romanian Patericon*, St. Herman of Alaska Brotherhood, Platina, California.

Bălan, Ioanichie, 2000: *Shepherd of Souls, The Life and Teachings of Elder Cleopa*, St. Herman of Alaska Brotherhood, Platina, California.

Berdiaeff, Nicholas, 1935: *De la destination de l'homme* [About Man's Destiny], Editions Je sers, Paris.

Bloom, Anthony, 1970: *School for Prayer*, A Libra Book, London.

Braga, Roman Archim., 1996: *Exploring the Inner Universe; Joy – the Mystery of Life*, HDM Press, Inc., Rives Junction, Michigan.

Cabasilas, Nicholas, 1977: *A Commentary on Divine Liturgy,* Saint Vladimir's Seminary Press, *SVS Press,* Crestwood, New York.

Calciu, Fr. George, 1997: *Christ is calling you,* St. Herman of Alaska Brotherhood, Platina, Califonia.

Camus, Albert, 1947: *La Peste,*[The Plague], Gallimard, France.

Climacus, John Saint, 1982: *The Ladder of Divine Ascent.* Paulist Press, Mahwah, New Jersey.

Colliander, Tito, 1985: *Way of Ascetics,* Saint Vladimir's Seminary Press, *SVS Press,* Crestwood, New York.

Coniaris, Anthony M., 1998: *Philokalia, The Bible of Orthodox Spirituality,* Light and Life Publishing Company, Minneapolis.

Coniaris, Anthony M., 2001: *Whatever Happened to Truth?,* Light and Life Publishing Company, Minneapolis.

Danielou, Jean, 1956: *Dieu et nous,* [God and us], Editions Bernard Grasset, France.

Eliade, Mircea, 1987: *The Sacred and the Profane, the Nature of Religion,* A Harvest Book, Harcourt, Inc., Orlando.

Every, George, Richard Harries, Kallistos Ware, 1984: *The Time of the Spirit,* Saint Vladimir's Seminary Press, *SVS Press,* Crestwood, New York.

Evdokimov, Paul, 1971: Poèmes (1953-1954), in Contacts, Paris, France, No. 73-74: 116-118

Evdokimov, Paul, 1973: *L'amour fou de Dieu* [The Passionate Love for God], Editions du Seuil, France.

Evdokimov, Paul, 1977: La Nouveauté de l'Esprit, Études de spiritualité. Spiritualité orientale, no. 20. Abbaye de Bellefontaine, Bégrolles (Maine de Loire), France.

Ferrini, Paul, 1994: *Love without conditions. Reflections of the Christ's Mind*, Heartways Press, Parrish, Florida.

Florensky, Paul, 1987: *Salt of the earth*, St. Herman of Alaska Brotherhood, Platina, Califonia.

Fudel, Sergei, 1989: *Light in the Darkness*, Saint Vladimir's Seminary Press, *SVS Press*, Crestwood, New York.

Gillet, Lev, 1976: *The Burning Bush*, Template Publishers, Springfield.

Gobry, Pascal-Emmanuel, 2015: *Why religion will dominate the 21st century*, http://theweek.com/articles/555371

Groza, Horia Ion, 2006: *Treptele de văzduh ale sufletului şi setea de Dumnezeu*, [The Ladder of the Inner Sky and the Thirst for God], Criterion Publishing, Bucharest, Romania.

Hamant, Yves, 1995: *Alexander Men: A Witness for Contemporary Russia, A Man for Our Times*, transl. Steven Bigham, Oakwood Publications, Torrance, California.

Irme, Simona, 2013: *A Life of Sacrificial Love: The Life and Teachings of Elder Justin Pârvu*, in *The Orthodox Word*, Platina, California, No. 292 –293, p. 209-248, 261-304.

Jackson Brown Jr., H., 1993: *Life's little instruction book II*, Rutledge Hill Press, Nashville, Tennessee.

Joantă, Seraphim, 1992: *Romania. Its Hesychast Tradition and Culture,* St. Xenia Skete, Wildwood, California.

Kuhl, David, 2002: *What Dying People Want: Practical Wisdom for the End of Life,* Perseus Books Group.

Lossky, Vladimir, 1997: *The Mystical Theology of the Eastern Church,* Saint Vladimir's Seminary Press, *SVS Press,* Crestwood, New York. Also, Vladimir Lossky, *Essai sur la Théologie mystique de l'Église d'Orient,* Aubier, Éditions Montaigne, 1944.

Malik, Charles Habib, 1974: *The Wonder of Being,* Word Books, Waco.

Nicodemus, Monk, 2001: *The Elders of Kolitsu.* In *The Orthodox Word,* Platina, California, No. 216, p.16

Noica, Constantin, 1991: *Jurnalul de idei* [Journal of ideas], Humanitas, Bucharest, Romania.

Polkinghorne, John and Nicholas Beale, 2009: *Questions of truth,* Westminster John Knox Press, Louisville, Kentucky.

Reardon, Patrick Henry, 2000: *Christ in the Psalms,* Conciliar Press, Ben Lomond, California.

Rose, Seraphim, 1980: *The soul after death,* St. Herman of Alaska Brotherhood, Platina, California

Ramakrishna, Shri, 1936: *Un des Chemins* [One of the Roads], Union des Imprimeries, Frameries, Belgique.

Scrima, André, 2000: *Timpul Rugului Aprins* [Time of the Burning Bush], Humanitas, Bucharest, Romania.

St. Herman of Alaska, 1989: *A Treasury of Saint Herman's Spirituality*, Little Russian Philokalia, St.Herman Press, Platina, California.

St. John Climacus, 1982: *The Ladder of Divine Ascent*, Paulist Press, Mahwah, New Jersey.

St. Nicodim Agioritos, 1996: *Apanthisma*, Constantinopol, 1799 (transl. in Romanian, 1817), edited by Virgil Cândea, Editura Anastasia, Bucharest, 1996.

St. Paisius Velichkovsky, 1994: *The Scroll. Field Flowers. Instructions*.Little Russian Philokalia, New Valaam Monastery, Alaska, St.Herman Press, Platina, California.

Staniloae, Dumitru, 2002: *Orthodox Spirituality, a practical guide for the faithful and a definitive manual for the scholar*, St.Tikhon's Seminary Press, *STS Press*, South Cannan, Pennsylvania.

Taushev, Averky, 1995: *The Apocalypse. In the Teachings of ancient Christianity*, St. Herman of Alaska Brotherhood, Platina, California.

Tudor, Sandu, 2001: *Taina sfintei Cruci* [The Mystery of the Holy Cross], *Caietele Preacuviosului Părinte Daniil de la Rarău*, Christiana, Bucharest, Romania.

Un moine de l'Eglise d'Orient [Lev Gilet], 1963: *La prière de Jésus* [Jesus Prayer], Chevetogne, France.

Vulcănescu, Mircea, 2004: *Bunul Dumnezeu cotidian* [The Good Daily God], Humanitas, Bucharest, Romania.

Walsch, Neale Donald, 1996: *Conversations with God, an uncommon dialogue*, G.P. Putnam's Sons, New York.

Ward, Benedicta, 1975: *The Sayings of the Desert Fathers*, Mowbray, London & Oxford, Cistercian Publications.

Ware, Kallistos [Bishop Kallistos of Dioklea, Timothy Ware], 1986: *The Power of the Name, the Jesus Prayer in Orthodox Spirituality*, The Sisters of the Love of God, *SLG Press*, Oxford, 1986

Ware, Kallistos, 1996: *Praying with the Orthodox Tradition*, Saint Vladimir's Seminary Press, *SVS Press*, Crestwood, New York.

Ware, Timothy, 1987: *The Orthodox Church*, Penguin Books Ltd., London, England.

Bibles quoted

The Orthodox Study Bible, **SAAS**™ , St. Athanasius Academy of Orthodox Theology, Elk Grove, California, 2008.

The Bible, King James Version, Ivy Books, New York, 1991.

The Bible, Revised Standard Version, Thomas Nelson and Sons Ltd, New York, 1952.

Reflection Publishing. P.O. Box 2182
Citrus Heights, California 95611-2182
E-mail: info@reflectionbooks.com
www.reflectionbooks.com

CPSIA information can be obtained
at www.ICGtesting.com
Printed in the USA
FSOW03n0219050916
24612FS